THE IDEA OF PROPERTY IN LAW

The Idea of Property in Law

J. E. PENNER

CLARENDON PRESS · OXFORD
1997

Oxford University Press, Great Clarendon Street, Oxford OX2 6DP
Oxford New York
Athens Auckland Bangkok Bogota Bombay
Buenos Aires Calcutta Cape Town Dar es Salaam
Delhi Florence Hong Kong Istanbul Karachi
Kuala Lumpur Madras Madrid Melbourne
Mexico City Nairobi Paris Singapore
Taipei Tokyo Toronto
and associated companies in
Berlin Ibadan

Oxford is a trade mark of Oxford University Press

Published in the United States
by Oxford University Press Inc., New York

British Library Cataloguing in Publication Data
Data available

Library of Congress Cataloging in Publication Data
Penner, James.
The idea of property in law / James Penner.
p. cm.
Includes bibliographical references.
1. Property. I. Title.
K720.P46 1997
346.04—dc20
[342.64] 96–44689

ISBN 0–19–826029–6

1 3 5 7 9 10 8 6 4 2

Typeset by Vera A. Keep, Cheltenham
Printed in Great Britain by
Bookcraft Ltd., Midsomer Norton, Avon

To John Penner,
Jean Penner,
and Rae McMillan

Preface

Although the views in this book were developed and refined over the last three years, its main ideas occurred to me during my three years in Oxford when I was doing my D.Phil. dissertation. So the book owes a kind of primary allegiance to Oxford and the resources and intellectual companionship which it provided. More specifically this debt is payable to the Master, Fellows, and Servants of University College, and to the undergraduate and postgraduate Members who were my colleagues when I was there. I cannot mention everyone, in and out of Oxford, who during this time was a source of support or inspiration, but I owe particular thanks (in no particular order) to John Finnis, Bill Sykes, John Albery, Christine Griffiths, David Bell, Leslie Mitchell, the late Herbert Hart, Jenifer Hart, Sandra and Ian Williamson, John and Norma Roberts, Jill Smith, Brian Langille, Malcolm Grant, Fiona Galton-Fenzi, Kate Vaughan-Neil, Laurence Hurst, Brian Gill, Eric Bates, Lee Beckerleg, Joe McCarney, Kristen Erickson, Jennifer Di Toro, Kimberly Crouch, Simon Joscelyne, Jesse Lander, Jonni Penkin, Carla Saint, John Lilly, Richard Barton, Michael McKinley, James Basker, Colin and Sally McColl, and Chisholm and Julie Lyons. Steve Sheppard, Strefan Fauble, and Jonathan Sutton deserve special mention for having read and astutely criticized previous versions of the arguments I present here.

James Harris supervised my work for a term at a crucial stage when officially on leave from University duties, for which I am deeply grateful. He has been a constant source of encouragement since. I am also grateful to him and to Neil MacCormick for their time and interest as examiners of this work as a thesis. Their criticisms exposed more flaws than I care to remember. I hope I have repaid their attentions with the revisions I have made here.

I owe most, of course, to my D.Phil supervisor, Joseph Raz. He was a severe critic of my work, and that was just what I needed. I cherish the fancy that the extremely rough and unpolished thinker he first faced became, through his attentions, something of a respectable scholar. If this book meets the standard of his worst paper I will be pretty pleased with myself.

Since leaving Oxford I have greatly benefited from discussions with Peter Birks, Peter Jaffey, Bernard Rudden, William Swadling, Lionel Smith, and Robert Chambers. Steve Smith provided valuable criticisms of some of the ideas in Chapter 9, and Michael Rosen was kind enough to look at what is now Chapter 11. Stephen Munzer deserves special thanks. His magnanimous willingness to read my work and provide insightful criticisms on several occasions has immensely helped my completion of this project. I must also thank Alain Pottage for inviting me to teach on his novel and stimulating property course at the LSE, and to the students in my classes there on whom I surreptitiously tried out many of these ideas over the last few years.

Needless to say, I am heir to all the criticisms which this work deserves.

My dear wife Elizabeth has borne my recurrent mental and physical absences over the course of this project with more grace and good humour than I deserve and can ever repay.

Finally, this book is dedicated to three people whose assisted and inspired me throughout my education. I shall ever be grateful for their generosity and interest through more years in education than any decent person should seek to spend.

Some passages in chapters 4, 5, and 6, were originally published in (1996) 43 *UCLA Law Review*, 711, under the title 'The "Bundle of Rights" Picture of Property'.

I am grateful to Richard Hart, John Whelan, Michaela Coulthard, and Kate Elliott for moving this through the publication process at OUP; they were understanding, patient, funny and professional. I hope this book justifies their efforts.

Contents

1
Introduction

Property is a bore. It rarely contributes meaningfully to a conversation. It's an annoying old idea that, given half the chance, will sit down beside you and maunder on about its past glory, its veneration by Locke and Blackstone, or its running battles with Marx and Proudhon. Ah, those were the days! Mention something topical though, and property will be at a loss; property suffers from a distinct collapse of self-esteem which attends any identity crisis. And not just any old identity crisis, property will be more than happy to inform you. Property has been on the couch for years now. It's been pulled apart and reassembled so many times it is a wonder it knows its own name.

Whatever *that* designates. 'You see', property will say, 'now I am not even my own idea. I'm just a bundle of other concepts, a mere chimera of an entity. I'm just a quivering, wavering, normative phantasm, without any home, without anything to call my own but an album full of fading and tattered images of vitality and consequence and meaning. I'm depressed.'

Despite an understandable reluctance, we might ask property how all of this happened. Can property not say a few things about itself, which in spite of all its tortures and travails, it knows in its bones to be true? Here, property, have a drink. Let us light your cigarette for you. Now just start with something simple, something we all understand. What sort of company have you been keeping? Come on, no idea is an island. You say your marriage to Gift has broken down? That's terrible. And been spending all your time with that hustler Contract, hanging around in the market place, have you? Well, well, well, that explains a lot.

To say that the idea of property needs a bit of therapy, a course of analysis as it were, may be somewhat fanciful, but it strikes the right note. In a recent, very long paper[1] I argued that while the idea we call 'property' has been with us a long time, it is looking pretty shaky these days, at least in what might be called mainstream Anglo-American legal philosophy. I attributed this to the fact that the generally accepted picture we have of property, that property is a 'bundle of rights', treats the idea of property as a kind of deficient concept, whose persistence in the language is to some extent inexplicable. For as I tried to show there, on the 'bundle of rights' picture, 'property' is not really a useful concept of any kind. It doesn't help judges understand what they're doing when they decide cases, because it doesn't effectively characterize any particular sort of legal relation. Property is pictured as a bundle of different

[1] Penner 1996.

rights, such as the right to possess, the right to use, the right to consume, the right to destroy, the right to manage, the right to give, the right to lend, the right to sell, and so on. Property, it is supposed, is a kind of aggregate or complex composed of more basic elements. One has property when one has some number of these rights, although it has proved exceedingly difficult to say with any certainty whether some rights are essential, or whether a certain critical number are. It is not even clear there is any workable notion of 'enough' rights to make up a property bundle. Hence property's identity crisis.

Nevertheless, I think property can be sorted out so that it may once again make a valuable contribution to society. If the paper I have just referred to constituted the negative project of showing why the prevailing picture of property is wrong, this book is the positive project, my attempt to characterize the idea of property to show how vital this idea is to the way we think about the world in moral and legal terms. The view I would like to defend here is that property is what the average citizen, free of the entanglements of legal philosophy, thinks it is: the right to a thing. Without a doubt that idea will require a lot of elaboration, and there are a number of sticky issues. But as it preserves an identity for the notion of property which the 'bundle' picture discards, it is surely worth the effort. If successful we may be able to say something interesting about it, and property may be able to tell us something interesting about ourselves.

Before outlining how I shall go about that, one preliminary matter, the title of this book, must be addressed. I might have used the term 'concept' instead of the term 'idea'. I use 'idea' because Hegel does, and like Hegel (see Chapter 8) I want to emphasize the fact that property is something which has an existence in the real world. Specifically, property is a practice, a way of dealing with things in which people actually engage. But it is simply a matter of emphasis. The 'concept' of property must refer to the same practice. This book also purports to be about the idea of property *in law*, which might suggest that this is a work of comparative law, in which I assess the way property is conceived and regulated in different legal systems. Not so. What I am exploring here is the idea of property in which it is understood to be part of a broader normative system, a legal system. As I shall explain, it is my view that property is to be understood, in part, by clearly distinguishing it from other normative practices, such as the practice of making binding agreements which the law treats under the heading 'contract'. Looking at the practice of property as it is conceived and dealt with by the legal system is, perhaps, the only way this can fruitfully be done. While there might be a moral practice of property, and while morality may consist of a network of rules, rights, and so on, so that we might speak of a system of moral standards, legal systems are institutionalized and the content of their standards is for the most part explicitly defined. So I suppose the book might have been called 'The Concept of Property in a Legal System'. But I think the present title is catchier.

If we stand back from property for a moment, and consider its society, we see that property has a lot of colleagues. Both morality and legal systems guide our behaviour in a number of different ways. We are counselled not to murder, to keep our agreements, not to interfere with the property of others, and so on. We can take a quite fine-grained approach to these different instructions, but to make sense of them we sort them into categories. One such category is property. This categorization is made explicit in the legal system. We group together a number of different rules, rights, and duties and say they make up the law of property. We do the same with contract, with tort (the law of civil wrongs), with the criminal law, with the law of taxation, and so on. Now, as presently sorted, these legal colleagues rub shoulders quite a lot. For example, the law of theft seems to depend upon the criminal law and the law of property working together, for theft is the criminal taking of property. Similarly, the law of sales involves both contract and property, for sales are agreements to exchange property.

Viewed in this way, property is a creature of its environment, the legal system. We make a mistake if we think we can just wrestle it to the ground, take its measurements and fingerprints, and set it on its way again, satisfied that we have done all we need to understand it. We must be ecologists, and see how it behaves in its environment, interacting with its fellow creatures. But we cannot go too far in the opposite extreme, either. Property is not just its interactions with others. If we are inattentive to the categories themselves, these interactions may make us lose a sense of where property ends and other legal concepts begin.

Now, the reader may accept the general point that a legal system presents us with a number of rights, duties, and rules, so that one has to come up with some kind of defensible systematic overview of the legal material in order to get a reasonable grasp on it, and this will, in practice, probably mean sorting it into categories, each of which can be said to identify a coherent branch of law. But why should we suppose that our overview must result in branches of law that interact with each other? Whence this metaphor of different species interacting in an environment? Even if this is a result of the way that this categorization has so far been managed in legal systems, that may suggest an insufficiently careful development of the categories, not a natural feature of legal material.

This is a crucial matter. Jurists have been at work categorizing the legal material into comprehensible parts for at least 2,000 years, but none, I think, has thought that the purpose was to produce a set of categories which avoided any interactions between the various branches of law they defined. Yet as far as I know it was not until H. L. A. Hart wrote *The Concept of Law* (1961) which Joseph Raz followed with *The Concept of a Legal System* (1970) that anybody thought it worthwhile emphasizing the interactions of laws as an essential element of the way that legal systems actually function. If this interactive aspect is essential, and I shall argue that it is, then any concept which forms part of a complex system of rules, rights, and duties will manifest it. Thus the environmental approach to understanding concepts like property, not to mention contract or wrong or crime, is the proper way of going about it, and that is rather important.

I shall argue that the best way of categorizing the legal material is to arrange it so that it reflects how it serves and protects our interests. An 'interest' analysis sensibly draws the boundaries of the resulting branches of law and illuminates the interactions between the branches of law as well. It is, after all, sensible that the scope of a right or a rule which serves a particular interest we have will be defined, at least at the limit, by the extent or occurrence of that interest. It is also pretty obvious that our different interests interact. I shall defend these views in greater depth in the next two chapters, but it appears natural enough. We generally recognize that we have different kinds of interests, but not an infinite number. We can devise a list of a reasonable number of different interests at a workable level of generality, interests which characterize the motivations for our actions. We can say, for example, we have an interest in survival, in our careers, in our close relations, in our friendships, in aesthetic experience, in education, and so on. In his restatement of natural law, *Natural Law and Natural Rights* (1980), John Finnis does something similar when he claims that there are seven basic goods or values which each properly lived human life should realize.[2] It is clear that these different kinds of interests serve as natural focuses for different areas of law, for these interests will be protected and served by different rules, rights, and duties, according to the nature of the interest in question. It is also clear that these interests, and thus the rules, rights, and duties that concern them, will interact. If I have an interest in deciding how I shall use particular things, i.e. a property interest, but also an interest in making binding agreements, i.e. a contract interest, on some occasions it is likely that I will have an interest in making an agreement about the disposition of a particular thing. I might sell you this word processor.

The categorization of different branches of law and the interactions between them form the subject of the next two chapters, in particular Chapter 3. This preliminary matter it vital for understanding property, not as an isolated moral or political or legal concept, but as a particular piece of a much larger structure. If I can show that it is right to take this perspective, the corollary is that most theorizing about property heretofore has been impoverished because it was unable to situate property in its natural environment, i.e. in a system of rules, rights, and duties. Not only legal philosophers

[2] Finnis 1980, 59-99.

dealing with property but all theorists contemplating the examination of similar concepts should find this result worthy of attention.

Following this process of situating branches of law and the concepts that define them in the larger legal system, I build up a concept of property with the resources extracted. I will have this to say by the end of the book: property is the right to determine how particular things will be used, but this right is not to be perceived as the right to live like a hermit and use things on one's own. Nothing in the legal idea of property counsels a retreat from society, so to own includes the right to share one's property and give it to others. This is explained by the fact that persons are capable of treating the interests of others as their own interests. I therefore claim that people can share interests in each other, typically in cases of friendships and family relationships, but elsewhere as well. In consequence, the ownership of property is intimately connected to giving and sharing. By contrast, property is not wedded to contract in any way, so having a right to property does not entail the right to sell what one owns. There is nothing about the right to property which stands *against* contracts, but contract arises from the recognition of a different interest, the interest in forming agreements with others. The way in which parties to contracts conceive their interests is completely different from the way they conceive them when they make gifts, and so bargains with respect to property do not slip into the ambit of property simply because both gifts and sales involve transfers of property. I spend Chapters 7, 8, and 9 pursuing the way in which property and contract have been mistakenly intertwined for a long time, which has led, in my humble opinion, to an unfortunate misdescription of both. I admit that in the world of property theorizing I am rather alone on this point, yet I fondly hope to change some minds.

I conclude by briefly attending to a much neglected aspect of the nature of property, which is what I consider its true distributional function. Most people, when they think about property and distribution, think about the distributive justice of who owns what. I think this has nothing to do with property. It has a lot to do with the nature of the economy one lives in, whether that economy emphasizes command, or gift, or contract (i.e. markets), but property goes merrily along in any system in which people have the right to determine the use of things. The real distributive question which property raises is this: why do we treat some things of value as objects of property, and deny the same treatment to others? Not a simple question. Perhaps I can whet the reader's interest in the question with an analogy: if we are interested in the concept of beauty, it is not terribly interesting to pursue why some people are beautiful and others ugly; there are any number of well-rehearsed stories about genetic and developmental influences, and different cultural attitudes to beauty. What is more fascinating is why we apply the predicate 'beautiful', or similar terms, to some objects rather than others. Why can a face be beautiful or ugly but the categorical imperative neither, while at the same time we speak of a mathematical proof as elegant? More to the point, perhaps: is anyone not bored by the project of justifying or decrying inequalities of property-ownership?[3] On the other hand, do we not need a fairly systematic investigation of why we do or do not treat our bodies, our body parts, other people, our families, our sexuality, our cultural heritage, and other things besides as objects of property? This distributional aspect of property has, I think, much more to tell us about the kind of people we are. Or rather: at this point the other distributional aspect has told everything it can about the kind of people we are, and it is time we looked to property to tell us something different.

[3] See Becker 1992.

2

The Elements of a Normative System

The first job we have before us is to elaborate in some detail how normative systems, like legal systems, are composed. In particular, in this Chapter I want to show how the elements of a normative system can be explained making reference to the interests they serve.

Norms and Reasons for Action

A norm is a standard which guides behaviour. In the context of morality or law, norms are those standards which guide the behaviour of people in ways which have moral or legal consequence. Probably the most typical example of a legal or moral norm is a rule, for example the rule prohibiting murder. This rule sets a standard which governs our behaviour, by guiding us not to commit murder. Norms interact: as I mentioned in the last chapter, different rules interact with other rules, for example the way the rules of the law of theft interact with the rules of the law of property. Similarly, rights, duties, and powers are norms, and they interact as well. Together with rules they provide the elements of a normative system.

Perhaps the single most important recent contribution to our understanding of norms, and of practical reason in general, is Raz's clear and persuasive explanation of norms in terms of reasons for action.[1] The study of practical reason is that branch of moral philosophy which seeks to explain how we go about deciding to act in day-to-day circumstances. What distinguishes the study of *practical* reason from moral philosophy in general is that practical reason is not concerned with ultimate reasons for action, say the structure of human desires or interests, or general theories of the way in which we ought to behave, such as utilitarianism.[2] When we attend to practical reason we assume that individuals have ultimate reasons for action, whether they be values, interests, or desires. Practical reason is concerned with the structure of reasoning at a more mundane, but nevertheless extremely important, level, that of day-to-day decision-making and action. For example, the study of practical reason is concerned with the way we make sense of decisions like the decision to go to the cinema with a friend because one promised, even if one is now not terribly inclined to do so. How does the

[1] Raz 1990, ch. 1. [2] Ibid. 33.

fact that one promised interact with the fact that one no longer desires to go, so that the decision to go anyway can be regarded as reasonable? Or, to take another example, how do rules influence the decisions we make? If I wish to get home quickly at one in the morning, and I am stopped at a red light, the fact that there is a rule that I may not proceed until the light changes conflicts with my appreciation of the fact that, since there is no other traffic around, there appears to be no reason besides the existence of the rule that I should wait until the light changes. How does the existence of the rule overcome my other rational reasons which weigh in favour of proceeding, so that I remain at the light?

Raz famously introduced the notion of an exclusionary reason to explain how reasons for action operate at different levels. Normally, where one is not subject to any valid rules or other standards which bear directly on a decision, one simply decides what to do on the balance of reasons. If I am deciding what to do of an evening, different considerations will favour my staying at home to read, or going out to visit friends, or going to bed early. What I decide to do will depend on weighing the different reasons for each option. Exclusionary reasons are different. Their characteristic feature is that they are reasons for action that bear on the action of making the decision itself. They function as second-order reasons not to take into account other first-order reasons for acting when making a decision. Exclusionary reasons change the way we make decisions by guiding us not to decide on the balance of first-order reasons, or by altering the balance of first-order reasons in characteristic ways.

For example, having made a promise to buy A a drink is a reason not to take account of other reasons when deciding to act on the promise, such as the fact that one now doesn't feel much like having a drink with A, or that one now has a better use for the money. Having made the promise is like having made a previous binding decision. One is not allowed to re-open the discussion and weigh all the reasons for buying A a drink; all of these reasons have already been considered. The promise excludes our acting on the basis of these reasons; what we act on now is the promise. This example illustrates how exclusionary reasons are also typically first-order reasons for action. The promise stands as a first-order reason for action, since it is a reason for buying A a drink. But it is also a second order reason, because it operates on our decision to buy A a drink by excluding our acting on the basis of other reasons.

This feature of exclusionary reasons accounts for the categorical nature of norms in practical reasoning. The existence of a rule is like the existence of a binding general decision. Rules are not to be understood merely as particularly strong reasons for action—while there are important rules like the rule prohibiting murder, there are also trivial rules such as the more arcane rules of etiquette—but rather as a *kind* of reason which obliges one to exclude acting out of consideration of other reasons simply because of the *kind* of reason it is, i.e. an exclusionary reason the purpose of which is to settle the matter in one way or another. So we see how this distinction between first- and second-order reasons elaborates how practical reason functions in many circumstances where we require a standard of action which is generally to be complied with: it works by shifting decision-making from a weighing of all the considerations to that of a straightforward compliance with an established standard. While this exclusionary function of second-order reasons is the most important one, one occasionally finds second-order reasons which are not exclusionary. An example would be the injunction to those adjudicating child custody cases that considerations of the child's welfare are paramount. This second-order reason influences the decision-making process by formally altering the way in which the normal balancing of reasons might otherwise occur. It works not to exclude reasons, but frames the consideration of reasons by making one kind of reason paramount, so that however the various factors are weighed up no decision will be taken in which the best interests of the child are significantly discounted.[3]

We should not mistake the categorical nature of exclusionary reasons with the idea that the presence of an exclusionary reason is an absolute guide to behaviour, which covers all circumstances. Exclusionary reasons have scope.[4] There is no reason to believe that exclusionary reasons must exclude all first-order reasons. A good example of this is one Raz gives himself, that of an order made by an officer to his inferior.[5] An order is an exclusionary reason for the inferior: he should act on the basis of the order, ignoring the general balance of reasons which determines whether complying with the order is the right thing to do. But if the order was to commit an atrocity, the exclusionary reason would not exclude the first-order reason, that of the sanctity and dignity of human life, which counsels one never to commit an atrocity. That first-order reason does not fall within the exclusionary scope of the officer's order.

The second major contribution that Raz makes to our understanding of practical reason is to show how this first- and second-order reasoning serves our interests. Interests are, along with values and desires, *operative* reasons for action.[6] Operative reasons are things we believe that give us what Raz

[3] Nowhere does Raz actually discuss this kind of second-order reason, which might be called a formal strength-affecting reason; his discussion of strength-affecting considerations refers to the force of reasons in different contexts. Ibid. 45–6. Nevertheless, I do regard it as a true second-order reason, for reliance on this kind of reason gives rise to the typical 'feeling' of unease that occurs when two opposing rational ways of deciding come into conflict: Ibid. 41. There might easily be cases where, on the balance of all the reasons, a child may best be placed with his mother, but where the paramount emphasis on the welfare of the child indicates that the child be placed with the father, and this is an apparent case of just the feeling of unease that deciding on the basis of second-order reasons explains.

[4] Ibid. 40, 46–7.

[5] Ibid. 38, 41–2, 46–7.

[6] Ibid. 33–4.

calls the 'practical critical attitude', the attitude that we ought to do something. In other words, our desires, interests, and values are reasons *for action*. If we desire food, then we have a reason for finding something to eat. Surveying our situation, other facts, such as whether there is a restaurant nearby, will, together with the fact of our desire, provide a complete reason for acting in a particular way, as in going to the restaurant for a meal. While interests and desires are both operative reasons for action, serving one's interests is not the same thing as satisfying one's desires.

The difference between the two is that we define our interests critically. If we have a desire, we just have a desire. When we speak of our interests, however, we manifest a critical attitude to the nature of our well-being, in which we regard some desires as more important, some as legitimate and others not, and so on. We can, of course, shape our own desires and those of others by various means, like education, and we usually participate or require the participation of others in practices like education as a result of deciding what is really in our interests. It is obviously a good thing if our desires conform with our interests. But our interests, unlike our desires, are necessarily related to a critical understanding of values, i.e. of those things which are truly of worth and those which are not. Underlying interests, then, is the existence of a critical practice which generates views about what our interests are, though this does not mean that there is any consensus about the ultimate basis of those interests.

The particular operative reasons we shall be interested in here are our interests, though as I have just stated, because our interests are understood critically, they will be bound up with our appreciation of values. I will not separately discuss values as operative reasons for action. Although they, like interests, are to be distinguished from desires because they arise through the critical appreciation of what is desirable, they may be distinguished from interests. In general, values are not localized to particular individuals; we speak of the value of art, whereas a person has an interest in aesthetic experience. There may be values which cannot be translated into interests, i.e. localized to individuals in this way, but I shall proceed on the consequentialist footing that all values, or at least all values which motivate the norms of a legal system, may be so translated. In other words, values are to be reduced to interests on the footing that something can only be a value if it (positively) contributes to the well-being of people, and is therefore in their interest to realize. The reason we will be interested in interests, as opposed to desires, is that the law's legitimacy rests in part on whether it guides our behaviour critically, i.e. rationally. The law should not be regarded as there to serve our desires, but to serve our interests.

Our interests are served by the way in which reasoning works at first- and second-order levels. The presence of a second-order level of reasoning in which exclusionary reasons do their work allows us better to *conform* to what is in our interests, better, that is, than we should do if we tried directly to *comply* with what is our interests.[7] This idea, while simple, has profound importance. In many cases, we will decide to do what we ought to do, that is, act in accordance with reason and serve our interests, not by weighing up all the reasons that bear on the decision, but by following an established standard which tells us what to do. Traffic rules confine our actions by requiring us not to make all our traffic manœuvres on the basis of our own judgement about what is safe, but rather in accordance with the established standards. We do better by trying not to weigh up all the factors in each case about what is a safe or desirable manœuvre, but rather by simply following the rule. Thus we *conform* better to what is in our interests by acting on the basis of an exclusionary reason like a rule, rather than trying directly to *comply* with the balance of reasons which would indicate what is best in the circumstances. Acting in accord with our interests is the ultimate aim of practical reason. We are not concerned, in the general case, that we do so *because* we have assessed the first-order reasons directly, but only that we achieve this result. Second-order reasons that bear on the reasoning process itself are one immensely powerful way of securing that achievement.

This achievement must often be measured in the long run. We cannot be sure that in every case complying with an exclusionary reason rather than directly balancing the first-order reasons will provide the better result. Consider the rule that promises must be honoured. We often regret particular promises, but we recognize that the peremptory force of promises protects the *practice* of promising. If promises were not binding, if instead people were to re-open their commitments to others and re-weigh all the factors bearing on performance whenever the promise started to bite, then a promise would not represent the kind of valuable commitment it is, and the practice would deteriorate. The rule serves our interests because the practice allows us to commit ourselves to others and to certain courses of action, and being able to make these commitments is valuable.[8]

The upshot of Raz's relation of practical reasoning to interests in this way is of the greatest importance, and the rest of this book, in a sense, relies on its cogency. This analysis provides a crucial standpoint for assessing both the legitimacy of the norms we live by and the very nature of the way that systems of norms function.

The legitimacy point is simpler. It is reasonable to take the view that a system of laws and any of the particular laws or other norms within it are only justified or legitimate to the extent that they serve our interests. There may be other reasons which justify a system of laws: the system may bring us closer to complying with God's will, for example. But all legal systems make the general claim that they serve the interests of those persons subject to

[7] Ibid. 178–86.

[8] See Raz 1977, 1982; Penner forthcoming-b.

them. In the case of a theocratic system, a claim that the system is justified because it produces conformity with God's will must be re-interpreted as a claim that it is in the interests of its subjects that they do conform to God's will, and therefore the system serves their interests. The ultimate defensibility of this view is not my concern here, but its plausibility is obvious.

But perhaps even more importantly, the very functioning of a legal system is revealed by this analysis. If Raz is right to claim that norms are a kind of reason for action, then subjects of a legal system must understand its norms as reasons for action with which they must comply if the system is to function at all. Thus the reasons must themselves be ones which are explicable to them, and interests are the most obvious plausible kind of operative reasons to fill the role; interests are localized to individuals, and they have been refined by critical assessment. In subsequent chapters I shall be trading on the idea that we can understand how property functions by elaborating the way it serves our interests, and I shall also show how we can divide up the total body of laws into branches of law in a principled way by, again, showing how these different branches of law serve different interests that we have. So there is an expositional advantage in relating the characterization of norms to the way they serve our interests.

If Raz is right, however, this way of characterizing the various norms within a legal system is not merely *a* way of doing so, but is the central or truest way of doing so if we want to show how the legal system and its norms actually work and are properly justified. If legal systems work because they provide reasons for action for their subjects, and these reasons *are* the interest of those subjects, or are reasons which are made sense of in relation to those interests, then the various norms of the system are shot through with a kind of interest analysis already. The rules, rights, duties, and so on are comprehensible and comprehended by the officials and subjects of the system on this basis. This is not jurisprudential or theoretical knowledge, just a practical familiarity with the way norms work. Even so, this knowledge frames the task of someone who wishes to elaborate the normative character of particular branches of law, like property, or the legal system as a whole. For to the extent that his concepts and categories he comes up with obscure the way in which those norms serve the interests of the legal subjects, to that extent his categories are defective. If such defective categories begin to permeate the 'theoretical' judicial and legal consciousness, i.e. the conceptual overview judges and lawyers and legislators rely upon when they consider troubling questions or issues, confused and unjust decisions in particular cases, and, worse, confused and unjust laws, will be the result. The confusion arises because the decisions and legislation will not relate to other norms in any coherent way, because their effect on serving and protecting the interests of the legal subjects will be obscured. The injustice follows, not only because confusion which will undoubtedly lead to like cases not being treated alike, but because, severed from the link to interests, the right justificatory relationship is lost. There will be a deficient vocabulary and conceptual apparatus to relate actual norms to the interests they affect.

Using the role of interests to tie up the theoretical analysis of norms with the much more grounded issue of carving up the legal material into substantial categories like property and contract and tort, in order to produce this sort of grand, unified foundation for legal analysis, seems a bit overambitious, if not far-fetched, I know. I propose it with some hesitation. I will shortly put much more flesh on these bones, which should enhance its attractiveness. But the wholly unconvinced reader may at this stage write 'Fat chance!' in the margin, and take it that the expositional advantages alone of the interest analysis of norms are what justify its use in my examination of property. Either way, we must now attend more closely to the way that particular kinds of norms work.

The Normative Character of Rights

The most interesting feature of rights is the way they relate to duties in the course of representing or protecting the interests of the right-holder.[9] Again, the starting point for discussion is the work of Professor Raz.

The essential claim Raz makes is that a person is the bearer of a right when a duty is imposed *in order* to serve or protect *his interest*. Thus it is the rationale behind the imposition of a duty which brings into existence a right—and so not any benefit brought about by the imposition of a duty will make the beneficiary a right-holder. His theory avoids making it an axiom that whenever someone benefits because of a duty, the beneficiary is said to have a right. If a duty not to interfere with others' property were imposed on people generally in order to serve the interests of owners, then owners have rights in respect of their property. If it were imposed instead in the public interest to avoid conflict or bloodshed, then the owners of property would merely be the beneficiaries of the duty without having a right. Furthermore, a right exists only when the reason for imposing the duty on others is a person's *interest*, as opposed to any benefit to him whatsoever.[10] While there are other reasons for imposing duties, the assertion of a right is the assertion that a person's interest is of sufficient weight to ground a duty.[11]

As one would expect, Raz believes that rights serve as reasons in practical reasoning. A right is an interest of sufficient importance to the person who

[9] Understanding rights and their normative character has occupied philosophers for a long time. One particular argument concerns whether rights represent or protect the interests of the right-holders, or whether they represent or protect a choice of a right-holder to take advantage of a particular benefit. I have argued elsewhere that the former 'interest' theory has the better of the argument, and will not review the reasons here. Penner forthcoming-a.

[10] Raz 1984a, 195, 199.

[11] Ibid. 211.

has it to serve as an exclusionary reason guiding the action of others. Thus, for example, since my bodily security is an extremely important interest of mine, this interest serves as an exclusionary reason guiding the behaviour of others. I have a right to bodily security, and others have a duty not to interfere with it. So rights indicate the existence of duties in an interesting fashion. When I have a right, that indicates that *someone else* (or some group of people, or the state) has an exclusionary reason for acting, i.e. a duty. Raz criticizes the view that every right correlates with just one duty which guarantees the enjoyment or possession of the right.[12] Rights correlate with various duties, any one of which may fall short of guaranteeing the right. For example, the right to bodily integrity is served by the duty not to assault others, but compliance with this duty doesn't guarantee that one's right won't be infringed in other ways.[13]

The interest underlying the right serves as the reason for the imposition of the correlative duties, but this does not mean that rights are the same thing as interests. No matter how important the interests of a solitary individual on an isolated planet might be, it would be odd to say that he has rights, for example a right to adequate nutrition. If there are no other persons who can serve as possible duty-owers, there can be no duties on them, and therefore he can have no rights. He has no rights because there is nothing a 'right', being a relational concept relating to the duties of others, can get a grip on. This is not true of interests. The solitary individual can have interests regardless of the presence of others. An interest grounds a duty or duties on others to respect that interest not only when it is of sufficient importance for the individual who has it, but because there is a relation of the right kind between that individual and the duty-ower such that it is appropriate that the latter should have that duty. The justification of rights is in this sense dual: not only is it dependent on a person's having an interest of sufficient importance, but it is also dependent on there being another person (or institution, or group) upon whom it is appropriate to impose the correlative duty or duties. We therefore conceive of rights as imposing duties on a determinate set of duty-holders: either an individual or a group or generally on everyone.[14]

How, then, do rights serve as reasons guiding the behaviour of these ordinary subjects of the law? There is obviously no difficulty in determining how the rights *of others* guide one's behaviour, since these rights correlate

[12] Ibid. 199.

[13] From this point onward I no longer rely on Raz's account of rights. See Penner forthcoming-a.

[14] Some interests, of course, are naturally 'relational', such as the interest in the love and care of one's parents, and thus recognition of the interest as sufficiently important to ground a right will, in a sense, automatically indicate the appropriate duty-ower. But this only confirms the relation between rights and duties, and the distinction between interests and rights. While many interests are not relational, all of the rights to them necessarily are.

with duties one has oneself (assuming that the right in question is one which imposes a duty on one). The harder question is whether rights are normative for the right-holder. Does, for example, the existence of correlative duties on others, which secure or protect the right-holder's interest, guide the right-holder's action?

First of all, there are a number of rights to things or states which do not involve any action at all on the part of the right-holder, and therefore there are no actions which they can guide in a straightforward way. Consider the rights to life and bodily security. These rights name states in which a person finds himself, i.e. alive and secure. Even so, one's actions are guided by whether one has these rights. One will act differently in a society in which one has these rights, especially if they are legal rights, from the way in which one will act in a society where there are no such rights. Presumably, one is simply less likely to come under attack if one has those rights. Without them, one would modify one's behaviour accordingly—carry a gun, perhaps, or stick with one's clan or tribe.

So, in this way, all rights are normative,[15] even rights that do not directly protect actions like the right to freedom of speech. They are normative because their correlative duties alter the situation in which a person may act on the interest the right protects. In this way the existence of rights alters the balance of reasons which contribute to practical decisions.

But rights which are rights to do something, that is, rights which concern the acts of the right-holder, are normative in a much more important way. These are rights to liberties, and many of our most cherished rights, such as the right to freedom of expression, are of this kind. Such rights are normative in the way that permissions are normative. Permissions are normative, but not because they guide a person's behaviour by requiring some decision or act; they guide behaviour by allowing, though not requiring, a person to alter the normal balance of reasons which would apply when he decides how to act,[16] usually by excluding reasons which are actually relevant but sometimes by supplementing them with reasons not normally considered relevant. Permissive rules typically apply to decision-makers who must consider a number of complicated reasons before rendering a decision or exercising discretion. For example, a planning authority in deciding on a particular building application may be permitted to disregard particular goals which have been identified by the authority in creating an overall plan for an area; for example, it may be permitted to disregard traffic implications where the proposed development is in a derelict area crying out for economic activity. Or it may be permitted to supplement the normal reasons, say by taking into

[15] Except the rights of those who are not agents, or not fully agents, such as young children, or animals if animals have rights. We should remember that the rights of children (and foetuses if foetuses have rights) are justified partly on the basis that they will normally become agents.

[16] See Raz 1990, 89–95.

account the nationality of the applicant in deciding whether a large re-development scheme should go ahead. Rights to liberties are explained in the same way. The balance of reasons the agent faces is altered by these rights because, focused upon and justified by the interests of the right-holder, these rights declare that, as far as the law is concerned, the right-holder *may*, i.e. is permitted to, consider only his interests in deciding how to act.[17] We can attribute a similar view to Raz by reviewing his explanation of supererogation.[18] Supererogatory acts are those which are praiseworthy if they are done, but do not attract blame when they are not. For example, it may be regarded as, on the balance of reasons, the best course of action for a person to throw himself on a hand grenade to save the lives of others, but no one is blamed for not taking this supererogatory course of action. The agent is entitled to disregard certain valid and relevant reasons for acting, the particular reason here being the possibility of saving many lives; absent that reason, it is clear that the balance of reasons dictates that one should not throw oneself on a live hand grenade, since it will almost certainly cost one one's life. Rights work in the same way, although they always permit one to discount reasons that regard the interests of others, for rights give pride of place to the right-holder's own interests. Thus, the normative function of rights is to allow the right-holder to exclude from consideration all reasons save his own interests (obviously within bounds established by other rights and duties which are valid within the system). This is what can give demands based on rights a selfish taint, for while rights, if justified, are not truly norms based on selfishness, they are intended to be self-serving from the right-holder's perspective. It should be emphasized that rights, having the normative structure of permissions, do not dictate that, as a right-holder, one *must* exclude all considerations except one's own interests. One is merely entitled to do so.

The Normative Character of Powers

A normative power is the *normative ability or capacity* to change one's own or another's normative position by modifying, creating, or destroying rules, rights, duties, or other powers. While legal powers like the power to enter contracts, the exercise of which alters or creates rights and duties of the

[17] While I have divided rights into two rough categories to reveal their normative influence on right-holders, into rights to states and rights to liberties, this is obviously crude. One also has rights which fall half-way on the normative analysis, such as a right to benefits, as under a contract or from the government—to the extent one has no control over the duties of those who owe the benefits, then one is normatively influenced as when one has the protection of a state: one simply acts taking into account the duties of others; where one has some control over the duty, where one can 'exercise' or 'waive' the right in a real way, the second kind of normative influence, analogous with the permission, operates. See Hart 1982, 174–93.

[18] Ibid. 91–5.

parties to it, or the legislature's power to create laws are often recognized, 'moral' powers are much less discussed. But there are obvious analogues: if we have a moral duty to keep our promises, then when we create that kind of duty when we make a promise we are exercising a moral power to alter the moral situation. Similarly, we may believe that there are moral authorities, like the Church, which can lay down moral rules. The normative character of powers has been well illuminated by Raz,[19] and here I will simply summarize his exposition and make a few further remarks.

The normativity of powers arises because they are created at law for the very purpose of enabling persons to make the normative changes they enable persons to make.[20] '[T]he law itself attaches legal consequences to an action in order to determine the considerations for or against that action on the basis of which the power-holder will decide what to do.'[21]

In other words, capacities are powers if the normative effects of their exercise are designed to enable the power-holder to achieve a particular sort of result, for example to make a contract or a will, to pass a law, or to administer an estate. In this respect, powers are normative, because they guide the choice of the agent by organizing the effects that actions will have so that one may achieve a particular result. They affect the balance of reasons by producing consequences which the law provides just so that the power-holder has reason to exercise the power if it is conferred on him. It therefore goes without saying that powers, like rights, directly refer to interests. For instance, the legal power to enter contracts is recognized because it is in our interest to be able to make binding agreements with others for various purposes such as co-operating with others on a project, or exchanging property. The power to transfer property serves, by giving legal means and recognition to, our interest of giving and sharing our property with others. Powers thus organize the normative consequences of pursuing interests which require the production of normative consequences if these interests are to be properly served.

Powers may be more or less specific, and specific powers are often geared to particular circumstances where other powers are insufficient for the purpose. For example, a person may wish to leave property to his children after his death. While there are many possible ways in which this change of normative consequence, this 'shift of rights', might be attempted, such as giving the property to the children prior to death, or giving it to others with the promise that they will pass it on to his children at death, the law guides acting on this reason by conferring the power to make a will. The existence of the power therefore contributes to the balance of reasons, providing a legally recognized set of consequences for acting in a particular way.

This is why powers cannot simply be reduced to the effects their exercise

[19] See, in particular, Raz 1990, 98–106, and Raz 1980, 224–30.

[20] Raz 1980, 228–9; Raz 1990, 104–6.

[21] Raz 1980, 228.

entails. One must consider the *raison d'être* for a power, the interest underlying its existence in the normative framework. Otherwise one cannot distinguish powers from the capacity to commit crimes or torts. Clearly, we do not regard as a legal power the ability to act negligently, the consequence of doing which is that a legal right arises in the victim to sue for damages. The difference is clear only if we consider the kind of purpose for which the power, but not the mere capacity to alter norms, is recognized. A legal power is created so that individuals can bring about the very changes in rights or duties which the exercise of the power entails. This is not the case with other acts that have legal consequences. The tort of negligence is not a part of the law in order that a person can endow someone with a right to damages. The purpose of the right to damages is to compensate the victim of a tort, and all subjects of the law are under a duty not to commit torts in the first place. While we can imagine some odd scenario in which someone committed a tort for the very reason that he wanted to be bound in law to pay his victim some sum of money in damages, this is not the purpose for which the duty to compensate was created. Understanding powers as distinct norms constitutes a recognition of the critical attitude that legal subjects, or at least law-applying institutions like courts, take to the legal effects which various acts can bring about.[22]

This is the gist of Raz's analysis of powers, but a few further remarks are in order, since they will bear on the analysis of property to come.

In the first place it is essential to distinguish the exercise of a legal power from the exercise of natural powers or capacities, which is protected or served by legal rights or duties. If my scratching my head happens to be protected by my right not to be assaulted, this does not mean that I exercise any legal power when I scratch my head. This is true even where I exercise a liberty where my interest in that liberty actually grounds a right to it, as in the case of the right to freedom of expression. The existence of my right to write political satire does not entail that when I write it, if I am capable of doing so, I am exercising any legal power to write political satire. The exercise *per se* of capacities which are protected by liberties to which we have a right has no normative consequences whatsoever, unless, that is, they otherwise produce legal consequences, say by fulfilling the terms of a contract I have with a publisher. Similarly, simply because the law may in certain circumstances recognize the exercise of other normative powers, such as the power to communicate using language, as constituting also the exercise of a legal power, as when a judge gives his decision or a person enters a contract, this does not in general turn these powers into legal powers.

Secondly, legal powers are the basis for explaining the idea which is incorrectly expressed by the idea of having 'the right to do wrong'. Legal

[22] On this function of the 'critical attitude', see Raz 1980, 151–4, 228.

rights constitute, for the actions they concern, the scope of legally valid activity. If we act within our rights, then we should be immune from adverse legal consequences (always remembering that there can be clashes of rights which will result in conflicts which the law must determine in favour of one right or the other). And the scope of validity cannot without some loss of coherence expand to encompass some measure of invalidity. There are legal rights to liberties which, as we have seen, may protect us in doing things that are, all things considered, wrong, because we are permitted to discount the interests of others. There are, however, no *legal* rights to commit *legal* wrongs. There are only rights to exercise natural powers or legal powers which may be exercised in ways that result in legal wrongs. The idea of power is conceptually distinct from ideas of rightness or validity.

It therefore makes better sense to say that a legislature has the power to pass any bill into law, but that it does not have the right to pass laws which infringe constitutional rights (e.g. the actual formulation 'Congress *shall* make no law respecting'[23] is to be preferred to 'Congress is *unable* to make any law respecting'), for the simple reason that that better depicts what actually occurs, i.e. better describes the legal events. The legislature goes through the same motions to pass an unconstitutional law as a constitutional one, and often the determination of a law's unconstitutionality occurs after many years of enforcement. If we regard the case as one where the legislature passed a law, i.e. exercised its power, but in violation of right, we may treat the history of the law's enforcement as a series of rights violations. If, on the other hand, we regard the scope of validity, i.e. the scope of right, as the scope of the legislature's effective action, then the law never really existed, which makes mysterious, if not inexplicable, the character of the reasons for which the various violations of right occurred.[24] The key to this distinction, which is admittedly a difficult one and which is not regularly recognized in legal discourse, is whether the power of the legislature is curtailed, or whether it is subject to duties in its exercise. The distinction is valid partly because of the nature of rights, since duties correlate with rights, not powers. But more to the point, we recognize a distinction between the absence of jurisdiction and the violation of a right. A constitution may remove an area of jurisdiction from a legislature, and this typically occurs in federal systems where, for example, only the national government may have jurisdiction over the criminal law. But in the case of a constitutional right to freedom of expression, for example, the legislature is not excluded from regulating expression, for example by regulating advertising, thus exercising

[23] US Constitution, First Amendment.

[24] I realize Hart, in explaining the importance of the concept of power-conferring laws, took the opposite view. Hart 1961, 68. On the view I am proposing, a legislature has a duty not to pass unconstitutional laws. The fact that that duty is not made more effective by a remedial rule which compensates those who suffer by the unconstitutional rule does not invalidate the analysis. A legal standard may exist without a sanction for violation.

its powers in the 'expression area'; it is only prohibited from acting in ways that violate the freedom of speech. Bad legislation is measured by whether it was wrong, i.e. violated a right, not by whether it was only purportedly made because in excess of its jurisdiction.

Another example is found in the law of agency. A principal may be bound by the contractual obligations undertaken by his agent even when the agent exceeds his rightful exercise of powers. The agent has a power to deal on behalf of his principal, which he may abuse in violation of right. Or consider the power of a trustee. A trustee has the power to deal with the assets of the trust, as legal owner. He can therefore do things which violate the rights of the beneficiaries, and which exceed his rights as trustee. But he still has the legal power to do them. When he signs the documents which transfer title to trust property it is still an exercise of his power even if in breach of trust; a buyer in good faith who has no idea that the property is trust property keeps it. The distinction is probably most importantly realized in the legal system by the power of courts to decide cases. If a court of appeal holds in the course of rendering a judgment that a previous decision of a lower court (that is, not the one presently under appeal) was wrongly decided, the original litigants in that case are not thereby entitled to treat the decision as a legal wrong to be remedied. The decision, while legally wrong, was made within the scope of the court's power, and it stands. This applies *a fortiori* when a court of appeal refuses to follow one of its own past decisions.

As these examples show, powers permit the law to recognize a version of the idea of 'abuse of rights', without the problems of 'nonsense', 'evasion', or 'devaluation of moral currency' to which that particular formulation can lead.[25]

Contingent Norms

Many norms of a legal system apply only at particular times to particular subjects of the system, unlike the right to life, which applies universally and all the time. For example, rules regarding the paying of income tax apply only to those people who have earned income. In other words, some norms apply only contingently. The clearest framework for understanding the effect of contingency on norms is provided by Hart. Hart addressed only the question of contingent rights, but contingency can be a feature of all kinds of norms.

Hart usefully divided rights into general and special rights.[26] General rights are those we have simply by virtue of our status as human beings, as subjects of the law or morality or whatever normative order we are con-

[25] On this point see Finnis 1971–2, 387–8.

[26] Hart 1984, 83–8.

sidering; standard examples are the rights to life, to vote, to the care of our parents; special rights arise because of particular events that occur in our personal history, such as making a contract, getting run down by a negligent driver, or being elected to Parliament. Special rights are contingent rights. They arise because of some event or human act, not as a matter of course for most individuals simply because they are born or reach full age.[27]

As we have seen, rights protect or serve important interests, and general rights can be justified because these rights secure important interests which all people are regarded as having, such as the interest in life. What kind of interests do special rights serve or protect? Are the rights contingent because the interests are, i.e. do the interests arise, as it were, *ex nihilo* on the occurrence of the event?[28] Or are contingent rights akin to the application of general rights in particular circumstances? In other words, should we regard the right, say, not to be executed without a fair trial as a right which stands on its own, or rather as the application in particular circumstances of the general right to life? The latter view is the better one, because it would not seem possible that particular events alone could generate rights, since particular events do not themselves *generate* interests.

Particular interests, i.e. those which arise only in particular circumstances, are explicable only in light of the more basic, general interests we already have, which do not arise in the course of any individual's personal history. We have a fundamental interest in nourishment, and a fundamental interest in certain types of pleasures, such as the pleasure of eating good food. But no one has an interest in eating a well-prepared dinner of roast lamb that can be understood apart from these more basic interests. Having an interest in nourishment *means* that one will have an interest in eating any particular piece of food nearby when one is hungry. In the same way, my general interest in a fulfilling career will be specified in different ways according to my talents and opportunities. Particular circumstances do not generate interests. Particular circumstances permit the specification of what serving an interest will require. The same can be restated in terms of reasons. Interests are the reasons which underlie norms. Therefore, particular events can generate special, 'operating' reasons (i.e. reasons to do specific

[27] We can be silly about this and say that our right to life and our right to vote depend on the particular events of our birth and our reaching the age of 18, respectively, and in this way show that all the rights we normally consider general are actually special, depending as they do on events like one's birth. But we reason, correctly, that the occurrence of contingent events giving rise to life itself is the precondition or presupposition of having rights at all, and the same is true of rights which arise upon reaching full age, since that makes having the rights of adulthood, like the right to get married or vote, possible. While contingent for any particular individual, reaching adulthood occurs as a matter of course in any normal life. The opposite is the case with rights like contract rights. The very idea of rights under a contract entails that an event that definitely does not happen as a matter of course, i.e. an agreement, has occurred. See Waldron 1988, 109–24.

[28] This is Waldron's view: Waldron 1988, 117–24.

things which operate because of specific circumstances) only because general reasons already apply.[29] Thus special norms arise in particular circumstances because general norms which only contingently apply, apply in those circumstances.

Two particular kinds of events give rise to special norms. The first we have already met, that is the exercise of powers.[30] If I make a contract with you, we now have rights and duties we didn't before. We may also frame this normative change in terms of special rules; the rules created by a contract may be said to govern our behaviour. Contingent norms arise on the occurrence of other events as well. Again, we saw an example in distinguishing acts which, though giving rise to norms, are not the exercise of powers. When I negligently injure you, I fall under a duty to compensate you. Another example is my duty to pay tax when I earn income. Lawyers generally make the distinction by saying that contingent norms of the latter kind *arise by operation of law*.

The contingency of norms explains the notion of 'liability'. In general, a 'liability' refers only to a contingent and *negative* normative change which may occur to us if particular circumstances occur, including the exercise of power. While I am, in a sense, liable to receive the benefit of a contract I enter into, we normally think of liabilities in terms of negative normative effects, so we normally think of our liabilities under a contract in terms of the contractual duties we may have. I am liable to punishment if I commit a crime, liable to taxation if I earn income, and liable to compensate those I wrongfully injure.

The last part of this Chapter deals with a distinction traditionally made between different kinds of right which has in the past very much coloured discussions about the nature of property: the right *in rem*/right *in personam* distinction. In the course of explaining the distinction, I will make the claim that the *in rem*/*in personam* distinction can be used to characterize all norms. Indeed, restricting it to rights has contributed to misunderstanding it.

[29] There is a very broad notion of a contingent right, which would take into account all the possible events which might occur. Thus, a British subject has the 'contingent right' to all the privately-held property in the UK, because any property holder might give him his property. No one, however, believes that such contingencies generate rights. Again, the fact that norms are reasons for action tells us why. No one treats these possibilities as reasons for acting in a particular way, or rather, there is certainly no social recognition of such reasons for acting which would generate norms: no one is expected to treat minute possibilities as exclusionary reasons for acting. The legal notion of certain contingent rights 'vesting' reflects the distinction between mere possibilities and those reasons which, though one may not, in the end, be able to act on them because of contingent circumstance, are regarded as having sufficient importance to guide behaviour. See Campbell 1992, 91; for the case of contingent remainders in land see Burn 1994, 276–80.

[30] The exercise of powers can also give rise of course to general norms, since the courts or legislatures can create general laws.

Norms in rem *and Norms* in personam

A right *in rem* is, roughly, a right in respect of a *res*, a thing. The classic example is a property right. Rights *in rem* are characterized as those rights which bind 'all the world', that is, rights which must be respected by all, or virtually all, of the subjects of the legal system; everybody must refrain from trespassing on my land. In contrast, a right *in personam* is a right in the behaviour of some person, such as the right to the performance of a contract. Rights *in personam* bind only specific individuals; only the other party to the contract has any obligations which correlate to one's contractual rights. While the distinction is quite intuitive, there has been a lot of controversy over the right way to describe it. Much of this controversy can be traced to Hohfeld, whose work is responsible for enthralling a generation of legal scholars with a bad, though appealing, characterization of the distinction.

Hohfeld famously argued that we should understand each right *in rem* as a multitude of more or less identical individual rights, each of which is held by the right *in rem*-holder against one of a very large and indefinite group of persons, essentially all subjects of the legal system.[31] In other words, rights *in rem* are to be conceived of as a myriad of rights *in personam*.

An example shows the implications of Hohfeld's view. Think of property rights in a piece of land, Blackacre.[32] If Hohfeld's description of rights *in rem* is correct, then whenever Blackacre is transferred from one person to another, everyone else in the world exchanges one duty for another. Since rights correlate with duties, when A sells Blackacre to B, all persons who previously had a duty to A now have a duty to B, since B now has the bundle of Blackacre rights. The alternative, and I think better, view is that no one's but A's and B's rights and duties have changed. Every one else maintains exactly the same duty, which is not to interfere with the use and control of Blackacre. It matters not in the least to C, one of the multitude, who owns Blackacre. It matters not one whit to the content of his duty in respect of Blackacre that B now owns it instead of A. Rights are norms, and the content of a norm must consist in its guidance of the behaviour of those subject to it. The duty not to interfere with the property of others is not owner-specific. We do not need to identify the owner in order to understand the content of that duty. Another way of putting this is to say that our duty to respect the property of others is not fragmented into a multitude of specific duties, each of which is owed to each owner in respect of each specific item of property he owns. Having said this, we can understand why Hohfeld's analysis of rights *in rem* is likely to leave much to be desired. Nevertheless, the grip of his general outlook, that the holder of a right *in rem* is the

[31] Hohfeld 1923, 72.

[32] In the common law world, a hypothetical piece of land is generally called 'Blackacre'. Whiteacre, Greenacre, and so on are the creative variations.

beneficiary of a multitude of duties, has been persistent, even among those who recognize that something is wrong with it. Honoré and Campbell may serve as examples.

Honoré argues the common-sense view that some rights can only be understood as rights to things: simply because such rights are protected by claims against individual people does not entail that their basic character is altered.[33] The reference to things is vital. If a thing stands between the right-holder and the duty-ower, then we can see how the normative guidance of the rights and duties can be impersonal. We do not have to frame the duty to respect property as a duty to particular individuals, but as a duty in respect of things. This will, of course, benefit the individual right-holders, but they need not be individually enumerated in order to understand the content of the duty. When the duty is breached, and the individual owner sues the individual trespasser, only then do we have a claim which is properly *in personam*, against a specific individual. But we must bear in mind that this is a secondary, or remedial, right which arises on the breach of the primary one. It is this primary one which we are trying to get to the bottom of here, and the distinction Honoré makes is absolutely on the right track. Yet when Honoré goes about describing the distinction himself he does so in terms that refer only to relations between persons, abandoning entirely the vital reference to 'things'.

Honoré rests the distinction on the idea that some rights are held to correlate to duties which are general, though there are specific exceptions; these are rights *in rem*. Others are generally held of no one, that is, there is generally no corresponding duty imposed on anyone, *except* where specific criteria are met; these are rights *in personam*.[34] In other words, in the case of a right *in rem*, unless a person is specified that person is held under a correlative duty to respect the right (the inclusive implication). In the case of a right *in personam*, unless a person is specified he is not (the exclusive implication). Thus the distinction essentially turns on the implication, either negative or positive, that any given individual will be a duty-ower in respect of the right in question. But Honoré adds that the black-and-white character of the distinction is lost because of the nature of claims that protect rights.[35] Rights *in rem* are *primarily* protected by claims against all others (with exceptions) and rights *in personam* are *primarily* protected by claims against others determined by particular title (specific criteria), but this is not always the case. Because of this, and also because *in rem* misleadingly suggests that such rights relate only to things, he suggest the terminology 'rights . . . to exclude primarily general and primarily particular'. Despite Honoré's starting point, where he insists upon the validity of the right to a thing, he concludes by producing what is essentially a refinement of Hohfeld's model.

[33] Honoré 1960, 463. [34] Ibid. 453–61. [35] Ibid.

Campbell's analysis of rights *in rem* also avoids reference to 'things'. His suggestion is that we must look at the existence of rights *in rem* over time: while it is true that rights *in rem* will generally correlate to duties held by all other subjects of the legal system, what distinguishes these rights is that the corresponding set of duty-owers will increase or decrease over time by operation of law in a non-substitutionally accretive way.[36] 'Non-substitutionally accretive' means that a person may be added to the set of duty-owers without replacing a person who is subtracted. The point is to capture the idea that as the number of subjects of the law fluctuates, so will the number of duty-owers. When a person becomes a subject of the law he will automatically, i.e. by operation of law, be added to the set, and when he leaves he will be subtracted.

It is, however, easy to come up with counter-examples which show that these conditions are not sufficient to distinguish rights *in rem* from rights *in personam*. The right of a state to tax individuals is completely general in most states. Such a right is also 'non-substitutionally accretive', as people come into and leave the class of taxpayers by operation of law. Yet no one regards the right of the state to raise taxes as a right *in rem*. Even if one wants to attempt the argument that the state's right to tax is like a right to the property of its legal subjects, and is in that sense a right *in rem*, a further example secures the point. The right of a state to demand that citizens serve in the defence of their country in time of war is certainly not a right to any kind of thing these subjects have; it is a right to demand their participation in a particular enterprise. It is not a right *in rem*, but it meets the criteria of being general and non-substitutionally accretive.

The problem here is that though they dismiss Hohfeld both Honoré and Campbell are captured by the idea that one should be able to formulate rights *in rem* purely in terms of relations between right-holders and duty-owers; this is a hopeless enterprise. To understand rights *in rem* we must not only discard Hohfeld's dogma that rights are always relations between two persons, but also the idea that a right *in rem* is a simple relation between one person and a set of indefinitely many others.

Rights **in rem** *and 'things'*

Hohfeld was mad for symmetry between rights and duties, and he based his notion of the correlativity of rights to duties on it. A right must have the same content as its corresponding duty; the only difference in content is the opposition in perspective achieved by framing the relation from either end. So B's duty to pay A £10 is a mirror opposite to A's right that B pay him £10. Hohfeld is therefore pretty much bound to describe a right *in rem* as a

[36] Campbell 1992, 87–9.

multitude of rights *in personam*, for only on that model do the contents of the rights show this symmetry with the contents of the duties. A, the owner, has a right that B not interfere with his house, and B has the correlative duty that he, B, not interfere with A's house. No one without a commitment to Hohfeld's views regarding symmetry need define correlativity in this way and, having no such commitment, I shall not. I want, since I think we need, a notion of correlativity which realistically captures the normative guidance which rights *in rem* actually provide; this means we need to explore the concept of a *duty in rem*, a task which as far as I am aware has never been purposely undertaken.

One may visualize the holder of a right *in rem* as standing at the hub of a spoked wheel, with the spokes representing relations to a multitude of duty-owers. Yet one may just as easily visualize the ower of a duty not to interfere with property, i.e. the ower of a duty *in rem*, in exactly the position, at the hub, so to speak, except that the spokes will represent relations to all those who hold property. These are lousy pictures, because a moment's notice will confirm that any trace of a *res*, like a bicycle or a pound note, is missing, which is something of a deficiency if we are trying to explain the normative relation which comprises property. The point, however, is that to conceive of a right *in rem* as a single relation flowing to some vast set of duty-owers, as Honoré and Campbell do, is to hold a quasi-Hohfeldian view of rights *in rem* that makes sense of the right only at the expense of treating the duty-ower as the holder of millions of duties, as many duties as there are property-holders and pieces of property. This is no improvement on Hohfeld. But if we pay attention to the fact that rights and duties *in rem* do not refer to persons, not in the sense that that property is not owned by persons, but in the sense that nothing to do with *any particular individual's personality* is involved in the normative guidance they offer, we may get somewhere.

Consider again A's ownership of Blackacre. Now while property rights and ownership are considered classic examples of rights *in rem*, it is clear that just because property is involved in a right does not mean that it cannot be a right *in personam*. If A owns Blackacre then he may grant any number of rights *in personam* to specific or specifiable people to make use of it, walk across it, and so on. But it matters to A who they are, and it matters to them who A is. It matters to A who they are because he must grant *to* them the licence to use his land. A does not deal with them *through* his property, like any passer-by who can only have an effect on A by somehow engaging Blackacre itself, by stealing some apples or throwing himself into the hedge. A deals *with* them directly *about* Blackacre. It also matters to the grantees who A is. In order to know the content of their licence to use a piece of land, they must know the scope of A's rights: what patch of ground does he actually own, and what is the extent of his rights to it? An occupier may be a mere licensee or leaseholder himself after all. Land or any other property does not usually wear the identity of its owner on its face, though of course it can be sign-posted or marked, and though we observe fences and the like, we know they do not necessarily reflect the boundaries of ownership. These truths are reflected in practice every day. A prospective purchaser, as a matter of course, has personal dealings with a seller (or his solicitor) to ascertain that he is the owner, the title-holder to the property, and thus capable of passing title.

A's relation with everyone else is different. They may never see him, or hear about him, or even know if he has died and been replaced as owner by his younger sister. Their only relationship to him is *through* his property, in the sense that they can affect A only by acting on his property in some way. To them, A is only represented as his property, and what's more, he is not even represented *as A*. He is only represented as 'owner', i.e. his particular identity is completely obscure. This is no relation *in personam* between them and A. It is exactly the same relationship that everyone has to all the property that is not their own. Indeed, in general, it is completely unknown to us whether any given amount of property is owned by one person or by several or many. Owing individuated, separate duties to particular property-owners would presumably require knowing what owners held what property in order to understand what those duties are. But we don't. And that's because our duty is not to trespass on the private property of others. We are under one duty to the plurality of property holders however their property is distributed amongst themselves. It is a simple, single duty, and very easy to comply with.

This duty would be just as easy to comply with if there were just one owner of everything. But that would not be a right *in rem*, for then the duty-owers could conceive of themselves as all owing duties to one person in respect of *his* things. While the duty would have the same content, i.e. not to trespass on property, it would be identified with the single right-holder, as a duty in respect of him, because all duties are at base imposed to benefit persons, and where the beneficiary of a duty can be easily identified, the duty naturally takes on the character of a duty *in personam*. The reason that we conceive of duties *in rem* is that it is wrong to conceive of a duty whose content is exhausted by the way one deals with a thing as a duty expressing a personal relationship; there isn't one. Therefore the idea of rights *in rem* to property *depends* upon there being many owners. If there were only one owner of all the things that were 'property', then he would have a right *in personam* against every other person that they not interfere with his things, and they would each have a single correlative duty *in personam*.

Although we have so far relied on property rights as the example of rights *in rem*, they are generally regarded as applying to more than property rights. Consider the right not to be killed and the right to bodily security. If we are to conceive of these security rights as rights *in rem*, then we must consider the correlative duty as a single duty which is applicable to all others because its content is like the single duty to respect property. We must be satisfied that a single duty *in rem* to respect the lives of others is the appropriate formulation; one duty, not a series of duties to respect the life of A, the duty to respect the life of B, and so on.

We can be thus satisfied, for two reasons. In the first place, the duties which correlate with these security rights apply in respect of all persons by virtue of general knowledge of what a person is and what counts as harm. They are easily conceived as duties 'to avoid harming others' in particular ways. No particular features of any individuals need be ascertained. Of course one generally comes into contact with others more or less individually, but the same is true of the way one walks past a single house or car.

Secondly, these security rights correlate with negative duties, the duties not to act in certain ways. They do not point to duties to do something *for* others, duties whose performance would likely require some more personal dealing with those others, giving rise in turn to a personal relationship which would colour the duty as a duty *in personam*. In these cases rights *in rem* to 'states' such as bodily security correlate with a duty not to interfere with a state of affairs that is an impersonal *status quo*.

So it is plausible to treat the rights not to be killed and to bodily security as rights *in rem*, where the 'thing' that interposes itself between the duty-ower and the right-holder is a state of affairs of non-interference with 'others'.[37] No personalities intervene to raise the possibility of rights *in personam*.

One can of course try to view these rights as special rights *in personam*. Rather than recognizing the duty not to interfere with others as an existing general duty, we can think of it as a general but contingent duty not to interfere with anybody who crosses one's path. This crystallizes into an actual, special duty not to interfere with X when X falls into the ambit of one's potential for causing harm. Taking this approach is just plausible because, unlike people's property holdings, people are naturally individuated into single persons, and so the boundaries of one individual's rights are generally fairly apparent. The individual one takes a swing at is almost certainly the individual whose security rights are in the course of being violated. So while, in general, one cannot determine whom one is benefiting when one goes around not interfering with property, in general, perhaps, this is not the case with security rights. Thus one could conceive of security rights as correlating with duties *in personam* not to harm the individuals one contingently comes across.

I hope this view fails to attract. In order to give rights *in personam* any meaningful content they should have as part of that content some reference

[37] The duty which correlates to security rights is not simply a duty not to interfere with a person's body, the corporeal thing; security rights protect the person, not just his body. For example, the threat of imminent harm characterizes assault, not the actual physical interference with a person's body. So the 'thing' is rightly characterized as the state of non-interference, not the person's body.

to the actions, intentions, or personal histories of the beneficiaries who are the correlative right-holders. Rights *in personam* should apply as relations between individuals where their individuality, i.e. their personality, is relevant to the right.[38] Simply coming across someone, or his or her property for that matter, is insufficient. Otherwise we treat any duty in which some individuals can be identified as its beneficiaries as a duty *in personam*, which makes nonsense of the idea of a duty *in rem*. Furthermore it suggests that whenever one happens actually to know who owns a piece of property the duty not to trespass is transformed from a general duty *in rem* into a duty *in personam*, but it would be insane to allow the determination of whether a right is *in rem* or *in personam* to fluctuate in accordance with closeness of the relationship between particular right-holders and duty-owers. The criterion is whether the duty is in any way specific to particular individuals in terms of its content. The general duties corresponding to the rights to life and bodily security are not. These are rights *in rem*.

'Things', then, whether physical things or states of affairs such as bodily security, mediate between rights *in rem* and duties *in rem*, blocking any content which has to do with the specific individuality of particular persons from entering the right-duty relation. How then, do rights *in rem* correlate with duties *in rem*?

A duty *in rem* is a duty not to interfere with the property of others, or some state to which all others are equally entitled. Thus a person is a holder of a right *in rem* when he benefits from that general duty. The holder of a right *in rem* benefits from the existence of an exclusionary reason, but one which does not apply to him alone. Note that in some sense the correlativity here is not symmetrical. The duty-ower's duty applies to more cases than that of the individual right-holder. That is not a failing, I hasten to add. Rather it makes sense given the way that the reasons work.

The more important result which the analysis shows is that the *in rem/in personam* distinction applies not only to rights, but to all norms. It applies to duties, and it is easy to show how it applies to powers and rules as well. Birks

[38] A lawyer might wish to challenge this view by citing the example of the duty of care in negligence. The content of such a duty is not dependent on any particular reference to the actions, intentions, or personal histories of the beneficiaries, yet the scope of the duty is cut down from all persons to a smaller class, those who might reasonably foreseeably be harmed by the defendant's lack of care. In this way, the duty of care appears to arise contingently and be shaped by the particular circumstances in which the defendant acts. The example, however, is not a convincing one. Restricting the scope of the duty of care in negligence law in this way is a mechanism by which 'but for' causation can be restricted in the application of secondary rules regarding liability for compensation. That is, the defendant's liability to compensate others who suffer by his lack of care is restricted to those individuals whose harms *have actually occurred* and are ones which a reasonable man would foresee as occurring due to the defendant's lack of care. The primary duty, however, identifies no specific class of people. Anyone might, for example, be the parent sent into nervous shock because of his child's death caused by the defendant's negligence.

provides a good example of a power *in rem* which arises in the law of restitution:

If you have obtained my car as the result of misrepresentation or undue influence, the car for the moment is yours. But that *res* in your hands is liable to be revested in me. I for my part have a right *in rem* which for a number of reasons is difficult to name and analyze. It could be said that I have a floating, or uncrystallized, ownership which I bring down on the *res* if I act in time. But it is probably better to say that my right is a 'power *in rem*', a power to change the legal status of the *res* owned by you.[39]

A rule *in rem* is simply a rule which applies to owners or holders of property simply by virtue of their ownership. The rules governing property tax are an example.

Norms *in rem* establish the general, impersonal practices upon which modern societies largely depend. They allow strangers to interact with each other in a rule-governed way, though their dealings are not personal in any significant respect. Grasping this point is absolutely vital to grasping legally recognized practices like property. We must recognize the error of treating a person's participation in the impersonal practice of property, which colours our behaviour from the minute we rise till the minute we go to bed, as a series of personal interactions with others. What we actually do is observe some very general duties about how we should act in respect of things we know or assume to be property. This is not to say that we cannot initiate personal exchanges with an owner, as when we wish to buy his property. But this point only makes sense against the background *in rem* practice which establishes the boundaries between owner and other which provide the issue of the exchange.

The appeal of Hohfeld's view lies in his observation that rights, and we should say norms in general, only operate between persons.[40] Reasons influence the behaviour of people, not things. Therefore we cannot have norms which operate on things as if a thing could be answerable at law. Thus Hohfeld's translation of rights *in rem* into bundles of rights *in personam*, however flawed, seemed a natural way of realizing the point that rights bind people, not things. The concept of exigeability, however, does that job much better. Exigeability is best explained by Birks. Though a right *in personam* will often relate to a thing, or *res*,

'it will be capable of surviving the loss or disappearance of that *res*. For to exact a right *in personam* you have to find the person, not the *res*. If you come under the obligation to give me the cow Daisy,[41] or to let me have the use of your theatre, it will be impossible to infer from the nature of the right . . . that Daisy's disappearance or the destruction of the theatre will discharge my claim. After all I can still find you, and it is still not nonsense for me to maintain that you ought to give me Daisy or to let me have the use of the theatre.

[39] Birks 1985, 66.

[40] Hohfeld 1923, 74–5.

[41] Goode calls this a right *ad rem*. 'An *ad rem* right is a personal right to the transfer or delivery of an asset or to a charge or lien on it': Goode 1991, 222.

By contrast a right *in rem* is one whose exigeability is defined by reference to the existence and location of a thing, the *res* to which it relates. A right *in rem* cannot survive the extinction of its *res*. . . . If you have wrongfully eaten my cake I can say I have a right *in personam* against you that you should pay for a cake which I once owned. But I cannot say in the present tense that there is a cake which I still own. [And] a right *in rem* cannot be exacted from anyone who has not got the *res*. It is nonsense for me to say, 'That's my cake', unless I can identify the cake in the hands of my addressee.[42]

Exigeability explains that while rights and powers *in rem* bind the world, and correlate to duties *in rem* which relate to property in general, not to particular pieces of property, nevertheless when there is a violation of a right *in rem* it is an individual that does it, and so remedial norms like claims to compensation will be personal, i.e. *in personam*. But that fact does not turn powers and rights *in rem* into a different kind of power or right *in personam*, because these powers and right continue to exist only so long as the *res* itself does,[43] and only against those who are in actual violation of the right *in rem*, i.e. wrongfully holding or harming the *res*. The example of property provides the clearest example of exigeability because not only can one harm or damage property, one can also take it, so the right *in rem*-holder may have to hunt down the person violating his right. But the same analysis applies to rights *in rem* to states like bodily security. If someone is in the process of violating one's security rights *in rem*, say by beating one up, one's bodily security is, in a sense, in the assaulter's hands. Once having been attacked, however, the *res*, one's bodily security during the time of the beating, is destroyed. Only a personal right to compensation remains against the assaulter.

This concludes my characterization of norms. The way I have gone about it emphasizes two things in particular. The first is that it seems both natural and important to show how norms serve underlying interests. The second, which has dominated my elaboration of norms *in rem*, is that the influence of norms must be appreciated from a practical standpoint, taking into account the sort of knowledge which those who comply with them are expected, in general, to have. There is no point treating a duty not to trespass on Blackacre as personal if nothing of the personality of the owner need be known or, if it is, it remains utterly irrelevant to understanding and complying with the duty. We can now move on to form an impression of the way that the legal system works through the institution and interaction of these basic elements.[44]

[42] Birks 1985, 49–50.

[43] Or a substitute *res* into which the prior right or power *in rem* is traced.

[44] I have assumed throughout this ch. that it is incorrect to hold that the normative character of rules depends upon their association with a sanction for disobeying them. See Raz 1980, 230–4; Hart 1963b, 720–1.

3

The Individuation of the Law of Property

To say that we are subjects of a *legal system*, or are governed (in part) by a legal system, usually means that our behaviour is guided and constrained by a system of social institutions, such as courts, legislatures, local councils, and enforcement agencies such as the police. But there is another meaning for 'legal system' which frames a particular focus for an inquiry that legal philosophers typically get up to, that is, the systematic body of laws which legal institutions create, interpret, and apply. It is common sense to believe that we are subject to a number of different laws: criminal laws, laws about consumer sales, road traffic laws, laws about citizenship, and so on. But it is also common sense to understand that these laws interact with each other. For example, criminal laws interact with property laws: one can only steal property, and so in order to convict someone of theft we must be sure that a taking of property has been committed, rather than, say, the fraudulent acquisition of a valuable service like hotel accommodation. Tax laws obviously interact with laws about citizenship, property laws, and contract law (since certain contractual transactions are taxed).

But these two common-sense observations give rise to a puzzle. If, as seems true, laws systematically interact in obvious ways, how do we understand the proposition that there is a plurality of laws? Are there actually a number of different laws which in some sense stand alone and are independent of each other? Or is there simply a seamless web, or tangled mess perhaps, of rules, rights, policies, and principles? If we dare to say that there are a certain number of particular laws, what would we give as an example of a single law? It is almost certain that the example we give will be a rule that is (1) subject to particular exceptions, (2) dependant on other legal material for a definition of its salient terms and concepts, and (3) related to particular rules about the legal sanctions or remedies available. Take what looks like a simple, single law, the law forbidding murder. Such a law is framed in statutes in various ways, often as a definition, followed by a direction as to punishment. So, for example, one might find something like: 'culpable homicide is murder where the person who causes the death of a human being means to cause his death. Every one who commits murder is guilty of an indictable offence and shall be sentenced to imprisonment for life.'

How many laws have we here? Have we one law respecting murder, which incorporates the legal rules concerning causation, the legal definition of homicide, the rules about the mental element requirement for criminal liability (*mens rea*), the rules about sentencing, and perhaps even the rules about probation? Or do we have a number of different legal rules, such as a straightforward prohibition against murder, which interacts with other rules about *mens rea*, sentencing, and so on which themselves interact with other legal rules? For example, the rules regarding *mens rea* define in part the prohibition on murder, but they also apply to define the scope of other criminal prohibitions, for example those against theft and assault. What part, then, of that great wealth of legal material, which comprises all the other rules regarding exceptions, definitions, and remedies, is properly considered to make up the law we have cited? Is it possible to disentangle the particular thrust of a particular law in a principled way?

At a different level, we may be concerned with the interaction of various *branches* of law, and the problem arises again. The criminal laws regarding theft depend upon the laws of property and so to understand how to apply the law of theft requires that one understands the law of property. But does this mean that the law of theft *incorporates* the law of property? Should we say that the law of theft and the law of property are really part of one big branch of law? Think of the law dealing with the sale of goods. Such a law clearly relies on rules both about the law of contracts (how contracts are formed, how we deal with breach, misrepresentations, etc.) and the law of property (rules about title, what property counts as 'goods', etc.) How do we decide what constitutes part of the criminal law, part of the law of property, part of contract law, and so on?

We may decide, as have several theorists we shall discuss, that these difficulties indicate that the idea that there are a number of determinate laws or branches of law must be confused. Perhaps we should not think of laws, but rather of 'the law', an amalgam of different rules, policies, and principles which are so completely entwined with each other that, instead of constituting a body of identifiable single laws, they form some kind of amorphous normative guidance system, a *resource* of considerations one might say, which can be drawn upon in different contexts so as to generate a specific legal standard for behaviour in any particular circumstance. If all the so-called 'laws' that make up 'the law' characteristically interact with other 'laws', why should we even be concerned to draw a line around part of the total body of laws and say that this bit is one law, or this bigger fraction one branch of law?

Joseph Raz was the first legal philosopher in this century to give this problem, which can be called the problem of the individuation of laws, any serious attention. (In the last century it troubled Bentham as well.)[1] In *The Concept of a Legal System* Raz argued that in order to understand how the law guides the behaviour of its subjects, it is necessary to understand the way in which laws interact. And in order properly to understand that, it is necessary

[1] See Raz 1980, 71.

to produce some kind of principle defining the scope of a single law: one cannot understand how individual laws interact if one cannot even describe the individual laws that do the interacting. From the perspective of 'general' jurisprudence, the 'individuation of laws' is about the theoretical problem of making sense of our common-sense belief that the law guides us in a number of more or less discrete ways, from prohibiting murder to enabling marriage to levying taxes. Devising 'principles of individuation', that is, the principles according to which one determines the scope of a single law, is a matter of legal philosophy, not a workaday task for lawyers, much less the responsibility of the individual subject of the law. Any lawyer, or his client, is only interested in what 'the law' says about a particular matter. They are not particularly concerned that it is one law or several which dictate what is legally required or legally acceptable behaviour, but only to ascertain what that behaviour is. Legal theorists, on the other hand, try to illuminate how the law works, and if we assume that one important aspect of this is to show how laws form an interdependent system, then they must either come to terms with the problem of the individuation of laws, or suggest reasons why doing so is unnecessary. Important theorists have done both, as we shall see in a few pages.

One approach to the individuation of laws is to show how there are different *types* of laws, and to explain how these interact to make the system function. The most famous division of laws in this way is Hart's. Hart argued that the key to understanding law is to recognize that law is the union of two kinds of rules, primary rules and secondary rules.[2] Roughly, this is the idea that the law is constituted not only by direct rules which govern the behaviour of legal subjects, but also by second-order rules which typically apply to officials, which direct them to apply the rules and also empower them to change the rules and adjudicate conflicts.

The individuation *of the substantive branches* of law like the law of property and the law of contract, however, is important not only to legal theorists, but to lawyers and the subjects of the law they advise. This concerns the identification and justification of broad conceptual categories like tort and contract, by which lawyers sort areas of human endeavour and social conflicts into manageable classes. This project has been going on for centuries, the first great (known) categoriser being the Roman lawyer Gaius; in the common law Blackstone stands as the most influential individuator.[3] The importance of this task is stated by Birks:

[2] Hart 1961, 79.

[3] See Buckland and McNair 1965; Birks 1995. The present branches of the common law were largely created by the great text writers of the 19th century: see Birks 1994; Sugarman 1986. For examples of recent work on the nature and correct boundaries of the major categorical divisions of private common law see Atiyah 1978; Barker 1995; Beatson 1991; Birks 1985, 1990, and 1992b; Burrows 1983; Calabresi and Melamed 1972; Friedmann 1991; Goode 1991; Hedley 1988; Jaffey 1995; McBride 1994; Penner 1993 and 1996; Samuel 1994; Watts 1995.

> [T]he most elementary principle of justice is that like cases should be treated alike, which supposes a stable basis of differentiation. . . . [T]he human brain cannot function in any field, or not in a predictable fashion, without some taxonomy of the relevant data. A defective taxonomy will produce actions and decisions which are open to criticism, but in the absence of a taxonomy decisions can only be intuitive and either good or bad according to the whims of the decider.[4]

Thus in order properly to understand any system of thought or practice is in part to understand the basic categorical distinctions which organize it. In the case of law, the basis of categorisation is not merely of academic interest, for these categorical distinctions daily impinge on the lives of its subjects. If one principal task of the law student is to learn to 'think like a lawyer', a central aspect of that is to learn to characterize situations of social conflict as legal problems in the right way, as a 'tort' problem, or as a problem raising 'property' or 'contractual' issues. To think like a lawyer is, in part, to adopt a particular perspective which divides areas of human interaction and conflict into a limited number of well-known kinds. This in turn results in a conceptual division of the law into various branches.

Not only is individuation of the branches of law necessary, it is of utmost importance that the categories it creates are sound ones. As a theorist, of course, one may sort the laws into any conceptual structure one fancies. An economist, for example, may sort the laws into categories which illuminate whether the law furthers or impedes wealth maximisation. But a legal philosopher does not find a *tabula rasa*, a mere litany of different rules upon which he may impose any old structure. Any existing legal system is worked by lawyers through categories which are already in place, and so the development of the law is shaped by the incumbent categories which inform it. The individual bits of the legal material are there, in part, because they once appeared advantageous or necessary additions to a structure already in place.

Obviously, the law is not static. While the law must, broadly speaking, have one and only one set of canonical categorical divisions of its subject matter if it is to function, these divisions are constantly pressed and disputed by both practising and academic lawyers. Cases in which the appropriate legal analysis is disputed are not infrequent. It matters, for example, whether one can treat confidential information as property, for then copying it may count as an appropriation of property so that one would be liable to conviction for theft. A difficult case of this kind asks: 'What is the nature and scope of this particular branch of law (property), and how does it interact with others (criminal law)?'

The legitimacy of these canonical divisions is also a matter of academic controversy. Nuisance law, the law governing the way in which one person uses his land to the detriment of his neighbours, provides an example.[5] Is the

[4] Birks 1995, 86. [5] See Penner 1993.

law of nuisance principally about the private law duty not to harm one's neighbours, or is it, or should it be, principally a public law matter of regulating competing use-rights in land? In other words, should nuisance be regarded as a matter of tort law, or of planning and zoning law? Or consider whether the law of tort and the law of contract are rightly distinguished as separate branches of law; they may better be perceived as coherent sub-elements of a larger but unified law of obligations. Atiyah in particular has long argued that the division between contract and tort is an artificial one which has obscured legal understanding and development.[6] Moving in a more disintegrating direction, we may feel it appropriate to individuate some branches of law at a finer level than at present. Collins, for example, believes the substantive law covered by the conventional category of contract can only properly be understood once it is fragmented into different types of transaction, each 'governed by its own distinctive standards'.[7] And the matter of individuation also arises in the context of recognizing, or re-recognizing, a branch of law which is to be regarded as independently complete in its own right. Birks's *Introduction to the Law of Restitution* largely consists of an exercise of re-categorization in which he argues that the law of restitution is an independent substantive branch of law which is not to be marginalized as a rag-tag set of rules and actions on the periphery of contract.[8] Understandably, the organization of the legal curriculum around these divisions is also a matter of current controversy.[9]

So we see that, however concerned we are that legal philosophers sort out the individuation of laws at the level of general jurisprudence, individuation of branches of law at the level of substantive law is not merely a philosophical romp. While of important theoretical interest, the categorical divisions of law significantly shape the day-to-day workings of the legal system. It is obvious that the conceptual apparatus which characterises social life in the law, so that some conflicts are dealt with as matters of civil law, some in terms of the criminal law, some are regarded as involving important interests of the state, while some are regarded as conflicts between private individuals, practically shapes the administration of justice.

Finally, and perhaps this is the area where I should hope that paying attention to the individuation of branches of law yields results not only for lawyers but for a wider community of moral and political philosophers who take an interest in property, understanding these categorical divisions should sharpen our sense of the true scope of concepts like 'property'. For not everything that people might discuss under the rubric of 'property' may actually concern property. I shall say further on that the right to make money by entering contracts is not a property right, and that, while taxation and the redistribution of wealth, may, in our society, depend upon the institution of property, the existence of property does not entail any kind of taxation

[6] Atiyah 1978. [7] Collins 1993, 29. [8] Birks 1989. [9] Birks 1992b.

regime or any particular distribution (or maldistribution) of wealth. In short, contract, taxation, and policies concerning the distribution of wealth are not part of the law of property, once its true scope is realized.

What the individuation of laws makes clear is that branches of law like the law of property are situated in a network of legal rules forming a system. Conceptual categories in law, like 'property', are only ever relatively independent from other categories, since the branches of law they give shape to interact in many profound ways. To say this is not to deny the validity of exploring the nature of property in its own right, nor to minimize the coherence and completeness of the notion. It is to point out that attaining an understanding of this coherence and completeness is in large part distinguishing property from other normative concepts which guide our behaviour, often in similar ways.

In making these claims, and addressing the nature of the categorical distinctions we make when we discuss wrongs or property or markets when we engage in political and moral theorizing, I am relying on the learning and genius of lawyers and writers of jurisprudence who over the centuries have incorporated their wisdom in drawing distinctions of just this kind in building systems of law, where these distinctions mattered in the most tangible way: in actual conflicts, upon the judicial and legislative determinations of which the wealth and liberty of the those affected has depended. This learning and theorizing is therefore grounded in 'real' laws.[10] The rules, principles, and other standards the legal system adopts as its own must be ones which its subjects are capable of understanding, and so can actually guide their behaviour. Therefore, if the legal system addresses the nature of property, or of contract, or of harm, in a particular way, that particular way is worth attending to for the simple, yet extremely powerful, reason that that way is constantly subject to the test of practicality. What I hope to show through considering the structure of norms and the structure of the legal system is that 'that particular way' is to address the various interests which the subjects of the law have, and in light of which their day-to-day actions are shaped and make sense. If, then, there is a coherent idea of property in law, its existence is of the greatest importance not only to lawyers, but to any moral or political philosopher interested in the standards societies adopt in their practices of dealing with things.

The rest of this book can in a very real sense be regarded as the individuation of the law, or the branch of law, of property. The goal of the remainder of this Chapter is to examine Raz's principles for individuating laws according to their normative function (which in large part will concern dealing with his critics) and show how they extend to the task of individuating different branches of the law. This task should be tackled, I shall argue, by individuating *branches* of law according to the fundamental interests that a

[10] See Honoré 1987, 69–88.

body of rules, rights, duties and so on serve and protect. For example, the norms of that branch of law we call 'property' should be revealed and characterized in terms of the interest we have in exclusively dealing with things. This scheme of individuation will make clear how the law of property can be a single, complete branch of law, identified by such an interest, and I shall show that it adequately meet Raz's set of criteria for a successful set of individuating principles.

The Individuation of Laws and General Legal Theories

As a particular topic in jurisprudence, individuation has only rarely been addressed since the publication of Raz's *The Concept of a Legal System*. There it was examined out of the concern properly to understand the claims, and hence the validity, of general theories of law, in particular those of Bentham, Kelsen, and Hart.

For Raz, the concept of individuation is primarily important because it forces the legal theorist to appreciate the truth of the thesis that, to understand the law, we must examine not only the structure of a single law, but its relation to other laws. The concept of individuation forces us to consider the way in which laws are parts of legal systems.[11] What makes any particular scheme of individuation valid is the extent to which it forms part of an accurate description of the way a legal system, as a social institution, operates, by revealing the way in which various laws function and interact with other laws. The operation of a legal system is primarily normative: laws work together to serve as reasons for action for those who are subject to them. Consequently, Raz individuates laws according to their normative function. He provides criteria for identifying single complete laws from the mass of legal material, which will be of certain normative types, such as duty-imposing or power-conferring rules.[12] In that book Raz was interested in the general jurisprudential question of the nature of law, not any specific branch of law like property. The point in referring to his thoughts on individuation is to see how one significant branch of law can be identified as a proper object of attention in its own right, without at the same time obscuring its status as an element of the total system.

Individuation by Norm-type

There are several distinct elements to Raz's position regarding the individuation of laws which must be appreciated separately. The first, bedrock point, is that the law exists as a system of individual laws. This bedrock point has

[11] Raz 1980, 121, 140–2, 145–7, 168–70. [12] Ibid. 181–3, 224–5.

been challenged by Harris, and by Dworkin to some extent. The second element of his position is that there are different types of law evincing different normative functions. Raz holds that each legal system will evince laws of at least two types, duty-imposing and power-conferring laws, both of which are norms.[13] This point has also been challenged by Harris, who believes all laws can be reduced to one normative type, duty-imposing (or duty-excepting) laws. It has also been challenged by Honoré, who argues that a great many laws are not norms. Thirdly, laws must have a structure which makes sense of the fact that they exist in a system which is capable of providing normative guidance. This element of his position has been challenged both by Dworkin and by Honoré. Since I shall justify my own position regarding the individuation of a branch of law, such as property, on the basis of Raz's position, I must deal with these fundamental objections in turn.

The Very Possibility of Individuation

Someone who believes in the possibility of individuation believes that the law somehow already exists in particular packages, which are just waiting to be identified. Individuation presumes that the organization of law, according to normative function for instance, is a feature of the law itself. This structure is something that is inherent in the legal material. Individuation presumes that the legal material will break along pre-existing fracture lines, so to speak.

Since someone who believes that laws can be individuated is committed to the idea that the law in force already exists as particular laws, he believes that a plurality of laws, rules, rights, duties, and so on, can be described within a range of variation for any legal system. Together these laws will be the total law in force in the legal system. The range of variation in description exists because it is a matter of judgement whether various bits of the legal material form single complete laws or parts of laws, e.g. whether one counts an exception to a rule as part of that rule or as a second distinct rule. Regardless of this range of variation, however, these laws and parts of laws will relate to each other in determinate ways. A theorist cannot arrange them or group them on any principle he likes.

It seems clear that Raz holds some version of this view. Although Raz claims no more than that individuation is a problem for legal philosophy in coming to the right account of the nature of a legal system, he must (I would argue) also believe that the individuation of laws along normative lines must inhere in the system itself, since he believes that the legal system is primarily an institution which actually guides the behaviour of legal subjects. It is submitted that the foundational critical insight of *The Concept of a Legal*

[13] Ibid. 147–66.

System is to take seriously the idea that we think of the mass of legal material in terms of individual laws that have constancy, laws which are not reconceived each time we look at the legal material with a particular purpose in mind.

Harris disputes the possibility of individuating laws in general, and of individuating laws according to normative function in particular. Harris's two arguments against the former are, if I understand them correctly, both about the way we commonly think of the law, and about what individuation would entail as a practical matter for the legal theorist.

Harris regards the law as 'the well of legislative source-materials' into which we may dip 'conceptually shaped buckets of many kinds'[14]. The legal system is a 'normative field of meaning'.[15] Laws do not exist 'in advance of any demand for information', but rather, the legal material is organized by the legal professional into units for particular inquiries.

'[R]ules are to systems, not as members are to a club, but as slices are to a cake'.[16] In other words, a rule has no existence apart from our decision to describe one part of the normative system as one. For his purposes, Harris organizes all legal content in the form of duty-imposing and duty-excepting laws,[17] because he holds that 'it is the primary function of legal science to give information about existing legal duties.'[18] Harris argues that his particular 'reductionist' approach is plausible because '[w]hatever the syntactic structure of sentences contained in legislative source-materials, the products of legislation are always reducible to a unique logical form, that of the conditioned imperative or permission.'[19] He accepts that his reductionist principles will not be suitable for the organization of legal material for many legal purposes—we are not always concerned with amassing all the legal material necessary to state in full the content of a legal duty, but nor for that matter, *pace* Raz, are we always concerned to emphasize the normative aspect of various rules.[20]

As I have said, Harris has, I think, two arguments about the possibility of individuating laws. In the first place, he argues that we think of the law as a normative field of meaning, not already broken up into units. This is why we can take different approaches to structuring rules for particular purposes. Secondly, he argues that someone who thinks individuating laws is possible is committed to the possibility at least of a massive reorganization of the legal material without reference to any particular inquiry about what the law on any point happens to be.[21]

It is difficult to assess the claim that we think of the law as a field of normative meaning. Most people, I would suspect, think that the legal system is indeed made up of a set of laws, that is, a number of particular legal instructions of some kind, even though they could not name a fraction of

[14] Harris 1979, 92. [15] Ibid. 89. [16] Ibid. 84. [17] Ibid. 92–106.
[18] Ibid. 93. [19] Ibid. [20] Ibid. 95. [21] Ibid. 101.

them. But Harris argues that most people associate 'law' with 'statute'; since there is certainly no one-to-one correspondence between laws and statutes, this 'common sense' of the plurality of laws is merely a sense of the plurality of forms in which the law exists.[22]

This seems wrong to me. The way we think of 'laws' as well as of 'the law' is important because it provides important evidence that we do not simply conceive of the law as a smear of normative force, or a field of normative meaning, or a well of legislative source materials that can be decanted into any size or shape of vessel. I should say that laymen understand the common-sense proposition that the law deals with different aspects of human life by addressing particular laws to particular act-situations. The laws addressing these different act-situations are individuable, that is, they can be described in a determinate fashion as relatively static, existing legal instructions, because the act-situations they address, for example the act-situation of one person killing another, are conceived by people in general as a relatively static categorical kind or way of acting. Not even the most benighted layman is going to accept the view that the difference between the law of murder and the law of corporate taxation is simply a matter of what one makes of the total body of law in these two different situations. We rightly understand that the law has already provided specific instructions to deal with these two cases. In this respect, at least, we cannot slice up the normative material any way we want; the slices are pre-cut. Or, at least, the legal material is criss-crossed with ready-to-tear perforated lines.

Harris presents a picture of law in which legal normativity exists somehow *as such*, without applying to any particular part of human experience. Yet we do not (and ought not) conceive of the law as being an injunction like 'act according to the golden rule', or 'act with justice on all occasions', or even 'act in the most justifiable way given this set of principles'. We expect the law to have made up its mind and to guide us in determinate fashion in respect of typical act-situations where concerns about what it means to do unto others as you would have them do unto you, or to act with justice, arise. This fact should not be confused with the fact that the law presents itself in many different documents.

Though this issue cannot be explored in any depth here, Harris's view also seems to adopt a very contentious characterization of the way the rules work.[23] For Harris, the legal material serves as a resource for making a statement about what the law requires; it acts as a basis for *reflection* about what a legal subject ought to do in any particular situation. But it would seem that we do not need to reflect or engage in any process of judgement, to know what the law requires in any number of standard cases. The law is already determined. Just because a rule applies to an infinite

[22] Harris, in personal conversation with the author, 20 Nov. 1991.
[23] See Penner 1996, 789–93.

number of particular circumstances does not mean that each application of a rule is a matter of conscious judgement. Those who understand the rules realize that they just apply in standard cases. Harris's view also seems to deny, or at least minimizes, the fact that lawyers bring to any particular situation a conceptual apparatus already in place. On his view they seem to treat every particular situation as somehow *sui generis*, i.e. as a novel matter which does not reveal to them any obvious relevant similarities to other commonplace situations.

Some similar view also seems to motivate Dworkin when he says that individuating laws makes about as much sense as (is as 'mad' as) asking how many facts there are in a geology book.[24] He seems to treat the genuine problem of identifying the determinate rules which make up the law as the insane exercise of counting the number of true descriptions one could make about what the law requires. But the point is that the law addresses a limited number of *types* of act-situation, and in consequence tells us to act or refrain from acting in a limited number of ways. That it is of course true that one may murder someone in an infinite number of ways does not mean we have an infinite number of laws against murder. Abstract norms like rules and rights, by their very nature, apply to an infinite number of possible act-situations. Though the number of rule-applications may be infinite, it does not follow that there is an infinite number of rules. The example of the geology textbook is, in fact, instructive. Such a book is organized into chapters dealing with a number of different topics. So are course syllabuses. Students do regard what they are supposed to know to take their examinations as having a determinate quantity, or scope, and this is determined, in part, by the *number* of specific topics addressed.

Similarly, one may break up the law into various branches, and study these in more or less *depth*: one may consider more or fewer applications of the rules, as in legal cases in which the rules have been considered, and one can consider secondary sources, texts, articles and the like, as well. But the notion of their being a 'quantity' of law, in the sense of a number of types of act-situations addressed, or in the case of a geology book, a number of topics considered, is not 'mad' at all and is in fact the way that the scope of such material is commonly gauged.

For these reasons, one should be persuaded that we do conceive of the law as already made up of particular laws with substantial characterizations, not merely ephemeral, formal or descriptive ones.

Harris's second point really relies on the first. Someone who believes individuation is possible is not committed to a massive reorganization of the legal material prior to having a particular purpose in mind, because he does not believe that enquiring into the legal material involves reorganizing it at all, at least when the inquiry is one about how the normative guidance of the

[24] Dworkin 1987, 75–6.

law is to work in some situation, as for example when a lawyer is advising a client. Now it is true that if one wants to describe the law with a different purpose in mind, for example to reveal its historical origin, or from a sociological perspective, those descriptive purposes will impose different structures on the legal material, reorganizing it. However, someone who believes that laws can be individuated believes that these different structures are a matter of *formal* description, or reorganization if you will, not substantial organization of the legal material into different laws. Harris's argument is akin to arguing that because a painter of pastoral scenes, a veterinarian, and a butcher will describe a cow differently, regarding it as they do from different perspectives and with different purposes in mind, that they will in turn have substantially altered what a cow is. The legal system with its individual laws is not just a descriptive concept, but an institution with a determinate social function and historical existence. It exists as much as a cow does, and in that respect is equally immune from transformation by description.

Individuation on Normative Grounds

Both Harris and Honoré argue specifically against individuating laws on normative grounds. I shall deal with Harris's arguments first.

The efficacy of *normative* individuating principles depends on the possibility of breaking down legal material into 'packages which are convenient for the purpose of giving . . . reasons [for action]'.[25] But, argues Harris, normativity, i.e. the concept of guiding behaviour, is a hopelessly indeterminate organizing principle because one is faced with the task of assessing each rule in terms of whose action it is supposed to guide:

> If [the class of subjects] include[s] draughtsmen, then any phrase in any statute would have to count as one law, since it could be contained in a sentence reading: '(phrase) is the law', which could be given as a reason for a draughtsman taking a particular course.

The point of this example is as follows: any particular phrase in any statute can be a reason for someone acting in a particular way: a draughtsman might be bound or inclined to adopt the statutory language in preparing a legal document, for example. Thus each phrase in a statute, and indeed probably many single words, counts as an individual law, since each guides behaviour on a particular occasion.

This view is mistaken. As a legal professional, a draughtsman stands in a different position to the legal material than would the ordinary subject of the law. This does not alter the normative character of the law. When a legal professional drafts contracts or offers advice to his clients he is not guided by

[25] Harris 1979, 101.

laws in the same way as they are. In these circumstances he is not considering or altering his own position as a subject of the law, but advising others with respect to theirs. Of course the law must be a source of information for constructing an opinion. That the law, and the forms in which it is authoritatively expressed such as statutes, provides practical guidance for the draughtsman's own actions should not blind us to the purpose of the exercise, which is to provide for the client just that normative guidance that is the general function of the law.

Secondly, however, this view does not discriminate between the intended effects of laws and whatever side-effects they might have. As our discussion of the normativity of rights and powers showed, simply because someone might commit a tort in order to bind himself to pay damages does not mean that we should think of committing torts as exercising legal powers. Any version of normativity which considers 'guidance of behaviour' in any way whatsoever is simply uninformative about norms. On this view, placing a door on one side of a courthouse (surely an element of the legal institution) creates a legal norm, since doing so guides the behaviour of those who wish to enter the building.

Honoré's objection to individuation on normative grounds is different. Even if we accept that normativity is the principle defining characteristic of a system of laws, Honoré argues that

> The social function of laws need not determine either their formulation or their technical function as elements in a legal system; and if laws are framed in a way which does not reflect their social function, we had better try to find out if there is some reason why they do not. The normative tail must not be allowed to wag the descriptive dog.[26]

So, as a methodological matter it seems we should begin with description, avoiding reference to our preconceptions about 'the ideology and social functions of legal systems'.[27]

Honoré argues that if we individuate laws along the lines that lawyers do, paying attention to 'real' laws, we find that very few laws are normative in any straightforward way. This has great significance. Honoré holds that the non-normative formulation of the great mass of laws supports the view that there are non-legal rules or principles that actually provide the normative force of law.[28] We are therefore to conclude that Raz has put the cart before the horse by individuating laws to reflect the normativity of law; this prevents him from realizing the truth about the law, i.e. that its normativity is socially, not legally based.

Honoré's description of laws, however, evinces little more than a prejudice against normative formulation: in the first place, according to him, we ought not to individuate laws primarily as norms referring to act-situations because

[26] Honoré 1987, 74. [27] Ibid. 69. [28] Ibid. 87–8, 110 ff.

act-situational rules such as the definition of murder are characteristically not norms; '[t]hey are what they purport to be: definitions of offences.'[29] Raz convincingly answers this by pointing out that it is part of the meaning of 'offence' that it should not be committed, and hence, the definition of murder as an offence is indeed a norm.[30] On this point Raz must surely be right. Honoré's argument can only mean that if there is not a deontic linguistic operator like 'ought' or 'must' in the formulation of the law, it cannot be a norm. On this view even the formulation '[e]veryone has a duty to take care not to harm others' is not a norm, because a stickler could argue that there must be some underlying norm that we comply with duties.

Honoré's second argument is that

> individuating laws according to act-situations or treating the non-act-situational laws as appendages to the act-situational laws . . . obscures the place of general principles in the operation of the system. It hides the fact that there are laws which protect people by invalidating transactions rather than by regulating the conduct of citizens. It reintroduces . . . a form of reductionism which . . . holds that, while not all laws are norms, the non-normative ones are significant only by virtue of their relationship to the normative ones. This is an elliptical way of asserting that the only social function of law is to guide the conduct of citizens; whereas, we have seen, at least some laws protect people's interests by invalidating transactions which would otherwise prejudice them. In so far as these laws operate as norms at all, they do so as norms directed to officials and others who are committed to teaching, enforcing, and advising about the legal system. They operate as norms only at a secondary level.[31]

For Honoré, principles like the *mens rea* rule are more important, generally speaking, than act-situational rules; such principles are more important because they 'generate legal change, progress, and adaptation.'[32]

Honoré makes two claims in the quoted passage. The first is that general principles are not act-situational. This is false. Principles are just more general, and therefore apply to a broader range of act-situations.[33] Even something as general as '[n]o man should profit from his own wrong' applies to act situations, viz. all those situations in which a man may profit from his doing wrong. The doctrines of *mens rea* and consideration, both examples of Honoré's, apply to crimes and the formation of contracts, respectively, both of which are act-situations.

The second, more important, claim is that to the extent that a law invalidates people's transactions, it is a norm directed to officials, and thus only operates as a norm at one remove from the subjects of the laws. The problem with this claim is that, for it to have force, a significant number of laws must be primarily addressed to officials, and Honoré misjudges the number of principles of law that are really of this character.

[29] Ibid. 76. [30] Raz 1980, 225 fn. 5. [31] Honoré 1987, 77.
[32] Ibid. 73. [33] See also Raz 1972, 838–9.

Principles of sentencing, or rules regarding the assessment of damages in civil cases may be of this type, for the intended normative impact of the law on its subjects is that they comply with their duties not to commit crimes or torts in the first place. Yet, as we have seen, on Honoré's analysis the law creating the offence of murder is not a norm but merely a definition, and since legal definitions will have more impact on judges than on the general subjects of the law, one might conclude that the law concerning murder is primarily addressed to officials. But of course, to say the law creating the offence of murder is primarily addressed to officials because its statutory form is definitional is absurd. The same may be said of many laws permitting officials to invalidate transactions. The rules regarding the invalidation of contracts for duress or undue influence certainly *ought* to guide the behaviour of the general subjects of the law, and almost certainly will if they are given to taking legal advice. That many legal rules are expressed as directions to officials reflects, for the most part, the fact that officials are charged with applying the law in courts. This does not mean that outside the courts there is really very little law, or that the law has very little normative impact. Drawing the entire normative significance of a law from the formal attributes of its expression is not a sound method. Honoré's claim that Raz's principles of individuation misdescribe many important laws fails for there is no good reason to believe that most legal norms, or the most important ones, are addressed primarily to officials.

The different normative character of powers, rights, and duties makes it important not to reduce them all to only one of the three if we are to appreciate the different ways in which the law works to guide behaviour. Raz convincingly argues that both Bentham's and Kelsen's general theories of law suffer for the fact that they each try to cast every law as a norm of a single kind.[34] The issue of whether any accurate general theory of law will reflect or entail or be compatible with the individuation of laws on normative grounds cannot be decided here. It is submitted, however, that Raz's main reason for making this claim is persuasive:

> Law is universally regarded as a special social method of regulating human behaviour by guiding it in various ways and directions. This function of the law, which is also the main reason for learning and referring to the law, should be made clear in its theoretical analysis.[35]

Limitations on the Structure of Laws

Both Honoré and Dworkin argue that Raz's concept of individuation does not properly account for the fact that legal material is not only made up of

[34] Raz 1980, 70–120. [35] Ibid. 145.

rules, but also includes principles. We have dealt above with Honoré's position regarding principles, so it remains to discuss Dworkin's.

Dworkin argues that it is not necessary to commit oneself to a particular scheme of individuation to advance general jurisprudential arguments. In his famous first attempt to refute legal positivism, he argues that a social rule of recognition cannot properly account for the way that legal principles are used in judicial decision-making.[36] For the purpose of this argument he makes a 'logical' distinction between 'rules' and 'principles'. He argues that legal rules do not conflict, or rather that while they may conflict, 'conflicts' between two rules are always dealt with as legal emergencies which are solved by treating one rule as carving out an exception to the other; the point is that the absence of conflict means that rules can be applied more or less mechanically. Principles, on the other hand, do conflict, and have different weights.[37]

Raz criticises Dworkin's argument on a number of points,[38] but the criticism relevant here is that he claims that Dworkin's distinction between rules and principles commits him to a doctrine of individuation that is clearly unacceptable. Now, as we have seen, Dworkin opposes the very possibility of individuation, on the ground that conceiving of the entire body of law as a set of determinate laws is like conceiving of a field of knowledge as a determinate number of facts. Assuming, however, that laws can be individuated, Raz argues that Dworkin's distinction between rules and principles entails an unacceptable implication.

Raz argues that while the law tends to have in place methods of solving conflicts of rules, this does not detract from the point that they conflict.[39] Dworkin's scheme of non-conflicting rules, rules that would each include all their exceptions that have been carved out to accommodate other rules, would require a set of laws each of which would be immensely complex, so complex in fact, that they could not be mechanically applied in the way Dworkin believes.[40] Dworkin's response to this is essentially just a reassertion of his view that the individuation of laws is merely a matter of exposition of the legal material; the distinction between rules and principles does not concern breaking up the legal material, but is employed to describe the way judges *use* standards in decision-making and, indeed, he admits that stated that way, it is sometimes impossible to tell whether a standard is a rule or a principle—it all turns on how they are treated in decision-making.[41] Therefore, he concludes, '[t]he distinction between rules and principles remains untouched.'[42] It is worth noticing that this essentially amounts to a version of Harris's 'law as a normative field of meaning' thesis; here the resources of law can be shaped into standards of different kinds by different judges on different occasions.

[36] Dworkin 1987, ch. 2, especially 39-41. [37] Ibid. 24-5, 72-4. [38] Raz 1972.
[39] Ibid. 829, 842. [40] Ibid. 831–2. [41] Dworkin 1987, 27. [42] Ibid. 76.

But I think Dworkin misunderstands Raz's criticism, thinking that Raz is either making an argument (i) that Dworkin's distinction between rules and principles is merely poor exposition, so Raz does not grasp what he means when he says rules do not conflict,[43] or (ii) that he is committing himself to an ontological position about what one law is, and Dworkin maintains that he is not.[44] But Raz's criticism, if I understand it properly, is as follows: Dworkin's theory is supposed to correspond to reality in the way it depicts how lawyers and judges deal differently with rules and principles; this has certain theoretical consequences, in the same way that someone's arguing that all rules of law can be reduced to the commands of a sovereign has theoretical consequences. The particular theoretical consequence Raz points out is a commitment to a concept of a rule which does not correspond to the way anyone thinks of a rule, that is, as an immensely complex yet at the same time mechanically appliable unit. This is not, therefore, merely a problem of exposition for Dworkin.

This is as much as I will say on the subject of the individuation of laws and general jurisprudence. I hope that I have achieved my ambition of showing (1) that the individuation of laws is a sensible project, and (2) that the criticisms which have been levelled at it, far from being conclusive, are pretty much misconceived.

Interests, Act-situations, and Laws

Laws should be individuated on the basis of act-situations. The reason for this is that law is practical, and therefore guides *behaviour*, voluntary human acts. But act-situations need to be grouped according to a principle, and the claim that I now make, which essentially underpins the rest of this book, is that the categorical divisions of law reflect the individuation of act-situations according to the fundamental human interests at stake. These interests are those recognized by law as of sufficient importance to generate norms in the legal system.

It goes without saying that act-situations, as generic types of acts, do not identify themselves. *We* identify them. We can do this in any number of ways. We could identify act situations in terms of how they affect the maximization of wealth. We could identify them on the basis of their illustration of principles of physics. When we categorize act-situations for the purpose of making them the subject of legal norms, however, we do so in terms of how they affect our fundamental interests.

This theory of individuation does not follow Raz's in that it does not replicate his individuation only on the lines of normative function, in terms

[43] Ibid. 73–4. [44] Ibid. 74–8.

of duty-imposing laws, power-conferring laws, etc. However, it does equally well reflect the normative functions of the law: indeed, it better reflects their normativity. Individuating laws in this way groups together all the duties and powers, rights and permissions, which relate to the fundamental interest or interaction of fundamental interests that are the basic operative reasons for action recognized by the law.

What truly counts as a interest that we have, much less a fundamental one, is clearly a very difficult subject, and I have no intention of developing a theory of interests here. What I shall do now is provide an outline of the interests in property and contract, both of which will be a particular focus of the rest of the book. The reason for doing this here is that having these examples before our eyes here helps show how interests can serve as a basis for individuating branches of law.

The Interest in Property

The interest in property is the interest in exclusively determining the use of things. The precise meanings of 'exclusively', 'determining the use of', and 'things' all have to be elaborated. But first we should remind ourselves that our subject is the *interest* we have in the use of things. We have a critically considered reason for wishing to engage the world of things outside us, in particular the material resources of the world. Not only is occupying some patch of the earth and drawing on its resources for food, shelter, and so on necessary for life itself, much of what humans do culturally depends upon forming our physical environment in ways that appeal to us. There are, of course, ways of dealing with things which serve our interests in no way whatever. Certain, unfortunately realized, architectural fancies spring to mind. But the freedom to determine the use of things is an interest of ours in part because of the freedom it provides to shape our lives. If we believe in any fairly robust interest in autonomy, then the interest in determining the use of things is in part an interest in trying to achieve different goals.[45] And we cannot reduce this interest merely to our interest in those determinations of use that turn out actually to be valuable. Our interests in exclusively determining the use of things may serve our interests even if we burn the roast or squander our money on a terrible holiday. We can benefit from our failures as well as our successes.

The interest in property is an interest in *exclusively* determining the use of things. This should not be regarded as a requirement that an owner or owners must use things on their own, nor that there cannot be co-ownership of property by a few or many people. The claim is that a right to a thing is a property right only to the extent that some others are excluded from the

[45] See Raz 1986, 407–12.

determination of its use. While people speak of 'common ownership' or 'collective ownership',[46] these can be regarded as ownership only through surreptitiously relying on some notion of exclusion. In the former, though individuals each have equal rights of access to the common property, at the minimum they have the right to exclude others while they are actually using it, if only to the extent that one commoner's cow excludes other cattle from the patch of pasture it is presently grazing.[47] It is clear also that those outside the common ownership are excluded altogether. In 'collective ownership', the use is socially determined, that is determined by some mechanism which is intended to reflect the determination of people in general on how the thing in question is to be used. But this is still exclusive: *individuals* are excluded from the determination of the use of the property, although the system is usually justified on the basis that collective determination of use serves their interests better than would a system of private property.

To 'determine the use of things' does not mean that one may decide upon any use one fancies, and insist that that use be made of the property, drawing upon any other people, institutions, and resources that are around. Owning a piano does not mean that one has the right to demand piano lessons just because playing it is the use one would wish to make of it. The right to property is, in Berlin's terms,[48] a negative liberty. It is a freedom from constraint, not the provision of a means to act. One's determination of the use of a thing is served only to the extent that freedom from the interference of others does so.

The question of what 'things' are proper items of property is a very difficult one, which will be tackled in Chapters 5 and 6. It is enough to say two things here. One, property may be tangible, like material objects, or intangible, like a copyright. Two, as a first approximation, what distinguishes things that can be objects of property from things that cannot turns on whether the thing in question is a (legally recognized) person, or is significantly connected to the individual personality of a person, like one's kidneys are; these things cannot be property, but everything else can.

The interest in property is incorporated into the structure of legal norms at two levels, as a general right and as specific rights. We have special rights to those items of property we own. Here the law protects our particular interest in the specific items of property we have and, recalling the discussion of rights *in rem* in the last chapter, we see that these special rights *in rem* correlate to a general duty *in rem* upon all others not to interfere with property. This idea of property will be developed in the next chapter. But we also have a general interest in all property, not only because we might, as the result of a transfer, own anything, but because we have an interest in the

[46] See, e.g. Waldron 1988, 37–46.
[47] See the discussion of use and exclusion in the next ch.
[48] Berlin 1969, 118–72.

practice of property itself. This is framed in terms of a general contingent right to participate in the practice by acquiring special rights to specific items of property according to the well-recognized modes of the practice, principally gift and contractual transfer.

The Interest in Contract

One of the central themes of the chapters to follow is that our understanding of property has been marred by a consistent failure to appreciate its distinction from the realm of contract. I think it has harmed our understanding of contract as well, but that is another story. In order to provide a basis for this point, I am going to define, roughly, the interest in contract. It is obviously not part of my purpose to explore this interest in anything like the same detail, but the essential features require elaboration. The interest in contract is the interest in forming co-operative relationships by making bargain agreements, that is, agreements in which each party provides a quid pro quo, which in common law is called 'consideration', for the benefit he is to receive under the contract. Contracts, then, are exchanges. Not all co-operative agreements between people are of this kind.[49] I can make an agreement with my wife to take a holiday in Edinburgh this summer, which will give rise to obligations between us, but it is not a bargain. We are not exchanging benefits, but deciding on a mutual project which will serve our joint interests. I can make an agreement with my daughter to give her £50 to buy the clothes she needs for school. This is not a bargain either. It is an agreement giving rise to obligations—I must give her the money and she must spend it on clothes for school—but this agreement crystallizes a pre-existing obligation that I have to provide for her, an obligation I had already but which is general and unspecified until I make this agreement. (I could of course have decided how to meet this obligation unilaterally, but being a child of the 60s I want us to agree about it.)

We have a general contingent interest in entering the practice of making contracts, and have a power to do so. The power is reciprocally linked to a general contingent liability to comply with those obligations we undertake by, or those changes in our rights (e.g. the relinquishing of title to property) which result from, entering contracts. Thus we bind ourselves as we bind others when we enter a contract. The exercise of this power may obviously result in the creation of special rights and obligations under the agreement.

It is worthwhile noting here that the practice of making and carrying out contracts, which essentially constitutes the market, may be regarded as in the interests of more than the individual contracting parties. The state may take an interest in the functioning of the market, and may regulate the

[49] See Penner forthcoming-b; Raz 1977, 1982.

practice of contracting by imposing duties such as the duty not to advertise falsely, or by creating laws regarding anti-competitive behaviour.

Individuation by Interest

The rest of this book constitutes an attempt to elaborate and defend a characterization of the legal idea of 'property' through the elaboration of the interest in property and its difference from the interest in contract. Roughly, then, the reader can expect a sustained elaboration of the different norms, different rights, rules, duties, and powers which together compose a coherent body of law, that branch of law which is called 'property'. By focusing on the exclusion and use of 'things', a term of art yet to be explained, I hope to do just that. The discussion of norms *in rem* and the right to 'things' in the last chapter is a taste of what is to come, although particular kinds of property like land and so on will receive attention in detail. What I must do here is to make persuasive the claim that understanding the particular branches of law within a legal system depends on understanding that these branches reflect a legal characterization of what is in our interests, or what interests we have. (Note that stating it that way almost makes the case, for it seems to be almost common sense that a normative institution like law can only produce meaningful instructions when these are organized to guide the actions of its subjects in situations in which they understand that their interests are at stake.)

In the first place, to repeat the point I made in the last chapter, if we find Raz's explanation of practical reason convincing, individuating laws in a way which reveals how they relate to our interests is individuating laws in a way which reflects how these norms actually function. Thus understood, the individuation scheme proposed is not simply any old take on the categorical division of laws which might attract our philosophical fancy; it is a scheme which captures the way in which particular laws in the legal system actually have an existence in directing the practices of the subjects of the legal system; it captures, in other words, the actual life of these laws. Objections to it must be dealt with in the same way as Raz did with those critics such as Honoré who wished to know why the 'normative tail should wag the descriptive dog'. The answer is simply that the law is a normative institution.

Secondly, it should not be difficult to swallow the idea that we do have interests which are socially defined as the result of critical reflection, or that such interests when appreciated at an appropriate level of generality may define a branch of law; these are the interests I call 'fundamental', and I mean no more by 'fundamental' than that. The characterization of these interests need not be ultimately defensible, and certainly we do not need general agreement on their ultimate rationale or justification in order for them to be recognized as practical operative reasons.[50] Thus we would be wrong to assume that fundamental interests necessarily reflect intrinsic values we all recognize. Consider healthcare. We can conceive of the interest as intrinsic: it is valuable in its own right to be healthy. Alternatively we may regard our life in bodies as a matter of circumstance with which we have to learn to cope. Healthcare is a means of preserving our capabilities to do what is intrinsically valuable and, on this view, healthiness for its own sake, without regard to the projects that a healthy body enables us to pursue, is mere fetishism. On this view healthcare is an instrumental interest. The same debate can occur in regard to the ultimate justification of our interest in not being harmed or wronged, or an interest in making binding agreements. Whether we treat these things as part of the good life (security from pain or injury, the formation of valuable relationships), or as means which we cannot avoid if we are to live the good life (security from the disablement pain and injury cause, functioning markets) is a matter of valuation on which persons may never universally concur. The idea is not that the ultimate justification of fundamental interests is uncontroversial and foreclosed from reassessment. It is rather that fundamental interests represent a point of agreement beyond which controversy begins. Note that the fact that we are able to disagree about their nature does not mean that we can alter what our fundamental interests are. Whether we perceive the value of our bodies to be intrinsic or instrumental does not mean that we can decide to do without them.

It is often the case that the law recognizes a fundamental interest long after it has recognized more specific interests which it is afterwards seen to entail. This is almost characteristic of the development of legal rights at common law. Because judges are presented with particular fact situations, not general hypotheticals, it is to be expected that many of the norms that are first recognized will be no more than partial recognitions of more general norms underpinned by correspondingly general interests; only later when a sufficient number of these partial recognitions are embodied in the case law will a court feel justified in elaborating a more general norm which reveals the fundamental underlying interest.

It is plausible to accept that we believe ourselves to have a plurality of different generic interests. The common law story just described may suggest that the process of partial recognition developing into a more coherent, more general one should continue to the inevitable point that all rights and duties are mere manifestations of some general overwhelming fundamental interest, such as an interest in autonomy, or liberty, or happiness. Perhaps, but I am not holding my breath. It seems pretty natural to believe that we have a number of different interests. No bill of rights, for example, guarantees only one right, like a right to autonomy (though it would be an

[50] See Raz 1984a, 208–10.

interesting experiment), and the very idea of conceiving all interests as mere manifestations of an interest in autonomy or some such general interest may be wrong-headed in principle. Perhaps the reason we recognize the various interests we do is partly that there are irreducibly different values which any person would wish to secure for himself, along the lines of John Finnis's list of basic goods, for example.[51]

It is tempting to think that all branches of law can be individuated on the basis of fundamental rights, rather than fundamental interests. It is hardly to be doubted that we have a plurality of rights, that many rights are framed at something like the right level of generality (viz. those found in bills of rights), and rights tend to name the very interest at stake, as in the right to freedom of expression, or the right to property. I have no objection to this in principle in the case of many branches of law, but one must be careful. While we may be able to frame every existing branch of law in terms of a fundamental right, every recognized right which we may think is 'fundamental' in some sense does not frame a branch of law. For example, just because there is a right to freedom of religion does not mean we have a well recognized branch of religion law. It all depends on whether the interest the right frames is one which has been adopted by the system as one which organizes a category of norms. It may well be the case that there is a true branch of law, 'constitutional civil rights law' we might call it; but that branch of law might reflect and be primarily shaped by an interest we have in the right sort of relationship with the state, not the interests the individual civil rights protect, across which it merely generalizes as points where the state would unjustly interfere with us. Furthermore, bodies of law are to be understood not only in terms of rights, but also according to other norms. Bodies of law arise because of the analysis of act-situations by lawyers. Some of these analyses frame the underlying interests predominantly in terms of duties, some in terms of powers, and some in terms of rights. There is no reason to suppose that the analytical understanding of act-situations, and thus the analytical description of the interests which make these act-situations fit objects of legal attention, must be done in terms of rights. Particular norms or groups of norms within a branch of law may largely be defined in terms of powers or duties and should not be reduced to other norms, even if they all relate to the same interest. Powers, rights, and duties are granted on the basis of a different kind of consideration of the way interests should be served. For example, the formation of contracts is best understood in terms of the legal recognition of a power to make binding agreements, whereas, once formed, issues of breach and damages can probably be framed equally well in terms of the parties' rights or duties under the contract.

The rights approach will simply not work in all cases, however, because it is plausible, and certainly conceivable, that there are some fundamental

[51] Finnis 1980, chs. III and IV.

interests that we have that do not generate rights at all, but only duties.[52] These 'interests of self-conception' are the interests which are emphasized in duty-based as opposed to right-based perspectives on morality,[53] although duty-based perspectives are not normally elaborated in terms of interests. The form of the elaboration goes like this: we have an interest in living up to our fundamental ideal conceptions of ourselves as good, or admirable, or loyal, or brave, or just, or, in the broadest terms, as truly human. Securing these interests cannot involve rights against others, except perhaps for the right not to be morally corrupted or deprived of access to one's culture. Securing these interests can only be achieved by recognizing a duty to act in accordance with the self-conception.

Generally, the duties which arise from these interests are moral, not legal, duties, such as the duty to respect art, to honour one's parents and country, to act with kindness. Such duties are only exceptionally made legal duties. But the criminal law provides an opportunity for the legalization of one of them. The duty of self-conception not to act viciously or maliciously coincides nicely with the right of others not to be harmed (with its *correlative* duty not to harm others), since acting maliciously or viciously implies attempting to harm or actually harming others. Briefly and roughly, it is plausible to claim that the criminal law is at least partly justified by a duty of self-conception because the criminal law *punishes* offenders. If the criminal law was merely in place to protect the right not to be harmed, 'punishment' would have to be regarded merely as a matter of deterrence, as a means of ensuring, in the long run, that the fewest right-holders were harmed. On the other hand, if punishment is regarded in the retributive tradition, the punishment is what the offender *deserves*. His sentence has nothing to do with preventing harm to right-holders or with compensating them, but is rather what he deserves for breaching the duty not to harm others *maliciously*. He is punished for failing in a serious and tangible way to live up to what is regarded as a minimal standard of human behaviour.[54]

The claim, then, is that, regardless of whether a particular branch of law appears to be best characterized at a normative level in terms of a general right, duty, or power, a basic or fundamental interest can be revealed to underlie that branch of law. Whether the general norm of the branch of law is best understood as a right, duty, or power depends on the way in which the

[52] Of course they generate rights in the truistic sense that, in the same normative system, having a duty to x implies the right to x.

[53] On this distinction see Dworkin 1987, 168–77; Raz 1986a, ch. 8.

[54] This characterization of interests of self-conception as giving rise to duties does not mean right-generating interests cannot also contribute to our self-conception, but they do so in a different way. Consider the right of freedom of expression and the right to bodily security. The right of freedom of expression is a right that others not interfere with one's expression. Expression can be regarded as a fundamentally important experience for humans, and extremely important instrumentally for the achievement of other values. Nevertheless, it is not generally perceived to be our duty to express ourselves. This analysis applies *mutatis*

interest is most properly served through standards addressed to the subjects of the law; that is, what kind of norm is most suitable for guiding their behaviour in order to serve the interest.

Interactions Within and Between Branches of Law

One aspect of individuating branches of law, rather than individual norms, is that there will be a relation between the branch of law itself and the norms that it comprises, for example in the way that the rules of title form part of the law of property. A useful distinction can be made here between the rules of a branch of law, and that branch of law itself. Lawyers generally distinguish between legal rules and laws. We speak of the '*rules* of contract', not the '*laws* of contract'; we speak of the '*law* of contract'. This distinction tends to be made in all areas of law, in the rules of the law of tort, in the rules of criminal law, in the rules of civil procedure, and so on.

Within a single branch of law, the rules show various complex connections. All of the different kinds of norms we saw in the last chapter may appear within the branch of law. Yet, at the same time, these interacting norms do seemed to be tied together into a whole. None of the rules of contract can be properly understood without some familiarity with the whole of the law of contract. Students, of course, have a layman's understanding of contract, and this is vitally helpful to them in the early days of a course. But because the rules of contract must be understood as a whole, there is no natural starting point. In England, for example, the study of contract law usually begins with the topic of offer and acceptance. In North America, conversely, it was fashionable in recent years to consider damages first, to show how the expectation measure of damages[55] distinguishes contract from tort. Students must just start where they start and slowly the whole body of

mutandis to powers like the power to make binding contracts. This would appear to be true even of rights like the right to bodily security; while bodily security would appear almost an essential part of a properly conceived human life, again we do not think of it as our duty to make sure that our bodies are always secure from harm. Indeed, doing things that genuinely risk their bodies is often the hallmark of what some people consider a fulfilling life. This does not mean that the right to bodily security is not essential to leading a life which matches up to our conception of the good life. The difference between the right and duty versions of these interests of self-conception is that the right version frames the interest as one of being free and able to act so as to experience various human values, the experience of which will naturally contribute to our self-conception. The rights enable, but do not require, us to take advantage of life's opportunities to create a fulfilling human life. Duties of self-conception, on the other hand, are either duties actually to experience those values, which generally are not enforced by law, or duties to avoid pursuing experiences which are either not of value or are positively harmful, which more than occasionally are.

[55] i.e., a damages award measured by the plaintiff's expected profit under the contract, rather than his loss through relying on it.

the material comes to make sense. This is true of all branches of law. To use a phrase of Wittgenstein's, light dawns gradually over the whole.[56]

Not all single complete laws reflect one fundamental interest. There is no necessary one-to-one correspondence of fundamental interests to laws. This is so because our interests interact, giving particular meaning to particular types of act-situations. For example, we have a fundamental interest in not being harmed by others. We have an interest in life and an interest in bodily security and an interest in property. As I have argued above, the interest of self-conception we have in not acting maliciously to harm others seems to underlie the criminal law, and thus the right and duty of the state to punish. These private interests work together with this state interest giving rise to (amongst others) the law of murder, assault, and theft.

This example also illustrates that the same act can be the subject of different laws in the way it is characterized according to interests. Many crimes are also torts. The law of tort is not concerned with malice[57] as the criminal law is; this suggests that the criminal law reflects a further interest than does the law of torts, and I have suggested that an interest in self-conception, i.e. in not acting with malice, is that further interest.

The example of the law of theft illustrates another important principle of this individuation scheme. Single, complete laws may contain other single, complete laws, as the criminal law contains the laws of theft and murder, because these laws, or branches of laws, are complete in different ways. This does not mean that single, complete laws can be infinitely subdivided. If that were true, this would not be a scheme of individuation at all. The laws may only be subdivided on the basis of fundamental interests. When various combinations of fundamental interests are found to be affected coincidentally by a particular kind of act-situation, and thus reciprocally such a combination defines a particular act-situation in normative terms, a different branch of law may arise. Thus single, complete laws may be nested within others, and so individuating laws on this scheme means that there will be more single, complete laws than fundamental interests.

Finally, some so-called branches of law depend on no level or focus of analysis which fits within the general scheme at all. In principle one may write a book or teach a course about the way the law deals with any aspect of life that strikes one's fancy. Professor Honoré's book, *Sex Law*,[58] serves as an example of this legal genre. But however important it may be, our interest in sex does not, I think, form the focus of a legal analysis which reflects the reality of the law's normative guidance in any way.[59] The same can be said

[56] L. Wittgenstein, *On Certainty* (G. E. M. Anscombe and G. H. Von Wright (eds.); trans. Denis Paul and G. E. M. Anscombe (Oxford, Basil Blackwell, 1979), para. 141.

[57] Except in exceptional cases, where the issue of exemplary damages arises.

[58] London, Duckworth, 1978.

[59] Cf. Birks 1985, 73–4.

for all those single purpose books aimed at layman in particular businesses or situations in life, 'law for medical practitioners' or a 'teen-ager's guide to law'. By attending to interests, then, we get not only a scheme for individuating branches of law, but also a basis for assessing whether some body of legal norms, which may be coherently organized for some purpose or other, is truly to be regarded as a real branch of law. We are counselled to ask—what conceivable interest draws these norms together, and is it plausibly one which the law uses to draw meaningful categorical distinctions about the act-situations it governs?

Proving the Scheme

I now propose to subject the individuation of branches of law by interests to the tests for an acceptable scheme which Raz proposes, and it will pass. But the proof of the scheme does not truly lie in that, for Raz's criteria test the acceptability of a scheme which underpins a theory of the nature of law, not a theory about the actual character of substantive branches of the law. It is important that the scheme passes because it makes the individuation of a branch of law a plausible one, plausible because it does not suggest an incoherent idea of a legal system. But that should not convince us that I am right to say that generic interests underpin branches of law. The only thing that will convince us of that is the exploration of different interests and the legal norms which they purport to organize and justify, and see if there is a fit. And this must be done for every branch of law. I shall only do that for property, though I will say a lot about contract too.

We should expect the individuation of branches of law that arises from the scheme to be conservative, reproducing the categories of private law, including the law of property, pretty much as they are found in Western legal systems. I regard this as an advantage, for if the legal system is comprehensible as a system of workable norms, these interests should already be reflected in the categories of law. An interest analysis that would radically reorganize the branches of law would suggest either that understanding the interests at stake is not an essential aspect of normative function, and I have said enough about that, I hope, to make swallowing it unpalatable, or that we have, for centuries as it were, misunderstood our true interests, and hence the norms we live by are truly lousy. Some I am sure will find this tempting, but I should like to point out that we are considering pretty basic interests here, like the interest in determining the use of things, the interest in not being harmed, and so on. Surely one must waver at the thought that a shiny new legal system willing extensively to displace this characterization of our basic interests has bright prospects for success. This point is not to be mistaken for a related one. Anyone looking at private law will recognize that the division into tort, contract, property, and restitution does not produce four species in the same genus. While we might claim that tort, contract, and restitution all fit into the same genus, that is, obligations, property is left outside, for property is usually regarded as establishing a *kind* of right which might become the *object* of obligations. A theorist might well think that we should distribute the norms of property amongst other branches of law, the same way that other rights, like the right to labour or the right to bodily security are only to be found in the law of contract or tort. Or one might do the reverse, and outline a series of constitutive rights or assets, and deal with the way they become subjects of tortious, contractual, or restitutionary obligations.[60] Each way might appear preferable to the *status quo*. I am not so sure. It seems to me at least plausible that 'it was mine' (property), 'but we agreed' (contract), and 'he harmed me' (tort), are reasonable and workable ways of practically capturing our interests and so defining categorical act-situations out of the maelstrom of human interaction. What we might sacrifice in terms of intellectually satisfying system might be more than compensated by the practical gains afforded by a widespread appreciation of the gist of the categories.[61]

The Role of Interests in the Development of the Law

The claim I have been advancing here is that the individuation of laws depends on our understanding of the different reasons for the laws that we have, and that these reasons are interests. So in order to understand legal norms we must be familiar with the interests underlying them. Most of the time we are not pressed to articulate those interests, but in hard cases we often do.[62] We rarely have to shift to the most general statement of an area

[60] Hedley 1988; see also McBride 1994, who reorganizes the map of private law purely in terms of generic duties.

[61] I have not a proposed a simple phrasal description for restitution, since I am not sure there is one which delivers the gist of the category in the way that the ones in the text do for contract, tort, and property. As a result, I am also less convinced that restitution is a stand-alone branch of law like the others, but that is another story. The argument in the text is not affected.

[62] By 'hard cases' I mean those which concern the meaning of a rule, i.e. those 'hard cases' which have engaged the likes of Hart, Dworkin, and Raz. There are of course other hard cases, which arise not because the meaning of various rules is in issue, but because the body of law has rules which are actually legally incompatible, where, in other words, the law is in a mess. It cannot be argued that the latter are reducible to the former on the view that it is always possible to devise some theory of an area of the law which will make all the rules and decisions compatible, for that would be to ignore the plausibility requirement. If all lawyers think one of two cases simply must be overruled in order to straighten out an area of the law, i.e. no theory of distinguishing one, or minimizing its effect is plausible, then this is not a 'hard case' of the kind favoured by jurisprudes.

of law[63] to articulate what someone familiar with the law will understand to be the correct character of a norm, since most particular questions of law concern fitting a case within the body of more or less particular norms which are justified, or nested, within an area of law carved out by the general interest.

The general claim that common law courts recognize interests is the claim that interests are those justificatory bases of legal norms that courts recognize. Interests are not recognized as norms themselves, as are rights or rules, and so on; they are recognized as the most basic *reasons* for which laws ought to be instituted. Thus understood, the recognition of interests, I claim, is like the recognition of various policies or principles. The recognition of interests thus forms part of the customary practices which make up what Hart calls the 'rule of recognition',[64] the practice by which judges treat particular standards as legal norms. Of course, many areas of law are not subject to judicial legislation, being administered by various tribunals and agencies, and so recourse to basic interests as guides to the development of the law is often effectively prohibited.

As our perception of our interests changes, the individuation of laws will change. For example, environmental law, if it was conceived as such at all, might once have been considered part of the law of nuisance, as a matter of private legal relations between individuals. As the collective interest in the environment has been recognized, environmental law is now regarded as the law pertaining to the right of the state to control pollution and development, and the duties of individuals, corporations, and other bodies not to harm the environment.

Raz's Criteria for a Scheme of Individuation

The proposed individuation of laws resembles in many ways the organization of subjects in the syllabus of a course in law. The law of contract, for example, constitutes one 'law', or one 'branch of law', reflecting the interest in making binding agreements. The law of taxation reflects the interest of a state in raising revenue. I pick the last example intentionally. The interest of the state in raising revenue is not normally the sort of 'fundamental' interest that immediately springs to mind. One of the benefits of this individuation scheme is that it helps us identify those interests a legal system treats as basic, basic in the sense of organizing a coherent branch of law. Of course, simply because a legal system identifies certain interests does not mean that

[63] *M'Alister (or Donoghue)* v. *Stevenson* [1932] AC 562 (HL) *per* Lord Atkin, is a famous example, where the scope of the duty in negligence law was determined in reference to the question 'who is my neighbour?'

[64] Hart 1961, 92–3, ch.VI.

it is justified in doing so. But to the extent that the law already recognizes some plurality of interests as an essential aspect of its normative functioning, any scheme which individuates branches of law on the basis of interests must to a large extent deal with the law as it finds it.

Raz has proposed in several writings desiderata for the individuation of laws.

> [W]e should adopt a doctrine of individuation which keeps laws to a manageable size, avoids repetition, minimizes the need to refer to a great variety of statutes and cases as the sources of a single law, and does not deviate unnecessarily from the (admittedly hazy) common sense notion of a law.[65]

Other desirable features of an individuation scheme are conceptual simplicity, that the laws be self-contained, that every act-situation is the core of a single law, and that the individuating scheme should make clear important connections between various parts of the legal system.[66]

It is submitted that the individuation of branches of law according to the interests at stake meets these criteria adequately. Respecting manageable size and repetition: the very fact that the individuation of laws here proposed corresponds in large part to the way the law is taught argues for its being presented manageably and without undue repetition. Over the decades the teaching of law has been developed precisely to present the law in a manageable way. Furthermore, the practice of law tends to divide along the same lines. Most lawyers specialize in one or a few branches of the law. This again suggests that the individuation proposed meets the criterion of organizational efficiency.

'Minimizing the need to refer to a great many cases and statutes as the sources of a single law' seems to be met in that the law is collected along the lines of the proposed individuation in texts, treatises, digests, and encyclopaedias. Indeed, the fact that the profession and the legal academy have seen the need to organize the law in this fashion suggests that, in the absence of these tools, reference to a great variety of statutes and cases *would* be essential to understanding a single branch of law. But the individuation of the laws proposed both meets and rejects this criterion. It meets it because the lawyers organize the material in a way which does prevent reference to myriad sources. But it does not accord with what seems to be the premiss of the criterion, which is that sentence-length statements of what the law is in cases and statutes are to be viewed as somehow indicative of the way laws are really understood.

In regard to conceptual simplicity, Raz writes:

> A law should be conceptually simple; it should have a relatively simple structure, easily grasped, and its meaning should be relatively easily understood. Understanding the meaning of a Kelsenite law is a task equal to understanding a legal

[65] Raz 1972, 832. [66] Raz 1980, 143–5.

textbook, and indeed, they are of roughly the same length. The structure and meaning of a norm like 'Do not steal' are much easier to understand.[67]

We should be wary of pursuing conceptual simplicity where it does not exist. The law of contract may be presented in what appears to be a conceptually simple formulation, essentially reflecting the fundamental right to make binding agreements. There is no problem with that. But the law of contract is not itself simple. It is fairly complex, though this is not to be overstated. The distinction between rules, i.e. the component parts of a branch of law, and complete individual branches of law which I have proposed is an attempt to combine conceptual simplicity with a respect for the complexity of the subject to which the law applies.

'Do not steal' is surely a problematic example. It is true that such a sentence is easily understood in comparison to a long sentence with dozens of subordinate clauses expressing exceptions and nuances of meaning. On the other hand, it is not the case that a short simple sentence accurately reflects a body of norms which guide a normative practice, even if a general principle or other norm provides a revealing overview of it. $E=mc^2$ is simplicity itself, and is grasped in its essentials by many people. But to apply it to a problem in physics requires an understanding of much more complex physical and mathematical concepts. While it would be stupid to try to state the law of contract in one long sentence expressing each part of it, it is not stupid to suggest that really to understand the law of contract one must cover the amount of material that would fill a book. As Harris states, '[a] complete enumeration of all the conditions of the duty imposed by [section 1(1) of the Sale of Goods Act 1893] would require a description of most of the English law of contract.'[68] If we believe, as lawyers do, that one's understanding of the meaning of various laws grows with the experience applying them to cases, then Raz's criticism of Kelsenite laws must be refined to apply only to those theories of individuation which propose that each individual rule is one law which must include all its relations, exceptions, etc, to other rules. With the individuation I have proposed, there is no question of stating the complete branch of law, with all its parts, in a single sentence, much less of stating each rule in a single sentence which elaborates all its relations with other rules. Whatever we say about individual rules, there is no reason why branches of laws should correspond to sentences, and the desideratum of conceptual simplicity should not be understood to require that. 'Do not steal' is therefore a dubious shorthand for the law of theft.

Regarding the criterion of self-containment, there is not much question that the individuation of laws I have proposed results in laws which (1) 'contain a relatively complete part of the legal system', (2) 'without combining unrelated ideas into one law' or 'dividing related areas into several

[67] Ibid. 143. [68] Harris 1979, 94.

laws for no good reason'.[69] The proposed individuation also takes care to organize laws around act-situations which are the core of a single branch of law, via the characterization of act situations according to the interests at stake.

Finally, does the proposed individuation make clear important connections between laws? I think it does. By individuating laws on the basis of fundamental interests, laws can be seen to interact when our interests interact with each other, both when they do so in some positive way, as for example when our interest in property and our interest in making binding agreements gives rise to an interest in selling property, but also when they conflict. This kind of connection between laws, when they must take account of each other because of the interaction of the fundamental interests they serve, is arguably the most important connection a law has with other laws.

Taking all of this into account, I would submit that the scheme of individuation I have proposed attains the standards demanded by Raz's criteria. What I want finally to do here is to sharpen the reader's appreciation of the significance of pursuing one scheme of individuation rather than another, by contrasting this interest analysis with a pair of different conceptions of the categories of private law. The first is that of economic analysis as characterized by Posner, and the second, Calabresi and Melamed's classification of laws according to the sort of remedial consequences which befall a person who breaks them. Both of these would, if taken seriously, require a significant reorganization of the way we think about not only property, but all of private law.

Posner

The economist's characterization of property can be dealt with very briefly, for in no way does it represent the legal idea of property. The point of mentioning it here is not to deride economists, nor the economic analysis of law, but to show how much there is to be explained about the legal idea of property that will not be assisted by economic analysis.

The economic view of property is very simple.[70] Property comprises any valuable resource in respect of which an individual has an exclusive entitlement. Exclusivity is vital, and serves economic efficiency because it allows an owner to invest in his property with the assurance that he will be able to capture the value of the proceeds, but economic efficiency is further enhanced if the entitlement, or property right, is transferable or alienable by contract. 'Efficiency requires a mechanism by which the farmer can be induced to transfer the property to someone who can work it more productively; a transferable property right is such a mechanism.'[71] This is not pre-

[69] Raz 1980, 144. [70] Posner 1986, 29–33. [71] Ibid. 31.

cisely right, for to be 'induced' to transfer here means induced to sell by being offered the right price, so a power to make contracts is vital as well.

What is so radically simple about the economist's view is simply that all valuable entitlements are treated as property. The substantive private common law, Posner tells us:

> can be conceived in economic terms as having three parts:
> (1) the law of property, concerned with creating and defining property rights, which are rights to the exclusive use of valuable resources;
> (2) the law of contracts, concerned with facilitating the voluntary movement of property rights into the hands of those who value them most; and
> (3) the law of torts, concerned with protecting property rights, including the right to bodily integrity.[72]

As we shall see, and as the reader is no doubt aware, not all valuable rights are regarded by the law as property rights. The rights to one's bodily security, to one's labour, and to one's life are not. For obvious reasons, determining why some exclusive rights to valuable resources are property rights and why others are not is about as crucial to the legal idea of property as any issue can be. Clearly, we shall find no help from economic analysis on this point. Secondly, as we shall also see, the emphasis on contract rights as the paradigm voluntary transfer of property obscures the much more central place of gift in understanding the right to property. But the main point here is that the characterization of property follows from the scheme of individuation, or vice versa. The implicit scheme of individuation only has its tidy three-part structure if every valuable entitlement counts as a property right.

Calabresi and Melamed

In 1972 Calabresi and Melamed wrote a clever paper which organized the entire normative structure of the law according to a pair of choices which any hypothetical system could make in guiding the behaviour of its subjects: the first choice concerned 'entitlements'. An entitlement is any value which can be held in some way by an individual, such as property or bodily security, and a system is to be characterized in part by the distribution of entitlements. We may all have the right to life, or only some of us. We may have rights to different amounts of property, and so on. Secondly, a system must choose ways of determining the legal scope and regulation of these entitlements in two contexts, those of voluntary and involuntary transactions; the concern is to regulate the way in which others may or may not take advantage of the entitlements one has.

Where the particular entitlement is subject to an *alienability* rule, A may

[72] Ibid. 29.

voluntarily, for example by a contract, alienate his entitlement to B for whatever price he wishes. This notion of alienate is very broad: if I waive my right to bodily security for £100 so that you may beat me up for laughs, I have alienated (to a certain extent) my entitlement to bodily security, for you are taking advantage, so the reasoning goes, of that entitlement which I have. Under an alienability rule such transactions are allowed; under an *inalienability* rule they are barred. For example, A may be prohibited from alienating his right to freedom by selling himself into slavery.[73]

Alienability and inalienability rules hardly cover all circumstances for, as we well know, 'transactions' in the broad sense are regularly involuntary from the point of view of the entitlement holder. It is in the case of involuntary transactions that *liability* and *property* rules make an appearance.[74] 'Whenever someone may destroy the initial entitlement if he is willing to pay an objectively determined value for it, an entitlement is protected by a liability rule.'[75] This is rather narrow, for the rule concerns any taking advantage of another's entitlement, not just its destruction. The important point is that the value the destroyer or taker must pay is determined on an objective standard, not on the true value of the entitlement to its holder. So, for example, when I 'take' your right to bodily security by negligently poking your eye out, I pay damages which are not measured by what the eye was actually worth *to you*, but on an objective scale by which society collectively determines what one eye is worth. Thus, under the liability rule, I may legally 'take' your entitlement so long as I am willing to pay the objectively-set price for it, regardless of how much you actually value it.

'An entitlement is protected by a property rule to the extent that someone who wishes to remove the entitlement from its holder must buy it from him in a voluntary transaction in which the value of the entitlement is agreed upon by the seller.'[76] Property rules effectively force would-be takers to bargain with the holders of the entitlements they want. This sort of rule comprises a number of variations in different contexts; in the case of continuing violations, B is liable to an injunction, so that if he wants to go on taking advantage of A's entitlement, he will have to make a deal with A which satisfies A. In the case of criminal law, 'an indefinable kicker', that is, an increase beyond the normal market price, is added to the criminal penalty on top of the liability rule measure of compensation to act as an added

[73] Calabresi and Melamed do not specify the consequence of violating inalienability rules, i.e. by purporting to alienate voluntarily something that is inalienable, but their examples, of contracts made while the transferor is drunk or otherwise incompetent, suggest legal nullity as opposed to punishment: ibid. 1093.

[74] This framework in which inalienability/alienability rules are restricted to the voluntary transactions realm, while property and liability rules are restricted to the involuntary transactions realm, is a slight modification of the original structure of the paper, but which presents its insights in a superior way: ibid. 1112 n. 44.

[75] Ibid. 1092.

[76] Ibid. 1092.

deterrent, 'which represents society's need to keep all property rules from being changed at will into liability rules'.[77]

The rationale for the distribution of entitlements and the imposition of the voluntary and involuntary transaction rules does not concern us. What is interesting about this characterization is that it constitutes a set of individuating principles for the law. The normative character of the system can briefly be outlined, to reveal the sort of normative guidance the system would deliver.

It is clear that the character of any entitlement, and thus the way in which subjects of the law ought to regard it, is wholly captured by the remedial consequences of the transaction rules in the voluntary and involuntary circumstances. A 'property' entitlement is an entitlement to the extent that it is protected by a property rule. It has nothing to do with the characteristics of the kind of thing the entitlement is. If, at civil law, I can only get damages, measured on an objective scale, from you for your theft and destruction of my car, then to that extent my car is not property. But this is a mere facet of a much more wide-reaching consequence of the equation of the character of a right with the remedies the law provides in the case of its violation.

Look again at Calabresi and Melamed's definition of the liability rule: '[w]henever someone may destroy the initial entitlement *if he is willing to pay an objectively determined value for it*, an entitlement is protected by a liability rule.'[78] The normative guidance offered to legal subjects under this scheme of individuating laws is to measure their own wants against a set of prices, and act accordingly. If it is worth the compensation plus criminal kicker you will pay, say £3,000, to give your next-door neighbour a sound thrashing, then go to it. The effect of the property rules of the criminal law, to the extent that they work, is to price most criminals out of the involuntary transactions sector.

This is all well and good as an exercise in theoretical speculation, but it should be obvious that it completely misrepresents the actual normative guidance of the law. In general, the law does not treat remedies as price-setting mechanisms for the violation of rights.[79] We are meant to comply with our duty not to act negligently, not weigh the benefit of acting negligently against the cost of the damages we will pay. We are guided not to murder people at all, not weigh our desire to do so against the objective price that has been fixed, say twenty years without parole. In other words, the normative guidance of the law is, in general, not to be equated with the motivational influence its remedies may have, but to insist that the primary duties be complied with. Hart pointed this out long ago.[80] A fine may have the same motivational influence as a tax

[77] Ibid. 1126.

[78] Ibid. 1092, italics mine.

[79] For an excellent discussion of the doctrine of efficient breach of contract from this general perspective see Friedmann 1989.

[80] Hart 1963b, 720–1.

in discouraging the behaviour in consequence of which they are imposed, but their normative guidance is not the same. I am supposed to refrain entirely from that for which I am fined, such as parking my car illegally, but I am not supposed to quit my employment because I pay tax on my earnings.[81] This individuation scheme, with its general price-setting approach to liability, cannot make such crucial distinctions. Neither can it make the distinction, discussed above in Chapter 2, between a power to create rights in others by contract and the breach of a duty, say in tort, which by operation of law creates rights in the victim to damages.

This equation of primary rights and duties with the motivational effect of the remedies put in place to deal with breaches is further complicated by the fact that Calabresi and Melamed analyse the connection between right and remedy in an insupportably narrow way. The claim must be that subjects of the law are not to be guided by the primary rights, duties, and powers that the law lays down, but by the consequences that occur when these norms are violated or, in the case of powers, misused. But why stop at property and liability rules, i.e the first-order of remedial rights and duties, i.e. secondary rights or duties. If I breach a contract, I am liable to pay damages. This duty arising on breach may be replaced by a court order to do the same. If I refuse to comply with that, the sheriff or bailiff may have a right to come round and seize my goods to pay off the judgment debt. Which of these sequential remedial measures is privileged as the right one to guide my behaviour? The first? The last? Any scheme of individuation which intends to equate normative guidance with motivational effect must, in actuality, be much more fine-grained than Calabresi and Melamed's, for one presumes that different persons will be differently motivated by different stages of the remedial sequence.

Finally, this scheme also prevents any sorting of entitlements into general kinds, like property, or personal rights, for as Calabresi and Melamed say: '[i]t should be clear that most entitlements to most goods are mixed',[82] that is, in different contexts and *vis-à-vis* different interlopers my ownership of my house will be protected by any number of different property and liability rules. So there is no basis upon which an entitlement holder can regard this entitlement as his property *per se*.

It is difficult to avoid the conclusion that the individuation of branches of laws in Calabresi and Melamed's analysis cannot but misdescribe the legal system, and in particular its idea of property. The examination of the views of Posner and Calabresi and Melamed make it plausible to suggest that the interest in property has some work to do in making sense of the idea of property in law, to which task we now turn.

[81] This is not an entirely general point, because occasionally taxes are imposed to deter behaviour, such as those on alcohol or cigarettes. ibid.; see also Raz 1980, 230–1.

[82] Calabresi and Melamed 1972, 51.

4

The Right to Property: The Exclusion Thesis

When in the last chapters I have discussed property, I have done so largely to aid our examination of systems of norms and the individuation of branches of law. Nevertheless, the astute reader will no doubt have a fair idea of what I think about property already. In this Chapter I commence characterizing property from first principles, as it were. I shall approach the task by examining the nature of property rights, or the right to property. This is an exploration of the way in which the law, through imposing duties on others who bear the right kinds of relationship to the owner, protects our interest in things. My contention is that property rights can be fully explained using the concepts of exclusion and use.

Exclusion and Use

The concepts of exclusion and use are more complex than they first appear, because, in general, they are intertwined. One can, of course, have a right to use something without having a right to exclude others, and vice versa. One can have the right to use a library, but no right to exclude others from it. Similarly a guard may have the right to exclude others from the library but no right to use it himself.

Yet rights purely to exclude or purely to use interact naturally, as it were, in the sense that use almost always involves some exclusion of others. As a rightful user of a library, I may not have the right to exclude others, but I would certainly have the right to occupy a desk, or take a book from a shelf. In this sense I have a right *not to be excluded* from the library, since use implies non-exclusion.[1] But what about the interaction of several rightful users? Does it count as an exclusion of other rightful users if I take the only copy of *The Concept of Law* and use it for a week? On one hand it would not seem so, since presumably they might as easily have taken it first—the book was not taken from their actual possession, so they were not *excluded* from it that way. But on the other hand, my acting as of right has effectively excluded them from the use of the book so long as I use it. They are prevented from using the book by my having a right.

[1] C. B. Macpherson is usually associated with the idea that, before the rise of 'possessive individualism' in political and moral theory, property rights were associated with a right *not to be excluded*, rather than as a right *to exclude others*: see Macpherson 1962, 1968.

So long as we conceive of a right to use in a social situation, in the real world, that is, the implications of that kind of right will raise issues about the rightfulness of excluding others, because the vast majority of the uses that a person will make of a thing are impossible if everyone tries to use the thing at the same time. Because we live in a world of scarcity there is an insufficient quantity of perfect substitutes for everything that people wish to use, and this cannot but give rise to conflict. Now, of course, some things are not scarce, and in some situations commons work (although in the case of commons, too, a large set of people is usually excluded), but this does not detract from the general point. The obvious solution is to link rights of use with rights of exclusion, and so we must look at the different exclusionary rights to which rights of use may be linked.

One can have a right to use so long as no one else was using, or wanted to use, something. This essentially amounts to nothing more than a right not to be excluded from something for no reason at all. This is the sort of right someone at the bottom of a hierarchy might have, who has to relinquish his possession of something whenever a superior person had use to make of it. This right has no exclusionary force over others whatsoever.

A second kind of right to use is the first come, first served version, the right to begin using any unoccupied thing and continue using it until one is finished. This sort of right is exclusionary, preventing others from using or interfering with one's use, but it is limited by the nature of the use one can make of it. Where the thing is generally used for a short time or intermittently, like showers or shoe horns, the exclusionary implications might be minimal. On the other hand, in the case of things which are used more or less continuously to be used properly at all, such as a house or flat, or in the case of things the use of which involves their consumption or destruction, as in the case of food or firewood, this right to use has the implication that the first to use is likely to exclude all others forever.

Finally, one might have the right to use whenever one wants. This is the sort of right the person at the head of a hierarchy might enjoy. With this right, all others must stop using a thing whenever the right-holder decides he wishes to make use of it. The exclusionary implications of this right are patent. With regard to the first come first served right, no one was actually forced to stop using something in the face of a right—they might only be prevented from beginning. Here, of course, the exclusion may work both ways.

Once these versions of the right to use are laid out, however, it is apparent that they can be framed as corresponding versions of rights to exclude having the same normative effect, so long as we remember that these rights are employed in a social setting. If the link between actual use and exclusion is the factual premise that using something characteristically requires that (at least some) others be excluded from it, the link between rights to exclude and use is that all rightful exclusions can be broadly characterized as serving the interest or purpose of putting a thing to use.

Now, clearly, one can exclude others from things for any reason at all, or for no reason whatsoever. Since we are concerned with *rights* to exclude, however, these non-reasons for excluding others are not candidates for interests that would underpin any such right. The guard at the library does not exclude persons willy-nilly, but only those without reader's tickets, so that the library can be used by those for whom it was intended.

The notion of use, however, must encompass those cases where one excludes others for a purpose without 'using' a thing in a narrow sense. Holding land as a natural sanctuary for wildlife, or hoarding gold to drive up the price are examples of a broader sense of 'use'. The sanctuary is a case of a use, a disposition of land, which accords with the owner's cultural or moral or aesthetic sensibilities. The hoarding of gold is a use of it given that there is a market in gold; it is a meaningful disposition of it. It is no more a use than that, but it is as purposeful and sensible a disposition of one's gold as, say, making jewellery out of it.

We do not normally wear all of our clothes at the same time, nor do we sit on all of the furniture, nor occupy all of the rooms of our house at once. Are they, then, not being used? In an obvious sense, they are not. That is the sense in which 'use' means active engagement of some kind. But in a perfectly valid other sense, they are. In this broader sense 'use' refers to a disposition one can make of something that is purposeful and can be interfered with by others. On the latter definition, use is still engagement with a thing, but it is simply of a longer term in which there is only intermittent physical interaction. Thus, the natural link of the right to exclude with use is simply that rightful exclusion of someone from a thing will always be purposeful, i.e. having some purpose in respect of the use to which the thing will be put. Were it not for its connotation with 'getting rid of', 'dispose of' would better describe this purposeful engagement with things.

The right to use something so long as no one else was using it or wanted to use it is equivalent to having no right of exclusion whatsoever. The right to use something so long as one got there first is a right to exclude others while one is using something, and the right to use whenever one wants amounts to a right to exclude others whenever one decides to use something. Yet once we have taken a broad view of use, these last two rights can amount to the right to perpetual exclusion. For example, it is certainly a meaningful disposition of land to hold it as a family seat for oneself and the heirs male of one's body, which use could last forever.

How do the right to use and the right to exclude explain the right to property? The right to property is grounded by the interest we have in using things in the broader sense. No one has any interest in merely excluding others from things, for any reason or no reason at all. The interest that underpins the right to property is the interest we have in purposefully dealing with things. Because we have long-term interests in respect of things, and interests in using them in many different ways the broad definition of use is the appropriate one. But because we are concerned with the *right* to property, we must be concerned with the correlative duties imposed on others. Because of the social setting in which we live, and the ways in which the things of this world are typically used, we see that any meaningful right to use is the opposite side of the coin to a right to exclude. Secondly, the right to use reflects our practical interest in exclusively using things, which correlates to duties *in rem* on everyone else not to interfere with our uses of things. Their not using the property is framed in terms of their duties to exclude themselves from it.

Thus at a theoretical level we understand the right to property equally as a right of exclusion or a right of use, since they are opposite sides of the same coin. Yet we can equally see that only one of these ways of looking at the right might drive the analysis in understanding the shape of the property norms in the legal system. It is my contention that the law of property is driven by an analysis which takes the perspective of exclusion, rather than one which elaborates a right to use. In other words, in order to understand property, we must look to the way that the law contours the duties it imposes on people to exclude themselves from the property of others, rather than regarding the law as instituting a series of positive liberties or powers to use particular things. This can be expressed as follows, in what I shall call the *exclusion thesis: the right to property is a right to exclude others from things which is grounded by the interest we have in the use of things.*

On this formulation use serves a justificatory role for the right, while exclusion is seen as the formal essence of the right. It is our interest in the use of property which grounds the right *in rem* to property and the correlative general duty *in rem;* yet exclusion is the practical means by which that interest is protected, and that makes all the difference to our understanding of property. However, treating the exclusionary aspect of the right to property as a 'right to exclude' involves a serious misconception which must be cleared up straight away. The essence of the exclusion thesis is that the duty *in rem* imposed on people generally is what provides the contours to the right. Any true right of an owner to exclude others must be understood to be an auxiliary right which enforces or protects the right to property. The right to property itself is the right that correlates to the duty *in rem* that all others have *to exclude themselves* from the property of others. It is a right of exclusion, certainly, but it is not the right physically or by order or otherwise (say by putting up fences) actually to exclude others from one's property. The fact that we may not have the right to throw trespassers off our land, and must call the police to do so instead, does not mean that we do not have a right to the land, but only that our means of effecting the right are circumscribed. The right to exclude is a right *in rem* like the right of bodily security. One may have various auxiliary rights which make the right to one's bodily security effective, like the right of self-defence, but it is not necessary to have those rights to have a right to bodily security. The essence of the right is that people generally have a duty not physically to harm others, including oneself. I shall hereafter employ the term 'the right of exclusive use' to refer to what we normally call a 'property right', and to refer to the element of right in 'having property' in something.

The exclusion thesis is a statement of the driving analysis of property in legal systems. It characterizes property primarily as a protected sphere of indefinite and undefined activity, in which an owner may do anything with the things he owns. The thesis is not a denial of the fact that an owner's use of property may be circumscribed in various ways, for example by planning restrictions on land use, or by speed limits on highways. What it does deny is that the law defines the right to things in terms of a series of well-enumerated and well-understood uses of things to which individuals have a right. Thus Harris, for example, regards as analytic of the institution of private property that there are 'trespassory rules' which provide the legal protection for the legally protected interests of ownership,[2] but says of any enumeration of specifically protected uses:

> The possessory owner has a prima facie privilege to do anything in relation to his land which the dominant culture of his society accords to a landowner. The set of privileges entailed is not a total set, because everywhere some things are excluded. It is, however, an open-ended set, since its present content could never be exhaustively listed: and it is a fluctuating set, because cultural assumptions about what an owner may do vary.[3]

Good reasons lie behind this way of shaping the practice of property. It is difficult in the extreme to quantify the many different uses one can make of one's property, so as to give a workable outline of what the 'right to use' property actually is. It is more practical to say simply that one has the *right* to dispose of property any way that one wishes, in the broadest terms, *but only in so far as those dispositions are protected by the specific duties on others to exclude themselves from the property.* The *right* to property is that normatively protected part of our interest in using property, and that part, i.e. that fraction of our uses of property, is determined by the extent to which others must exclude themselves from our property. Thus we are provided with the specific contours of the property right over the many different things that can be objects of property. Nothing in the world is naturally of exclusive interest only to the one most closely associated with it. I can take pleasure in your body simply by seeing it, or in your conversation simply by listening. I can similarly appreciate the beauty of your garden sculpture as a passer-by. I

[2] Harris 1986, 144–5. [3] Ibid., 160.

can even have an interest (the exact nature of which is interesting) in your not destroying the Poussin which hangs in your hall, even though I may never actually have the chance to see it. There must, therefore, be defined limits to property rights, that is to the owner's exclusive rights to the things he owns. The driving analysis underlying legal property norms defines these contours in terms of the general duties *in rem* that people have not to interfere in the property of others; it does not specify rights to use or dispose of property. Although I may desire to capture all the benefits of my beautiful garden because it resulted from *my* use of *my* property, even those gained by passers-by that look upon it, the law of property will not help me to do so, for there is no duty on those passers-by not to look. The right to property is thus a right to a liberty, the liberty to dispose of the things one owns as one wishes within a general sphere of protection. It is not the right to any particular use, benefit, or result from the use of property. The duty *in rem* of property correlates with the right to a liberty to dispose of property, not to a specific right in the value of property, or a right to any goal one may set on one's use of it, and so on. And to repeat the point I made in the last chapter, the right to property is not a right that others facilitate or ensure that one is able to use a thing in the particular way one would wish. In the same way that having the right to drive a car does not mean that the state is obliged to teach would-be drivers to drive or provide all of them with cars, the right to use is not the right to be given materials to build a house on one's land if that is why one bought it. It is a negative liberty.

Treating the notion of exclusion as underlying the driving analysis of property is also supported by the analysis of norms *in rem*, in particular rights and duties *in rem* from Chapter 2. If I am right in my analysis of duties *in rem* as correlatives to the more familiar rights *in rem*, then for these duties to be practical they must be relatively simple. They would not be simple in the right way if they referred to various uses that an owner might make of his property. The general injunction to 'keep off' or 'leave alone' the property that is not one's own defines the practice of property much better than a series of specific duties which work to facilitate particular uses of others' property. The law does not enquire whether, or to what extent, the trespasser or the thief impinged upon the owner's dispositions in respect of the property in question. The duty *in rem* that correlates with the right to property is the negative duty not to interfere with the property of others, i.e. the duty to exclude oneself from the property of others. The concept of exclusion, not use, dominates the legal analysis.

This is manifested in the common law when the court is faced with claims to novel kinds of property, such as property in news, sporting events, or information. It does not ask the question whether the claimant has the right effectively to exclude the putative trespasser or thief from the supposed property, by not publishing news stories, or by building a wall obstructing the view of an event, or by keeping information secret: it asks whether the putative trespasser or thief has a duty to exclude himself from it.[4] The fact that the putative property-owner is acting within his rights in gathering the news and publishing it, or putting on a sporting event, does not answer the question. The fact that he is using a resource of some kind in a legally acceptable and even admirable way does not solve the problem.

We therefore find that many of the most fundamental constitutive features of the law of property are actually found in the law of wrongs, both civil and criminal. This makes perfect sense once we grasp the fact that property introduces rights into a legal system which are akin to personal rights like the right to bodily security. The contours of the right to exclude others from one's body are the product of legal and moral ingenuity in recognizing appropriate general duties *in rem*. We must exclude ourselves from others by not touching them, for instance, but do not have to exclude ourselves by not looking upon them. The right to property, as much as the right to bodily security, is determined by the extent to which the law of wrongs will treat certain acts and omissions as causing a significant harm to the interest, and for that reason impose a duty on people generally.

This is all quite straightforward and accords fairly easily with our intuitions about the way that property norms are structured in a normative system. Now I am going to claim that something further follows from the exclusion thesis, which neither is straightforward nor obviously accords with our intuitions, that is, that the owner's power to share and even transfer his property is part and parcel of the right of exclusive use.

The Social Use of Property

An owner has the right to exclude others, and the very idea of property depends on the idea that others are to be excluded. It is essential that 'property' does not describe the situation where a thing is held by everyone. There is, of course, co-ownership in varying degrees. All that is required is that *some* persons are excluded.

One of the traps that an analyst of property can fall into is to mistake the nature of this exclusivity. The right to property is like a gate, not a wall. The right to property permits the owner not only to make solitary use of his property, by excluding all others, but also permits him to make a social use of his property, by selectively excluding others, which is to say by selectively allowing some to enter. The exclusivity that attends the ownership of prop-

[4] See *International News Service* v. *Associated Press* (1918) 248 US 215; *Victoria Park Racing and Recreation Grounds Co. Ltd* v. *Taylor* (1937) 58 CLR 479; in some cases the court defines a putative thief's excluding himself in terms of not depriving the owner: see *Stewart* v. *The Queen* [1988] 1 SCR 963; *Oxford* v. *Moss* (1978) 68 Cr.App.R 183.

erty is variable by the owner. By varying this exclusivity the owner can actually confer rights on others by licensing them to use his property.

In order to appreciate this, we must once again remind ourselves of the social setting in which the practice of property takes place. It would be absurd to suppose that when it comes to understanding property we must begin with the idea that individuals *qua* owners live in a social vacuum, and that their interest in using property is confined to using it alone, i.e. making dispositions of it which do not involve other persons. The property system works to exclude people generally from interfering with the property of others; it is not there to ensure that people live like hermits. There is thus no reason to suppose that people must somehow overcome the strictures of ownership in order to allow others access to what they have. Permitting others access is part and parcel of owning property, and therefore understanding the social use of property by the owner with others, or by the grant of the use of the owner's property to others must be as fundamental to understanding property as understanding the way in which property excludes. The important feature of property is the individual's *determination of the disposition* of a thing, not any requirement that he use it on his own.

There are two aspects of the social use of property which must be grasped. The first aspect I shall call the mechanistic one, that is the way in which the structure of property norms works to permit sharing and transfer. The second is the motivational aspect, which concerns the way in which different interests of people can be served by the sharing and transfer of property. When I come to the second aspect, I shall make the claim, which is perhaps counter-intuitive, that the right to property comprises the right gratuitously to share or to give away property, but does not include the right to sell it or contract to share the use of it.

The Mechanistic Aspect of Sharing and Transfer

The key to understanding the mechanism of property norms which underpins this is realizing the general impersonal nature of the duties *in rem* which correlate to the right to property. In Chapter 2 I pointed out that properly understanding these duties cannot involve knowing anything about the personality of the owner of the property to which they apply. As I walk through a car park, my actual, practical duty is only capable of being understood as a duty which applies to the cars there, not to a series of owners. For all I know, all the cars are owned by the same person. The content of my duty not to interfere is not structured in any way by the actual ownership relation of the cars' owners to their specific cars. By the same token, if one of the cars has just been sold, so that there is a new owner, or if one of the cars has been lent to the owner's sister-in-law, again, my duty has not changed one whit.

Thus transactions between an owner and a specific other do not change the duties of everyone else not to interfere with the property.

The nature of these transactions can once more be understood by reference to the normative structure of liberties and powers. Property is like a gate, not a wall, because the owner may open the gate, selectively allowing particular persons to enter, while at the same time leaving everyone else who is outside in the same position as before. As we have seen, a liberty is a freedom from restraint, and one may have a right to a liberty. A liberty *per se* is not a norm, but a matter of fact. Similarly, a power is a capacity, whether a natural capacity or a social capacity, which works to change the relationships between persons. And as we have also seen, there are also purely normative powers which rely upon the existence of a normative system to be operative, which work to alter the existence of norms within the system. We have no trouble understanding that the right of exclusive use protects our liberty to use, i.e. the freedom from the interference of others when we go about using the things we own. In that sense property protects the exercise of our natural powers, our intellectual and physical capabilities. But by the fact that we have the right of exclusive use these powers are not elevated into normative powers; no norms of the system are altered when we eat a sandwich or dig a ditch on our land. The case is markedly different when we attend to our social capacities to deal with property. The existence of our ability to communicate with others, the existence of society itself, and reasonable freedom from interference are all that is necessary to found our social capacity to share the possession and thus the use of our property, and transfer possession and use to another absolutely. These 'social' powers, then, are really no more difficult to understand than the capacity and liberty to use our property on our own. But in the case of sharing and transfer, the law does elevate these powers to normative powers for, obviously, these powers work a practical change in the way the norms of the system operate. The right of exclusive use protects the use of property, and thus in so far as it protects the use of someone other than the original owner, that person benefits from the right. Now, as we recall from our analysis of rights, only the person who is intended as the beneficiary of a duty may claim to hold a right, and so even if we accept that the owner has a right to property, we are not thereby entitled to say that those who are permitted the use of his property, either because he shares it or gives it to them, are *ipso facto* intended by the law to stand in his shoes as it were, as the intended beneficiaries of the duties *in rem*. This claim requires further justification, and I shall provide it below when I discuss the motivational aspects underpinning sharing and transfer. For now, it is worth pointing out that it is simply the case that the legal system of property norms does give legal recognition to the exercise of social powers, allowing them to alter the existence of norms in the system. They thus become legal powers.

All of this goes for the sharing of property, granting the temporary exclusive use of it, and for the absolute transfer of the property away from the owner. Absolute transfer, however, raises somewhat different concerns because there the owner permanently relinquishes his rights to the property, so sharing and absolute transfer will be discussed individually in turn.

At common law a distinction is made between transactions in which an owner retains possession of his property while giving others access, and those cases where he temporarily parts with his possession entirely to another. The first case is generally called a licence; in the case of chattels, a 'bailment' describes the case where the owner (the 'bailor') gives possession to someone else (the bailee); as regards land the boundaries are somewhat muddy, but in general the recipient of exclusive possession of land is a tenant (holding under a tenancy or lease or 'term of years'), while someone with the right to enter land or occupy it but not exclusively is a licensee (holding under a licence). I shall use the term 'licence' generally to cover all of these situations, and to distinguish these cases from transfers, in which the owner permanently relinquishes all of his rights to another. I shall use 'alienation' as a general term to cover both licences and transfers.

Licences

Licensing others to use one's property might may seem capable of overwhelming the very concept of exclusivity, because a licence can be general. An owner may allow everyone to use his property, for example letting everyone walk in his beech wood in autumn. We should, however, treat a general licence as a special case where the owner declares that he shall hold his right of exclusive use in abeyance (not enforcing it at all) rather than it as a conferral of use-right on everyone. This characterization is actually closer to the nature of such a grant, for it is in practice a declaration that the title will not be enforced by the rules of exclusion, rather than a grant of a right *in personam* to use to each and every person who might conceivably take advantage of it. Most licences, of course, are precisely grants of rights *in personam*, to specified individuals allowing them to use the property of the grantor.

Unless they are party to the licence, holders of the general duty *in rem* to exclude themselves from the property of others are not affected by a licence of any particular piece of property, for the duty on them is exactly the same as ever. Nothing is changed for them. Licensing use amounts to lifting the licensees' duties *in rem* not to interfere with the owner's property. Those who are not licensed, that is, everyone else, do not gain any duties or lose any rights as a result.

Because the mechanism of licensing is the selective use of the right to exclude, 'licences' can be very extensive, and should be taken to include all grants of lesser interests in the property one owns, from non-exclusive licences at will to contractual exclusive licences, rentals, and leases. Licences, therefore, can encompass any partial transfer so long as the transferor retains an interest in the property, no matter how small.

In this way the right of exclusive use serves one's use of one's property in the social context. Exclusion can be directed or relaxed to protect or facilitate any particular use, by any particular persons, for any particular length of time. The owner can use his right to exclude to protect any of his own uses but, more than this, he can use it to protect the use of anyone else who uses his property, *because the tool is the exclusion of others*.

Furthermore, since the licence can be as broad in its extent of use as the right of exclusive use itself, minus some increment retained by the grantor, the licensee can sub-license others. A licensee is a user by right, and there is no conceptual bar to his using the property socially any more than there is on his grantor. It all depends on the terms of the grant. A grantor need not grant a licence which permits the licensee to sub-license the property to others, but he may.

Alienation of the Property in its Entirety

A fundamental aspect of the property relation between an individual and a thing is its asymmetry. The individual is not on a par with the thing. The individual has control of, or over, the thing, as far as an individual is capable, and not the other way round. Furthermore, this control is absolute in the sense that a person's influence over the thing is unbounded in principle. He may destroy, modify, or leave the thing, to the extent that this is actually possible. (One cannot, for example, destroy land.[5])

'Leaving the thing', in one way or another, is our present concern. If a person is unable to free himself of a thing, then to that extent he is controlled by his relationship to the thing, if not by the thing itself. Such control is antithetical to the idea of property. This is not to say that while one holds something as property one may not be under various obligations imposed by society; even abandonment is unlikely to be free of social obligations, as laws regarding waste disposal and pollution show. It is, however, central to our idea of property that one is not bound to hold any thing as property. Not only is the property right conceived in terms of an interest in dealing with the things of this world without interference, but it is an interest in dealing with them *or not dealing with them*, as one chooses. Since one can choose never to

[5] Generally speaking. Land at the seashore diminishes with the erosion of the sea, and one can of course destroy parts of the land, such as buildings, which, as fixtures, are treated as part of the land itself.

deal with a thing again, it follows that one should be able to sever one's relation to it.

Abandonment

The simplest way of severing one's links with one's property is to abandon it. Abandonment is purposeful, unlike loss. It normally involves relinquishing possession of something that is no longer wanted, in respect of which the right of exclusive use is no longer of any value to the owner. Abandonment is a permanent decision not to take advantage of the general duty *in rem* prohibiting interference in respect of a particular thing abandoned.

Do we have the right to abandon the things we own? Under the civil common law,[6] property cannot be abandoned *de jure*, if that means that an owner may by his act alone destroy his title in a thing. An owner may only relinquish possession of a thing, whereupon any subsequent person's possession may give him a good root of title. Although the legal view respecting title might suggest otherwise, it is submitted that we do have the right to abandon property. It is surely part of a right to determine how a thing is to be used that one may make no use of it at all, for evermore. One ought not to be saddled with a relationship to a thing that one does not want, and an unbreakable relation to a thing would condemn the owner to having to deal with it. It would indeed be a funny turn of events if the norms serving our interest in property in essence gave the things a person owned a power over him.

Implicit in this notion of abandonment is partial abandonment as well as permanent and total abandonment. This is not, strictly speaking, what we call 'abandonment' normally, for nothing of normative consequence is normally recognized when we simply decide to leave off using our property for any particular period. We are naturally more concerned with the decision to do so permanently. But clearly, if we regard the idea that a *right* to exclusive use permits us to decide never to use an object of property again, then it must encompass the lesser decision to forego using it for a day or a month or a year. Such a decision is as much a disposition of the property as is its total abandonment.

Yet while the interest underpinning property incorporates the interest in getting rid of things one no longer wants, people also have an interest in not being harmed by the way that people deal with their things. This is both an interest that all individuals have, and a social interest, in that the maintenance of the environment is a collective good. The rules of title, specifically the rule that one's title is not extinguished unless another takes possession

[6] Abandonment is recognized under the criminal law of theft—one cannot steal that which has been abandoned: Hudson 1984.

and acquires his own title, either gratuitously or for a fee, provide a means of ascribing responsibility to a person for the harms which his property may cause, even though he might wish to sever his relation to it. The rules of title, therefore, reflect both the owner's right of exclusive use and the general right not to be harmed. An owner may relinquish possession, and therefore put his property in the position that any new title to it may be created, but by relinquishing possession he may not avoid responsibility for the effects of his ownership, say the creation of hazardous industrial wastes. It is predictable that rules about how one goes about disposing of things, for example by pouring toxic chemicals into rivers, will arise in any society in which citizens wake up of a morning feeling they no longer want part of what they own, and have a pretty clear idea that no one else wants it either. Thus the rule of the civil common law by which abandonment cannot be recognized may serve a different function from merely ensuring that a person maintain his use or possession of a thing.[7]

Transfer

I shall argue here that either the right to abandon a thing or the right to license others to use a thing can be elaborated to show that the right to transfer property is an inherent feature of property rights. I shall describe the abandonment route first.

We should remind ourselves that, since property is conceptually framed in a social context, abandonment does not occur in a social vacuum. In particular, part of the context in which property rights exist is in respect of rules of title, i.e. rules which deal with how a person comes to acquire title in something. So far I have just elaborated two rules of title that are inherent in the concept of property: the first purely negative rule is the rule permitting abandonment—it provides for an owner's relinquishing of his title, but it has nothing to do with the acquisition of title. The second rule is the rule permitting licensing. This is in a sense also a negative rule because it essentially involves an owner's relieving particular persons of their duty *in rem* in respect of his property. But it is positive in the sense that it creates rights *in personam* in licensees. In order to elaborate the right to transfer from the right of exclusive use we must first recognize the following further rule of title: where a thing is unpossessed, a person may gain title by taking possession of it, and over the course of time or in respect of the reasons for which a thing is unpossessed, e.g. that a previous owner intentionally abandoned it, this title may become good against all the world, i.e. be the best title to the thing. This is a plausible recognition, for that is the actual common law rule,

[7] See Hudson 1984.

but it is also the only rule which is conceptually plausible given the asymmetrical nature of the property relationship between person and thing. A thing has nothing to say about the relationships it has, and therefore only one party to the relationship has a say in whether the relationship will be formed. In other words, persons may acquire unowned things by simply taking them up and holding them as property. An individual alone has all that is required to possess a thing, that is, personality. The only reason a person should refrain from taking control of a thing is that his possession would interfere with another person's. In that case his taking control of a thing is not only a matter of his relationship to a thing; his taking control amounts to a battle for control with another, and such battles are inconsistent with the very nature of the practice instituted by the general duty *in rem* that correlates to the right of exclusive use. Thus the rule that taking possession of unowned things is to acquire title to them accords with the nature of the practice of property defined by the right of exclusive use.

It may appear extremely contentious simply to adopt such a rule: disputing and defending the justice of 'first appropriation' is almost an industry in moral and political philosophy. This appearance, however, is misleading, since the context of that dispute is entirely different from the one under discussion. The interminable dispute regarding the justice of acquiring property by appropriation from a world without any prior ownership is a dispute about distributive justice, which I have already pushed to the back burner for now. It essentially concerns the kind of advantages any individual may get by his own actions, by appropriating unowned things without the consent of others. It is only important when the claim about the justice of first appropriation is intended to shape the general distribution of all things, of parcelling out the lot. A right of *first* appropriation in these contexts is a notional right the exercise of which in a parable about the justice of property rights inevitably leads to, i.e. *creates*, the property system. We are much past that point as regards the appropriation I am talking about. We are already in a world where most things are owned. Appropriation in this context is acquiring title in the sense of adding one title to a system of titles or, indeed, re-adding one title previously abandoned. It does not concern first appropriation as the basis for the system of titles itself.

A more pertinent concern is raised by Waldron. Are there *general* rights *in rem*, which give rise to *special* rights *in rem* (which are what particular property rights in the things we own are, after all)? No one has any general right to the property he particularly owns, despite the fact that these particular special rights correlate to general duties *in rem* not to interfere with the property of others.

Waldron holds that both (i) the right *in rem* to property which arises from a first appropriation of an unowned thing and (ii) the right *in rem* to property that arises when title to a thing is transferred to one by gift or sale are to be viewed as special rights *in rem*.[8] They are special rights because both arise contingently, in consequence of the events of appropriation or gift or sale. Now, while it is true that both of these rights are special in the sense that they arise upon the occurrence of an event, they may be distinguished because of the way they correlate to the duty *in rem* not to interfere with property.

Let us deal with the second right first, the 'special' right *in rem* to property which arises as a consequence of transfer. As I have rather laboured above, the duty *in rem* not to interfere with the property of others makes sense because the duty-ower's exclusionary reason not to interfere with the property of others applies to all things that are property, not to each individual property-owner in respect of his particular goods. Of course the result of honouring the duty is indeed that each individual owner's goods are not interfered with. Thus when property is transferred either by gift or sale or succession or court order or taxation the duty not to interfere with the property is not changed in the slightest. If someone violates the duty there will of course be a different owner pursuing a remedy of some kind against the violator, but the particulars of the ownership do nothing to alter the duty *in rem*. The content of the right not to interfere with property is identical before and after the transfer as regards everyone who is not a party to the transaction.

In this way the right *in rem* attaches as much to the determinate piece of property which is the subject of the transaction as it does to any individual owner. As long as we restrict our consideration to transfers of a particular thing from one owner to the next, we can visualize a chain of title, in which the thing always remains property. Upon the passage of title, we do not conceive of the new owner as having to re-establish Blackacre *as* property. Passing title means that one person takes the *property* Blackacre from another. So in one sense it is correct to say that no right *in rem* arises upon the transfer of Blackacre. We say that the right has 'passed'; we say that title passes upon a legitimate transfer, or that title cannot pass by way of theft.

But property rights, of course, are not attached to things in the sense that things themselves have rights. We can conceive of the transfer of property as the transfer of the same right *in rem* because of the way the correlative duty *in rem* works. The duty is not to owners in particular, but to owners as those persons which stand behind the property; the property is the direct focus of the right. Who owns is irrelevant as long as someone does. The truth embodied in the idea of passing title is the fact that Blackacre remains the same property as it is transferred from one owner to the next because, as far as the duty-owers are concerned, it is the same property. It is the same property for them because it is the same thing, and their duties are directly related to things. Interestingly, conceiving of Blackacre as the same property

[8] Waldron 1988, 108–9.

though it passes from owner to owner is one example in which our conception of the right–duty relationship is from the duty-ower's perspective.

A right *in rem* that one's own actual piece of property not be interfered with that arises when one gets title from another *is* a special right, but a special right of a particular kind. It arises contingently from the general right *in rem* that one's property not be interfered with, i.e. the general right one has to participate in the practice and benefit from the general duty *in rem* as regards one's own property, yet its scope is not restricted to the actual parties to the transaction which gives rise to the special right. The new owner's right *in rem* correlates with a duty that all others have, one which already encompassed the particular item of property in question. Because of the nature of that duty, it is correct to say that the transaction has not changed the duty that all others have. The right *in rem* to the property one has acquired is special, but no *special* correlative duties arise; they are just the same old duties *in rem* as before. No special duties arise even for the transferor, who is now one of the multitude who must not interfere with the property. The ex-owner has merely relinquished his special right. He has not acquired a new special duty with respect to the particular property he has transferred. The property now simply falls within the immense class of things which he does not own and with which he may not interfere. There is no legal basis whatsoever for treating his ex-property as in any way subject to any particular duties which make refer to his historical ownership; it retains no earmark of his past relation to it. What comes out of this analysis, then, is that the right to property, that is to a specific piece of property, is special, but it does not correlate to any special duties at all; rather it correlates to general duties that we all already have.

The right *in rem* that unowned things that one has appropriated should be treated like property raises a further matter, for here there is an addition to the pool of things which draw on the duty *in rem*. Because the duty is conceived of as a duty toward things, any addition or subtraction of the things that are property affects each duty-ower. But any significant difference between the two situations disappears because the duty not to interfere with property applies generally to things in well-recognized categories. Conventions about what types of things are generally owned will determine which things are objects of the duty *in rem* and those which are not. For example, we take all cars and houses we come across to be owned, though not most pigeons. Thus the appropriation of unowned things in these categories merely brings into the property system items which in a sense belong there already. The insignificance of these appropriations turns, of course, on the fraction of property in the system which is traceable to this kind of appropriation. If we are in reality or notionally dealing with a situation where the bulk of property is being put into the system through first appropriation, we are dealing with the establishment of a particular distribution of property as a means of establishing the system itself which, as I have said, raises much different issues.

This raises an important point similar to one raised in Chapter 2. There I said that there must be a sufficient number of owners before there can be rights *in rem* to things. The impersonal nature of the correlative duties *in rem* depends on that. But not only must there be a sufficient number of owners, the bulk of the things that fall into various categories of things which can be owned *must be owned* for a right *in rem* to property to exist. The duty not to interfere with the things owned by others or, rather, the duty not to interfere with all things in conventionally recognized categories of property only makes sense in a context where, for all practical purposes, all of these things are owned. If the duty is not to be a duty *in personam* the duty-ower must not have to inquire every time he comes across a piece of land or a car or a sandwich whether or not this particular one is owned by someone. If that inquiry was necessary, it would amount to determining who the owner was, and thus dealing with him personally in a way which would negate the *in rem* character of the duty.

This point applies as well to the right to life or the right to bodily security. Imagine a society where there are many individuals who do not have such rights, because they are slaves for instance. Now if there are obvious visible marks of one's status, such as the colour of one's skin, then no problem of determining who has which rights is posed, because all the persons of one colour will have such rights, and the others will not. But where there is no such indicator, one may actually have to deal with a stranger to determine whether he has such a right. If these circumstances were the norm, then the sense of such rights being *in rem*, rather than *in personam*, would start to break down.

The Transfer of Property

The elaboration of transfer from abandonment proceeds as follows. An owner may abandon his property at any time and in any place (if it is movable) that he likes. At the time and place of the abandonment, any person who takes possession of it gains a title in it. Since abandonment is entirely up to an owner, he can mark his abandonment of a thing by communicating it to others. It is now apparent that, should anyone wish to pass his title to anyone else, all he must do is abandon it to him in circumstances where that other is well placed to take possession of it. This can indeed be assured by licensing that other person to take possession of it, and then abandon it while he has it in his possession. 'Take this: it's yours'. The common law has recognized the taking of possession as essential to the transfer of title in various ways, in the delivery of chattels, for example, or in the ancient common law ritual of 'livery of seisin', in which the transferor of land picked up a piece of the earth and placed it in the hand of the transferee before witnesses. The concept of this directional abandonment is reflected most clearly in linguistic use when we say that a person *leaves* his property *to* someone in his will.

The second route to transfer, through the power to grant licences, is somewhat more complicated. The method of alienation is obvious: the owner must simply grant an exclusive licence to the entire use of the property (or part of the property, if he is only giving away some of it). The obvious drawback to this method of transfer is that such transfers formally encumber the title of the property. The owner takes the use of his licensee-transferee to be his own, as a granted right to the relaxation of his right to exclude, and therefore the transferee's use conceptually counts not only as his own, but also as the adopted use of the transferor. Thus the title to the property is formally encumbered by its historic train of transactions, such that the right of exclusive use of the licensee in possession is recognized only through the history of transactions up the chain of title to the first licensor.[9]

In a recent paper Gaus argues against the validity of just this notion of transfer. An owner's 'waiving' of his rights in respect of one individual, i.e. licensing a non-owner's use of property by releasing him from his duty not to exclude himself from it, cannot amount to transfer. Gaus accepts that, by waiving the right to use his property and agreeing to allow the first licensee to do likewise with sub-licensees, an owner may allow a string of licensees to use the property in question in the same way as he would, benefiting as they would from the general duty of exclusion. Relying on Hart's theory of rights, however, he argues that the licensees are not themselves right-holders, but merely third-party beneficiaries of the duty of exclusion; therefore, this kind of licensing cannot amount to transfer: the original owner remains the holder of the property rights.[10]

This argument is unsound. In the first place, Hart's view is mistaken, or at least incomplete.[11] A third-party beneficiary of a right may be a right-holder himself if the right is conceived of as being imposed in his interest, i.e. if the reason, or part of the reason, for the existence of the corresponding duty is the third party's interest. As I have explained, the reason for property is not to enforce seclusion; the exclusionary duties of property are justified in part because they facilitate an owner's disposition of his property in a way which benefits others. If, as we shall see is the case when we discuss the motivational aspect of alienation, the interest of the owner in the use of his property

[9] Which is not to say that such a notion of title through transfer is impossible to deal with, for such a conception is essentially the one that lies behind the notion of good root of title to land at common law.

[10] Gaus 1994, 216–20.

[11] See MacCormick 1977; Raz 1984a; Hart 1982, 174–93.

is understood to include his interest in seeing the interests of others served by the use of his property, then the third party in this case, the licensee, is as much contemplated as a beneficiary of the duties as the owner himself. The logic of the duty to exclude oneself from the property of others reinforces this view, of course—one need know nothing about the identity of those who benefit from one's complying with this duty; one's duty not to trespass is not altered in the least if the houses on the street are owned by one person, by many, or are occupied by licensees.

Secondly, Gaus seems to assume that this transfer falters because he supposes that only the original owner may exercise remedial rights, by pursuing an action against a trespasser, for instance. But this is to beg the question. If the licensees are regarded as having rights, then that is the end of the matter, for we are only concerned with whether the owner can put them in the same position as he himself was in as regards rights to the property, rights conceived of as correlative to the duties *in rem* of non-interference, and clearly he can. That is precisely what his licence does. The question of remedies is an entirely different matter. My right not to be murdered is not diminished by the fact that I (for obvious reasons) have no remedy against my murderer. The licensee's rights may be protected by the terms of the grant from his predecessor, in that predecessors in title may bind themselves to exercise their remedial rights in favour of their licensees, up the chain to the original owner; or licensees may have these rights in law themselves. While these remedial distinctions are important ones, they are just that, distinctions concerning the remedies available. The foundational point is that licensees are considered to be proper beneficiaries of the duty of exclusion.

The two routes to transfer I have described show how the right of exclusive use intrinsically embraces transfer. It is clear that the holders of general duties not to interfere with the property of others are not affected in the least by any transfers, save where they themselves are party to the transaction. It makes no difference to the individual walking down the street that the building he passes has just changed hands. The system of property rights as it exists is in this sense distribution-insensitive.

It is worth reiterating here the different nature of the two routes to the transfer of property that I have described, for the difference has important implications for the discussion of gifts and contracts to follow. The abandonment transfer is conceptually founded not on the exercise of the right of exclusive use, but on the severing of one's relation to property, and thus the relinquishing of the right. The right to abandon is not *a part of* the right of exclusive use, but is rather entailed by it, because it is underpinned by the same interest. The licensing transfer, on the other hand, is an expression of the right of exclusive use, in which the use of others is treated as one's own social use of property. The right to license is therefore conceptually a part of the right of exclusive use.[12]

The Motivational Aspect of Property Sharing and Transfer

How far does conceiving of the right of exclusive use as comprising the right to use one's property with others, or to let others use one's property on their own, take us to 'full-blown' rights of alienation, in particular the right to sell it or exchange it, so that we arrive at what Christman calls 'full liberal ownership'.[13] Not as far as some might fear. While I shall argue that the analysis so far does support treating the right of property as comprising a right *to transfer* as well as to abandon, nothing in this implies that the owner has the right to bargain in respect of his powers of alienation; as a result, the right of exclusive use entails, and comprises, a right to give, but not a right to sell. However, it should also be clear that there is nothing in the nature of property which would lead us to *deny* that a person should bargain in respect of transferring his property. If persons are allowed to bargain or make agreements generally, then there is no obvious reason why their property rights cannot be the subject of a bargain. The characterization of property I propose is completely neutral on the question whether one should be able to sell one's property; that concerns not only the right of exclusive use, but the limit and extent of the justification of the power to make bargain agreements which is, as we have seen, a very different matter indeed so long as we pay attention to the different interests which underlie these norms. Neither does the right of exclusive use place any necessary limits on the power of the state to transfer property from one person to another by operation of law. If the state has legitimate claims on its subjects, then there is no reason it cannot have legitimate claims on their property, in the same way that a contracting party may have legitimate claims on the other party's property by virtue of the contract.

Different interests motivate, and thus underlie, the transfer or sharing of property, and lead to a characterization of transfers as gratuitous (gifts),

[12] We should note a distinction between waiving the specific special right to particular property, which occurs when we abandon something, and waiving the general right to property, i.e the general right to own property, which is not usually possible. By saying that the right to abandon is not a part of the right of exclusive use, I mean that it does not count as the *exercise* of any particular right to a specific item of property. In one sense one can say that it is a part of the general right of property, since the general right to participate in the property practice captures the 'right' not to be bound to hold any object of property against one's will; if the case were otherwise the rights serving our *interest* in using things would be defeated. So I am not double dealing with the idea of what is comprised in the right of exclusive use when I say that alienations by licence are conceptually part of it while abandonments are not, for the level at which the distinction is made is the level of the special right in respect of particular items of property, not at the level of the general right to property which clearly contemplates both kinds of alienation.

[13] Christman 1994a, 6–8.

contractual (sales, remuneration, trades), or by command (taxation, expropriation, judgment orders). I will address these in turn.

Gifts

We understand gratuitous sharing and giving only when we understand how permitting someone else to use one's property counts as one's own disposition of that property as, in a sense, one's own use. First and foremost, when I permit someone to share property that is mine that permission is my decision. To that extent it appears obvious that I have adopted the shared use as 'mine' in some sense. But, of course, it is not my own use at all in another sense, as I am not the one who directly benefits from the use of the property; the person I permit to use it is. Nevertheless, my claim is that this second person's use is my own use as well.

In order to understand this, we need accept nothing more than the perhaps mysterious fact about humans that they may be better off simply because other persons they care about or love are better off; our lives are so connected. This is clearly most easily understood in the context of family members or close friends. I may do better, be happier, or have more of whatever one takes as the indicator of one's well-being, when someone I care about has this glass of whisky rather than if I drink it myself. Being able to experience this kind of enhancement of one's well-being through the enhancement of the well-being of someone else is indeed constitutive of a relationship of friendship or love. I am fully aware that there are instances of what passes for sharing and giving in which the well-being of the donor is not in this way related to the well-being of the recipient. On occasion perhaps we all treat a gift as one move in a tacit bargain, and some despicable people probably do so regularly. I am certainly not claiming that all cases in which we share our property with others or give it to them manifest this taking on board of the recipient's enhanced well-being. But I do claim that this characterization of sharing and giving captures what might be regarded as the standard, uncomplicated case and how we should think about it. To deny this is simply cynically to deny the sympathetic character of much of human interaction. If this is roughly right, a law of property which did not accommodate an owner's social use of property in which he shared the use of it by taking on board the interests of his recipients as his own interests would be an odd and atrocious law (which of course does not mean that one could not devise such a law, which odd and atrocious people would prefer). If one thinks about how much of our daily living revolves around the shared use of property one can imagine the severe estrangement of people from each other that such a law would work.

The premiss underlying the view that the right to give property absolutely is a right entailed by the right of exclusive use is that, when we give something to someone, we treat the use of the donee *as our own use*. A gift constitutes the ultimate adoption of another's use as one's own. It is the largest expression of the social element of property because it transfers with finality the totality of a right of exclusive use. The important point about gifts is that, even though final and ultimate, they essentially *refer* to the donor's intentions and purposes, and so are to be regarded as dispositions of *his* property. Even though we may later be disappointed or annoyed with the way a gift is used, and would renounce it if we could, that does not undermine the intention with which a gift is given, which is a matter of historical fact. Many of one's own solitary uses of property do not turn out as intended either, and are regretted. That does not make them any less one's own disposition of the property.

The treatment of gifts manifests the donor's intentions, even though the donee is generally entitled as of right to dispose of a gift as he sees fit. Gifts are regarded socially in a much different light from sales, for example. In the first place, persons generally feel somewhat restrained in their disposition of property they have been given, as anyone who has ever received an unwanted gift knows. It is considered bad form immediately to turn round and sell it. Gifts are honoured and acknowledged in a way that sales are not. It is the name of the benefactor who gave the £10 million for the new library whose name is above the door, not that of the contractor who built it, nor that of the person who sold the land it sits on. We respect the fact that gifts arise solely because of the intention of the owner who made them, and recognize in our treatment of them that the intentions of the donor linger.

The reader will be forgiven for raising two related objections at this point, which seem to refute this view of gifts. How is it that one can regard the use of the donee as the donor's use, when the donee can do whatever he likes with the property, even if the donor would wish him to do otherwise? Secondly, even if what I say is true about how we *socially* regard gifts differently from sales, how does this translate to the *legal* situation, where buyers and donees are equally able to do what they want with their property?

In the first place, it is of course not strictly true that in law a donor cannot have a say in how his donee uses the property he has been given, for there are conditional gifts and marvellously restrictive family trusts, after all. But the general point is well taken, and requires a brief foray into the way we can be interested in others.

No one would doubt that I have interests in my children and how their lives go, for I love them. I love them so much in fact, I regard it as deeply in my interests that they grow up to be capable, autonomous individuals who have a reasonable facility for managing their own lives. There is no way that I am going to contribute to this development by devising ever more sophisticated ways of manipulating the way they 'choose' to act. They must actually choose. I may shudder to think of the choices that they will certainly make as they grow up, but unless one of them is about to make a disastrous choice, I must, as a general rule, refuse to intervene in most of their significant choices or they will never understand what making significant choices is all about. I am nevertheless deeply interested in those choices, though I have no control over them, and when I provide them with the means to make such choices it is nevertheless the case that I have provided for those choices, and indeed may share part of the responsibility for them because of that fact, even though the results may be ones I would not myself have wanted or chosen. *That* is what I mean by taking on board the uses of my property that my donees make. It is not my use in the sense that I used up or directly physically engaged the property, or that I decided precisely how it was to be used, but *my* use in the equally robust sense that *I* provided *my* property to others I care about to dispose of in a way which implicates *my* interests. It falls just as well within the general interest I have in property, the interest I have in disposing of things in a way which affects my interests. Giving is not mere abandonment of property to others, involving no interests of the donor.

If we then understand that there are ways of taking on board the interests of others which commit us to not interfering with the way those others act,[14] in this case how they dispose of things, the fact that the law treats donees and transferees for value in the same way, i.e. there are no legal limitations on their disposition of the property, tells us rather little. There is simply no good reason in either case for post-transfer legal restrictions on use, for they would in each case equally defeat the purpose of the transfer contemplated. We note in passing that property transferred by judicial order is likewise subject to no general restriction on its use, even in the case where damages are awarded in a civil case. The successful plaintiff *may* spend them on medical care or rehabilitation, that is, let us say, on the purposes for which they were awarded, but there is no law stopping him from buying lottery tickets instead. We do not simply assume in view of the absence of such restrictions that the law did not award the plaintiff damages with a particular view as to how they ought to be spent, or with a particular purpose in mind. The reason the right to give is to be regarded as within the right of exclusive use, but contractual transfers without is that, on the view I have expressed, the interest underlying property rights encompasses the social uses of property like sharing and giving. In contrast, in general I could not care less what a contractual transferee does with the property he receives from me in an exchange, since his use does not implicate any of my interests, as I shall now explain.

[14] See Raz 1986a, 407–12.

Contracts

In transferring property by contract, the seller relinquishes his property precisely on the condition that he will not exercise any right to dispose of it whatsoever. The seller does not make use of his property, but rather abstracts from the use of his property some measure of value, and compares it with the value of the contractual consideration offered to him, whether it is property, or services, or something else. The important feature of this valuation is that it is not a prelude to using the property, which use is protected by the right of exclusive use, but is rather a prelude to never using it again. This valuation establishes the particular property right as a possible object of exchange. The owner shifts from treating the property as something to be used to enhance his interests to treating it as something to be traded, either for some other property he can use to enhance his interests or for something else entirely, like a haircut. In contrast, therefore, with the way in which a gift refers to a disposition of the owner through the uses of his donees, a contract essentially refers to the decision of the owner to relinquish his interest in disposing of the property altogether.

As a consequence, a seller has no valid interests in the disposition of the property once sold; any intentions or interests he may have have no normative force whatsoever. Thus we feel no obligation to consider the wishes of the persons from whom we buy things when we decide how to use them. They have relinquished their intentions regarding the property by trading it as one value for another. The intentions of previous owners do not bind after a sale.

Because property rights are so often the subject of contracts it is often supposed that property and contract are intrinsically linked, or that one is the basis of the other. This single misconception has probably done more to confuse the understanding of both subjects than anything else. The concept of property does comprise alienability, but the concept of property does not depend on the existence of a right to create binding agreements.

Neither does the concept of contract depend on property rights. There can be any number of contracts with objects that are not property. 'If you scratch my back, I'll scratch yours', for instance. Believing that contract conceptually requires the exchange of property rights of some kind leads to believing that all benefits of whatever kind are species of property, which gives rise to the absurd belief, among others, that one's labour is something one owns.

Now, given the fact that we do have the right to make binding agreements, it is certainly arguable that we ought to be able to make binding agreements about licensing or transferring our property. No aspect of the right of exclusive use indicates that property rights should *not* be the subject of contracts. Even so, the right to exchange property rights is not entailed by the right of exclusive use. It arises because we have both property rights *and* a generally unlimited right to make contracts. These are very different rights, however, protecting very different interests, as we have seen: the former concerns the protection of our interest in exclusively determining the disposition of things, whatever the category of 'things' comprises; the latter protects our ability to enter a particular kind of voluntary relationship by which people can, for consideration, act co-operatively and consensually exploit each other's advantages of whatever kind. That we can treat our property rights as one kind of those advantages is hardly surprising. But to say that any of these advantages, whether institutionally bound ones like property rights, or naturally occurring ones like our good looks, talents, or abilities, *entail* a right to trade them with others is to say something which requires much more foundation than merely citing the fact that property is a common subject of contracts.

Commanded Transfers

Clearly, property is not only transferred in a legal system because an owner makes a gift or enters a contract. Some transfers, while still the act of the owner, are made to satisfy obligations which did not arise by his own agreement, such as transfers made to satisfy the demands of the Inland Revenue or to comply with orders of the court. Furthermore, some transfers are not intentional at all, involving no act of the owner whatsoever. Such movements of title, from one person to another, are effected by operation of law. An example is the medieval rule by which an owner's land was forfeit to the Crown on his commission of treason.[15] No act of transfer on the part of the felon is required; the title just moves by operation of law.

In essence commanded transfers are those which occur upon the exercise of normative powers by authorities of some kind, or by operation of rules in the system. There can be powers to transfer property directly (e.g. the power of a department of government to expropriate land), to order an owner to transfer property himself (e.g. the power of a judge to issue a court order), and so on. There are also powers to create rules in the system which operate, on the occurrence of certain facts, to transfer property or to give rise to an obligation on the owner to transfer property (e.g. laws of taxation requiring the transfer of money on the earning of income). The existence of these powers reflects the interests of the authority, whether to use the transfer of property as a means of punishment, as a means to support its activities, as a means of doing justice, or simply as a means of directly affecting the distribution of property among its subjects.

[15] Simpson 1986, 19–20.

Even more clearly than in the case of contractual sharing and transfers, the 'use' of the property by the authority does not count a use protected by the right of exclusive use. These 'uses' are obviously not the use of the owner and, indeed, are an interference with his right of exclusive use, albeit one which is embedded in the normative system.

We can return here to a point raised in the discussion of Gaus's objection to licences. Given the nature of gifts, we see how the uses of an owner's property by his donees counts as a use in his own interests. Consequently, the interests of the beneficiary can easily be regarded as interests which the system recognizes, as a vital aspect of the way that property serves the interests of owners generally. Thus there is no problem according the donee property rights, for only by doing so are the rights of the donor properly vindicated. Given the nature of our interests, which reflects our social nature, there is no good reason to privilege the solitary uses of property that serve our interests, treating the others as somehow objectionable. Indeed, one should go further, and say that there is no reason why the system cannot be regarded as protecting the interests of donors *qua* owners and donees *qua* owners equally, given the ubiquitousness of the gratuitous sharing and giving of property in our practice of dealing with things. If we treat sharing as the norm, which it is, there is no reason to take an owner-as-donor centred view of the way in which the system protects interests, for if the assumption is that most property will be used collectively, albeit subject to greater or lesser dispositional control by the owner/donor, all whose interests are served by that practice should be recognized, and this recognition should shape the system of norms.[16]

The Transfer of Property and Hybrid Branches of Law

Having looked at the motivational aspect of the alienation of property by examining the interests underlying different kinds of alienations, I would now like to point out how gratuitous transfers naturally cohere with the licensing explanation, while contractual and commanded transfers do so with the abandonment route. The conceptual model of the licensing route depicts the owner as inviting his licensee into the sphere of protection afforded by the general duties *in rem*, releasing his donee from those duties with which he would otherwise have to comply, so that the donee now takes advantage of them himself. By contrast, in the case of contractual transfers and command transfers, the owner relinquishes his rights of ownership to his transferees, so that they in effect take their own ownership by bringing the

[16] *Khorasandjian* v. *Bush* [1993] 3 All ER 669 may represent belated recognition of this kind in the law of nuisance in England. See also *Motherwell* v. *Motherwell* (1977) 73 DLR 3d 62.

particular property within the sphere of property protection by virtue of taking up what the transferor gives up. Gratuitous alienations work by the extension of the owner's interests to include those of others, all within the right of exclusive use; in the case of contractual and command transfers, contractual obligations or the operations of law work to extinguish the transferor's rights in favour of someone else, and these transfers naturally accord with the model of directional abandonment. It is the transferor's power to relinquish any individual property right which is the focus of the transaction, not his right to make use of a thing to serve his interests.

This characterization helps to reveal how the branches of law governing contractual alienations and command alienations are hybrid sub-branches of law. The law of sales exists because we have a law of property and a law of contract. We have the right to sell our property because we have both a general property right comprising a power to abandon any specific item of property, or in other words to waive any specific right to the exclusive use of a particular thing, and thus relinquish our rights in the property, as well as the power to make binding agreements which can, in general, concern any of our rights, powers, talents, or abilities.

Similarly, command transfers depend upon both our right to property and the rights and powers of various authorities to serve their interests by making particular orders or by creating various rules of law. Taxation is not simply an aspect of property, but a hybrid branch of law in which the property of subjects of the law is dealt with by authorities having particular constitutional powers of great importance. Thus both property and constitutional law are implicated in the law of taxation.

Nothing similar can be said of the law of gratuitous alienations. The law of gifts is not a hybrid branch of law. That is to say, 'gratuitous transactions' does not name a category of law in the way that contractual transactions, i.e. 'contracts' does. The law of gifts, such as it is, concerns only property; it is *not* concerned with other kinds of benefits we can cause other people to have or experience, in particular benefits caused by our acting in a particular way, like cooking someone a meal or giving someone advice on how to minimize his tax liability. Gifts are an essential element of the law of property because the right to property comprises, as we have seen, the right to give property away; by contrast, there are no general rules concerning 'gratuitous transactions' of services. In general the law could not care less what one does to benefit someone else, unless one is otherwise obliged to do it, i.e. that action fulfils a term of a pre-existing contract or complies with a command like a court order. The law takes a decided interest, of course, in those actions one performs which injure other people, i.e. torts, or those which otherwise fail to comply with one's obligations, like a breach of contract. But if, just to make you happy, I sing a song for you nothing of legal consequence occurs (unless of course I sing negligently and cause you harm by splitting your eardrums). By contrast, the law recognizes and characterizes every possible transaction concerning property, from the most trivial to the most significant, from the implied licence the postman enjoys to bring the mail up the path to one's door, to the bailment when one lends a book, to the outright transfer of land by sale. If I give you a penny to make you happy, we have a well-defined act of legal significance, a gift. If I save you from drowning, the common law yawns and has nothing to say.

This is not as arbitrary as it may look. Gratuitously performing a service is conceptually quite different from sharing or giving away property. There is a fundamental asymmetry between the two: when we share we take advantage of a thing in the world in respect of which we both stand equally; you and I will do essentially the same thing when we eat a loaf of bread or drive a car or live in a house. But taking advantages of a service is not partaking of a thing in the world, but receiving a benefit from another's action. I can sing a song for you gratuitously, but if I do we are not 'sharing' the same thing. I am experiencing my action of singing, you are experiencing someone else's singing, i.e. mine. When I share my property with you, I take on board your use of it by proxy as it were, since it serves your interests in a way in which it might identically have served mine. But if I do something for you, I do not take on board your appreciation of it the way I myself do—I put myself in a particular position so that you can have a valuable experience which is necessarily ontologically distinct from mine. This goes as well for things people do together for pleasure, such as sex. However much pleasure I may give you if I have sex with you, what I am clearly not doing is providing you with an experience I might have had myself had I chosen not to 'share' it. The underlying reason for this conceptual distinction is apparent. Doing things for others, or performing services, remains a part of the agent's experience, and thus his life, even though they enter into and, one hopes, beneficially contribute to the experience of others. The agent does not give up or trade away his experience in anything like the way an owner can transfer his property. His experiences remain a part of him, and note: they remain so even when he acts to fulfil a contractual obligation, as in a contract of employment; when one sells a word processor, it makes sense to say one relinquishes it to the buyer, but what precisely does one relinquish when one waits at table or teaches a class?

The benefits of my actions which I confer on others gratuitously are analagous to gifts of property, but their ontology is obviously distinct. The fact that they are gratuitous does make them identical in one respect, and may seem to provide a reason for thinking that together they form a category of transaction in the law, but they do not. Benefits conferred through actions or services rise to legal significance only in reference to contracts or commands which create definite legal obligations to perform them. Thus, instead of establishing a legal category of 'gratuitous transactions', our analysis points out that there is a law of obligations or, rather, that there are several branches of law, contract and tort and public law, which can give rise to obligations, including, though not restricted to, obligations to transfer property. Property rights are therefore peculiar and special. The benefits of property, however they are distributed, are 'exhaustively' characterized by the law, unlike benefits of other kinds, which find legal recognition only via the law of obligations.[17]

Overlapping Economies

Each of the different kinds of transfer of property will lead, if practised widely, to a different distribution of property. Gifts will result in a distribution of property which ultimately derives from the bonds of shared interest between people. Contracts give rise to a distribution based upon agreements under which people are motivated by their own individual interests, and commanded transfers will reveal a pattern of distribution which evokes the interests of various authorities. We can thus speak of a gift economy, a contractual or market economy, and a command economy.

Economies, of course, concern all values, not only property. Services, what we may *do* for others, not only property, are valuable and they make up part of an economy. The distinctions between gift, market, and command economies apply just as much to actions as they do to things but, as I have said, if not excessively dwelt upon, that does not mean we can then just treat services and property together as different species of the genus 'value' as if there were such a category in legal systems.

To a greater or lesser extent, all advanced nations manifest a mixed economy in which the three overlap to create the ever-changing distribution of property. The different kinds of economy operate at different levels and in different contexts. Within commercial organizations, the resources of the business that are applied to production are distributed by command of the managers, but these resources, whether labour or other factors of production, are acquired through contract. Gift economies may typify transfers within families, but may also typify systems of class or tribal patronage. One may be interested in the well-being of others for no other reason than that they are members of one's class or tribe.

[17] This is not precisely true. Some benefits arising from our interactions with things are not legally recognized; this is the case in our standard example of the passer-by who takes pleasure in seeing my well-tended garden. More precisely, the point is that being a branch of law that creates special rights to a kind of value, i.e. property, the law is in a position to recognize all kinds of movements of that value, through gift, abandonment, loss, tortious interference, contract, and command. This is not the case for actions or services, and so only when the law creates an obligation which involves an action or service is the value of that action or service given legal recognition. This is discussed in much greater detail in Penner 1997.

Furthermore, it is obviously the case that transactions may partake of the character of different kinds of economic distribution, because different interests can be implicated in the same transaction.[18] One can, for example, be in a sense obliged to give, mixing command and contractual motivations with gratuitous motivations.[19] The best example of this is the gratuitous transfers of property we make to our children. In one sense they are clearly gifts (my interests thoroughly incorporate those of my children), but similarly, by reason of the relationship I have to them, I am also obliged to provide for them. Similarly, one may, for example, rightly regard the use of one's taxes for various purposes as being one's own use of one's property to advance one's own society, in which one is of course deeply interested. Again, the compliance with contractual obligations may serve one's interests not merely as the *quid pro quo* for the consideration one reciprocally receives, but as a way of furthering a relationship with the other party in order, for example, to undertake true joint ventures in which the interests of the parties are really shared.

Given human nature and the complexities of society, it would be difficult, if not impossible, entirely to eradicate any of the gift, market, or command motivations for transactions. None is privileged in terms of necessity. What raises gifts to a constitutive feature of the right of exclusive use is the way in which they implicate the interests of the donor as regards the property he gives. He simply does not lose contact with its use as he does when it is transferred by sale or command. By contrast, contract and command drive a wedge between the owner and the use of his property, requiring his relinquishment of it. This is perhaps captured by framing the transactions as unilateral and bilateral. Gifts are unilateral acts of an owner, counting as his disposition of his property. Contracts are bilateral, in which the influence of the transferee is to make the owner relinquish his interest in the property.[20] Commands, like gifts, are unilateral, but are not the act of the owner at all, so could hardly typically count as an act by which the owner serves his own interests.

Ownership and Death

We own properly indefinitely. More precisely, there is, in general, no fixed period attached to the ownership of any particular thing. This raises another old problem of the justification of the property system, viz. why do we have

[18] I have elsewhere written on the different kinds of agreements which can give rise to obligations, and only some are pure bargains: Penner forthcoming-b.

[19] For example, Mauss's depiction of what he calls a 'gift' economy clearly includes notions of reciprocation which very much import an aspect of exchange: Mauss 1990, 1–46.

[20] I discuss the distinction between the unilateral nature of gifts and promises and the bilateral nature of agreements and exchanges in Penner forthcoming-b.

the time limits on property rights that we do? Why should it be the case that once something enters the practice of property, in particular land, it can be passed around through transfers indefinitely? After all, it must be an act of a person which brought it into the system in the first place. That person can certainly have no rights which extend beyond his own lifetime, and yet we clearly trace titles to things like land for centuries. How possibly could an act of first appropriation by one individual settle the status of a thing as something within the practice of property for all time? The key to this issue is the context of appropriation, specifically the prior existence of the practice of property. The individual does not by appropriating a thing make that thing a candidate object to be brought into the practice. As we have seen, it already is an object 'within' the practice, so long as it falls within a well-recognized category of things which are objects of property. Such a thing is already a reference point for the general duty *in rem* that people follow when they do not interfere with things they do not own. In other words, the first appropriator takes advantage of the factual non-ownership of the thing in question, not the absence of property norms. This case is radically different from that where a person claims ownership of a thing by claiming the existence of property rights in a *novel* category of objects, as, for example, were one to claim ownership of an event because one witnessed it (however an event might be incorporated as a 'thing' into the practice of property). Thus, we again draw a distinction between two kinds of 'distribution' questions that the practice of property raises. One has to do with the distribution of conventional items of property amongst the subjects of the law; this is a question appropriately framed in terms of the effect different kinds of economy have, not as a matter of property *per se*. As far as the idea of property in law goes, the practice of property is insensitive to the justice of this distribution, and it would be anomalous if the most trivial aspect of distribution in this context, that is the appropriation of the odd unowned thing, were to be singled out for special treatment. The second question, however, is very much of the essence of property, for it concerns the *kind* of things to which the norms of the practice apply. What we have, then, is a system in which the general rule for the status of a thing is: once in *qua* proper object of property norms, it is in before or after it is appropriated, and it remains in until it no longer exists. Only when the thing expires, as when we drink up our wine, does the property in it also expire.

Interestingly, the same is not quite true of our property rights when we expire. They do not disappear entirely, for we can control our property after our death, through things like wills and trusts.[21] Gifts have been analysed here as the transfer of property with a certain kind of significance: a giver takes as his own use of property the use of another. As we have seen, the way

[21] This is true as well with our contractual obligations involving property. Our dying does not get us off the hook when it comes to paying off our debts.

that recipients treat gifts shows that the giver's 'presence' remains in the holding of the property by the recipient. Ought we to honour gifts to the extent that they take effect after the death of the donor? After all, we can hardly say that the gift is serving the interests of the deceased if we believe, as I think we do, that dead people have no interests.

We must first decide whether there really is still some sort of presence of the giver in the transferred property after he has died. It is apparent that even after death recipients treat gifts in much the same way as they do gifts when a person is alive, except perhaps in the case of a testamentary gift that is conventionally expected, as where a man leaves his estate to his wife and children. The reason for this is simple. All gifts contain an element of futurity in the sense that the intention of the giver toward the property is in respect of the use that the donee will make of it. This future can as easily be contemplated as occurring or continuing as much after his death as before. It would, at first glance, seem idiotic to extinguish the continuing validity of a gift simply because the donor has died. Should the law make a distinction between two birthday presents because the giver of one is run over by a car on his way from the party? In such cases the donors are unlikely even to have considered whether their intentions regarding the gift are supposed to run, for the purposes of the law, *post mortem*. The intentions behind testamentary gifts on the other hand clearly run to the time after the giver's death, and many gifts *inter vivos* are made wholly or in part to benefit others after the giver's death. This is a sort of present taking on board of another's future use of a thing, where the future extends to the time when one is gone. These facts about our intentions colour, but do not determine, the question whether we ought to respect these intentions.

The argument against doing so does not deny the validity of another person's treating as his own use the use of another, but doubts the status of this 'taking on board' of another's use when one is dead. How, possibly, can the 'use' of a dead person, albeit through the use of another, have normative force? Though we appear to respect the intentions of the dead, we may be fools to do so.

This is a complex matter, which I shall not attempt to resolve here. The common law, however, does give a helpful insight, by focusing on the extent to which the donor's intentions are to control the use of his gift. Are the intentions open-ended, essentially simply choosing the recipient of the gift and impliedly adopting whatever he does with it, or do they not only choose one or a number of recipients, perhaps a number of possible recipients, but also control the kinds of uses to which the gift property can be put? The law cares little about who is chosen, but places severe limits on structuring the use of one's property after death by means of various rules like the rule against private purpose trusts and the rule against perpetuities. In this way the law limits the extent to which the use of property can be controlled from the grave. We might say that the law, being distribution insensitive, is tolerant of gifts which remain valid after the death of the donor, for once again, the property just *is* in the practice and it is not really a matter of interest who has title to it—but at some stage the intentions of the owner fall away and the gift becomes valid along the theory of directional abandonment, rather than the licensing model of transfer; at this stage the right of exclusive use is once again shaped only by the intentions of the present owner of the property. This transition is realized in law through the complicated rules governing the limits beyond which a dead ex-owner may not stipulate the uses to which his donees may put the gift property.

For the sake of completeness, we might mention intestate succession here, that is, the passing of property by rules of law, rather than by will, following an owner's death. There is nothing in the idea of the right of exclusive use which leads to any particular law of succession. Lawson and Rudden point out that the law of succession is nowadays geared to providing the transfer of property after death that is likely to have occurred had the deceased made a will.[22] At one time, however, at least in respect of land, the law worked to preserve a certain class in society through the doctrine of primogeniture. The most basic rule regarding the disposition of property after death is simply that it should count as abandoned. Nature severs the relationship between an individual and his things, and if he has nothing to say about the matter, there is nothing to be inferred about where they ought to go from the right of exclusive use alone. Of course, property-ownership does not occur in a vacuum. The concern of people to benefit and look after those close to them after they are gone is timeless, and the transmission of things is a tried and true method of achieving this. Rules of succession may be justified as default provisions covering cases where persons die without expressing their intentions regarding transfer. But almost any rule of succession can be justified as a means of avoiding the skulduggery that might precede, and the chaos that might follow, a person's death should his property become ownerless at that moment. While a right to transmit property by will may be comprised in the right of exclusive use, being related to gifts *inter vivos*, no particular rules of succession appear to be indicated by it.

Restrictions on the Use and Alienability of Property

The question to be dealt with here is this: to what extent can the scope of property rights be cut down before a right to a thing is no longer considered a property right? We are concerned with legal restrictions, such as a law against the sale of body parts, or speed limits on the highway, which impinge on the way we deal with things. The position that I will defend here is that

[22] Lawson and Rudden 1982, 208–9.

restrictions on the scope of property rights diminish one's recognition of a right as a property right only where the purpose of the restriction is just that, to prevent holders of the right from treating it as a property right.

Uses of things are regularly restricted by legislation for the purpose of preventing harm. Highway speed limits restrict the legal use of cars, there are legal codes dictating the way houses must be built, and so on. These restrictions, however, are not intended to alter the relationship of the owner to his property *qua* owner: he is still the only person who has the right to determine the use of the property with infinite variation. They concern the way that anyone may deal with things of that kind, whether they own them or not. I am not permitted to exceed the speed limit simply because I have borrowed the car I am driving from its true owner. These restrictions, while affecting the right of exclusive use, are not intended to strike at the property-like character of the right. An owner does not have a property right in each conceivable use that can be made of his property, so each limitation on his right to determine the use of his property does not necessarily constitute an expropriation of his property. It only does so if that is the intention of the legislation. The legislature may, of course, do something of just that kind. It might by operation of law turn all freeholds into ninety-nine-year leases from the State. Such a law would alter the thing that was held, destroying a fee simple estate and replacing it with a long lease, and that would be its very purpose.

Another sort of restriction that may be envisaged is one on the destruction of property. The listing of historical buildings strikes at the right to property, because it is meant directly to impinge on the relationship of the owner *qua* owner to his property. It can be interpreted in two ways. As a restriction on the use of land, the right to property is indeed diminished, because the right to use land in the normal way by building and rebuilding on it is replaced with a kind of duty of stewardship. Listing can also be interpreted as the law's replacing one object of property with another, like the proposal to replace fees simple with ninety-nine-year leases: the property right to a piece of land is replaced with a property right to an historic building with certain positive and negative obligations. The latter is what a sensible subsequent buyer would regard as the object on sale.

Restrictions on use-rights are also common in private dealings, and determining what someone holds as property often turns on them. For example, if a lease of land purports to grant the right to extract oil, but in reality requires the lessee to extract the oil on the land and use the land for no other purpose, it is clear that the lease does not grant a property right in land which includes the right to extract oil, but is in reality a kind of contract to extract oil. This contractual right may, of course, be an assignable right, in which case it will have the character of a property right to extract oil under certain terms, but the lessee does not have a property right comparable to a regular lease of land with full use-rights. The terms of the lease-contract are intended to avoid just such a interpretation.

Restrictions on alienability have great potential to alter the character of rights, but the reason the restriction is imposed remains crucial. If a government imposed a ban on the sale of land by the Crown, it would depend on the intention of the ban before one could decide whether the Crown still held its land as property. If the ban was conceived as a measure to prevent administrators squandering public wealth, for instance, it would have the effect of a measure, albeit a severe one, restricting dealing with property. On the other hand, if the measure was intended to create a new relationship of the State to its land, in which, say, the land was treated as actual property of the Crown's subjects, over which it was merely a bailee (not even a trustee), then such a measure would change the character of the Crown's right from being a property right to something else.

A ban on the sale of houses may be difficult to assess. If the intention of the legislature was to prevent contractual dealings in houses, in order to shut down a branch of the market, on the ground that market dealings in houses produced inequitable distributive results, then the right to property in the houses would not be diminished. Only the right to transfer the houses in a particular way, by contract, would be eliminated. As I have argued, contract rights do not fall under the right of exclusive use, and therefore no diminution in the sense of the right as a property right would necessarily follow. But the problem here is that a selective ban on market dealings which only applied to houses would remove property in houses from the general range of property in respect of which market dealings still applied. There is thus likely to be a taint of property diminution, in which the true intention of the act is to render property-holders mere occupiers of some kind, who would require some sort of state approval or intervention should they wish to withdraw from their property and take some of the value of it with them. If the ban extended to gifts of property or, even more extremely, to sharing it, one might conclude that the latter kind of intention was patent. Such very general restrictions on the scope of property use could hardly be regarded as not striking at the property-like character of the holding, unless there was an obvious reason of a different kind. A complete ban on any kind of transfer or sharing, imposed for an indefinite period, would not strike at property if the reason was, for example, to prevent the spread of an infectious disease. Though the latter ban is likely to be temporary, it would be a mistake to say that, even during its effect, owners had lost their property rights.

To take a final example, a ban on the sale of human organs might indeed be intended to characterize the right to one's organs precisely in order that they should not be regarded as property, since property rights are normally transferable in the market.[23] In the same way, a ban on surrogate mother-

[23] Honoré makes a similar point; Honoré 1987, 180.

hood contracts might be a legal attempt to prevent relationships of human reproduction being conceived of as market relationships.

Even direct expropriation without compensation might not be correctly interpreted as an attack on property. If owners can insure against expropriation, then a legislature might regard expropriation without compensation as working as a general tax on land ownership, since the cost of expropriation would be spread over all land owners through insurance prices.[24]

Conclusion

In the foregoing I have argued that the right to property should be conceived as the right of exclusive use. The discussion of alienability involved the greatest complexities, but the conclusions I have drawn are reasonably clear: first, the right of exclusive use comprises rights to license property and to give it away, and perhaps to leave it by will. The nature of the right also entails that property can be abandoned, and that property rights may be the subject of contracts and the operation of law. There is, however, no right of the owner entailed by his ownership to sell or exchange property, nor does the existence of property rights entail that the State or any other authority has the right to expropriate it. Finally, I have explained that restrictions on use and alienability strike at the right of exclusive use not so much by their extent, but in view of the purpose for which they are instituted, interpreted in light of the prevailing normative context.

We can now reformulate the right of property, or the right of exclusive use, to take account of the element of alienability: it is the right to determine the use or disposition of a thing in so far as that can be achieved or aided by others excluding themselves from it, and includes the rights to abandon it, to share it, to license it to others (either exclusively or not), and to give it to others in its entirety.

It is clear that, on this definition, no help will be given to one who wishes to extract some moral about distributive justice from property rights *simpliciter*. It has been my contention throughout this Chapter that property rights can be the subject of claims in distributive justice, but only because, like other items of value, property rights can be the subject of different kinds of economic transactions, and therefore they get distributed, sometimes justly, sometimes not. Thus it is also my contention, *pace* Waldron,[25] that recognizing the interest we have as individuals in exclusively determining the disposition of things does not lead to the conclusion that there is a certain minimum amount of property we ought to have, at least in so far as this interest is embodied in the idea of property in law, in so far, that is, as it grounds what we recognize as property rights. The right to property is no

[24] See Kaplow 1986. [25] Waldron 1988.

more a right to subsistence than it is a right to wealth. This is not to say that our interest in things may not ground a right to own some minimum amount of property, but we may remain sceptical; we must always remember that economies operate on all values, not just property; it is not obvious that to provide a decent minimum of value or wealth, a person need have any property at all, especially given the extent to which I have emphasized how owners may share the things they own.

So far we have treated the 'objects of property', the 'things' we own, as if that were an unproblematic concept. This is far from the case, and the nature of the things we own, and how we own them, is the subject of the next chapter.

5
The Objects of Property: The Separability Thesis

If property is a right to things, we must provide some characterization of the things that can be property. We can start by noticing that there appears to be a significant distinction between the uses we feel justified in making of 'things' which lack personality, whether objects, space, ideas, and even particular concretely specified relations between people, such as debts, and 'things' which do have or significantly involve personality, such as people, their actions, and their ongoing, dynamic relations with other people. If the distinction is of consequence to us, then one understandably expects it to be reflected in our concepts. 'Property' refers to a particular human practice, the practice of dealing with things, which stands in contrast to our practices of dealing with other people and dealing with what I shall call our 'personality-rich' relationships with other people. This can be further explained by examining the nature of things which can be objects of property, which I outline through a second thesis about the character of property, the 'separability thesis'. In the next chapter I return to the exclusion thesis, bringing the objects of property and the duty of non-interference together.

Objects of Property

At this stage, it is worthwhile giving a brief outline of what the law treats as property in conventional terms. Most persons familiar with philosophical treatises on property are never faced with the task of thinking about why some things are objects of property and others are not. Typically, philosophical works purporting to concern property start with a kind of justifiable evasion of this task. Here is Waldron's, which is laudable just for mentioning choses in action, a type of property much neglected by legal theorists and philosophers:

> I have defined property in terms of material resources, that is, resources like minerals, forests, water, land, as well as manufactured objects of all sorts. But sometimes we talk about objects of property which are not corporeal: intellectual property in ideas and inventions, reputations, stocks and shares, choses in action, even positions of employment. As we say, this proliferation of different kinds of property object is one of the main reasons why jurists have despaired of giving a precise definition of ownership. I think there are good reasons for discussing

property in material resources first before grappling with the complexities of incorporeal property.[1]

Waldron defends this with essentially two arguments: first, that the distribution of material resources is more basic, and thus universal, and so one suspects that incorporeal property arises, perhaps by analogy with property in material resources, only once corporeal property has been sorted out conceptually;[2] secondly, that, even in modern industrial societies, the ownership of incorporeal property can be regarded not as a right to some abstract object of property, but rather as a complex right (mediated via a complex private property system) to those same old material resources, which are ultimately the basis of wealth even now.[3] This move is justifiable given the fish Waldron wishes to fry; he is interested in examining the justice of a right to an unequal share of social wealth; 'property' is just a shorthand for that.[4] He therefore has no reason to distinguish between those economic advantages which are actually property and those which are not. My rights under my present contract of employment matter much more to my economic position than do any of my property rights (alas); call them property if you will, but that is simply a stipulated definition which attempts to fix someone's right to his economic situation and treat it as analogous to property. For most philosophers the actual objects of property are uninteresting, and the real meat of the question about property is how we can justify unequal holdings. As I have said, one of the themes of this work is that understanding property does not enlighten one on this question, any more than understanding what beauty is will allow one to justify why some people are beautiful and others ugly. What is essential to understand, and fascinating to boot, is why we think it appropriate to characterize some things in the world as beautiful or ugly, but not others. I shall charitably trust that the reader who has stayed with me so far is willing to take his property neat, unwatered by everything else that commonly adulterates it in the realm of philosophy.[5]

The menagerie can be categorized in different ways, and the divisions of English law are instructive.[6] Its most basic division is between real and

[1] Waldron 1988, 33. See also Christman 1994a, 24; Coval *et al.* 1986, 460–4.

[2] Waldron 1988, 34.

[3] Ibid. 37. Waldron regards the insistence that the nature of incorporeal property be addressed stems from 'a desire to preserve a link between the concept of property and "economic reality".' The appropriate desire is to preserve a link between property and legal and moral reality. It is significant from the normative, i.e. legal or moral, point of view that patents are regarded as property. See my discussion of the distributive character of property in Ch. 10.

[4] Although he called his book *The Right to Private Property*, I think a perusal of its contents shows that he primarily addresses the question of economic inequality, and the purported justifications of it, and not really the right to property *per se*. Waldron can hardly be faulted for this however; arguments about economic inequality have traditionally been framed as arguments about property: see Ch. 10.

[5] See, for example, the papers in Pennock and Chapman 1980.

[6] The best introduction to the kinds of property that English law recognizes can be found in Lawson and Rudden 1982, ch. II.

personal property, that is, into land and everything else. The use of the word 'real' originated in medieval law and described the legal remedies the system provided: the owner of a freehold interest in land could get the land itself back from a dispossessor—so the remedy provided the owner with the actual or *real* thing back again.[7] The owner of a chattel, that is any moveable corporeal thing like a cow (which is what the word 'chattel' originally meant), benefited from duties *in rem* prohibiting interference, but the remedy at common law was merely a payment in damages; the owner did not get the actual thing back again. Originally, one could not regain possession of leasehold interests in land, so[8] leases counted as personal property, under the oxymoronic nomenclature of 'chattels real'. Thus the legal analysis of the division between land and everything else was originally based on a distinction between the kinds of legal remedies available to the owner, rather than on any defined characteristics of the things themselves.[9] While leaseholds now count as real property, the situation regarding the right to repossession of the thing itself reflects to this day the real and personal property division. If one has been wrongly excluded from the occupation of land, one can regain occupation by legal action, but if one sues someone who has wrongfully dispossessed one of a chattel, in general the remedy is money damages.

Over the centuries, there has been a great growth in forms of personal property, and so new divisions have arisen. The most important one is that between tangible and intangible property, but there are also interesting combinations of both. This distinction is sometimes framed as the difference between 'choses in possession' and 'choses in action': things one owns because they can be physically held, and those which one owns only because one has a right to prosecute a legal relation by bringing a court action against some other person or persons.[10] Choses in action, therefore, unlike property rights in land or chattels, are not rights *in rem;* they are rights *in personam*

[7] Simpson 1986, ch. 2.

[8] The 'so' here is intentionally ambiguous; it is not clear whether leasehold interests were regarded as personal property *because* leaseholders did not have the benefit of the real actions, or whether they were denied the benefit of real actions because leaseholds were regarded as a kind of economic investment by landowners conferring rights which did not fit into the feudal system of tenure, and thus were not considered true interests in land. See Simpson 1986, 71–7.

[9] Another example of a classification of property based on legal forms rather than the object of property itself is that of Roman law between *res mancipi* and *res nec mancipi*. Goods in the former class, principally land, slaves, and cattle—were those that originally could be transferred only by the formal action of *mancipatio*; all other property was *res nec mancipi*. See Nicholas 1962, 105–5; Buckland and McNair 1965, 60–1.

[10] I use the term chose in action here to refer only to those rights which count as personal property. The term can be applied to cover all rights in action, whether assignable or not, which if successfully prosecuted give rise to a judgment for the delivery of property or money damages. An excellent discussion of the history of the term and its application to various kinds of intangible property is found in the early issues of the *Law Quarterly Review*. See Elphinstone 1893; Williams, 1894; Sweet, 1894; Pollock, 1894; Brodhurst, 1895; Sweet, 1895.

held against specifiable individuals, which should appear surprising at first glance. How they acquire a property-like character despite the fact that they are in essence personal rights will be discussed in detail in the next chapter. Although the division between choses in possession and choses in action applies to personal property only, we can treat land as a chose in possession as well, as a material thing to which one can maintain a physical relation. 'Occupation' captures this relation better than 'possession', though possession is the term of art in English law.[11] Some choses in action are 'pure' intangibles, like debts, and some are 'documentary', embodied in paper, like cheques. Pure choses in action are, roughly, those legal rights *in personam* to pay a certain sum of money or deliver specified property, which the right-holder can transfer to someone else by 'assigning' them. The requirement to do so in writing does not mean that the right, say to the payment of a debt, becomes attached to the writing. The writing is essentially evidence of the assignment, even if there is a legal rule that only written assignments are valid. A 'formal' requirement of this kind exists so that the difficulties of proving oral assignments are avoided, and perhaps also out of the fear of allowing individuals to bind themselves legally by making casual oral assignments. The debt remains a purely intangible, abstract legal relation. Documentary intangibles are legal rights *in personam* 'reified' or embodied in paper, like a cheque or promissory note which reifies a right to the payment of money, or like a document of title such as a bill of lading which reifies a right to the receipt of chattels.[12] The owner can transfer the rights embodied in these documents by indorsing the documents and delivering (i.e. transferring possession of) them to the recipient. They thus partake of the nature of both chattels and choses in action.[13]

Negotiable instruments are those documentary intangibles which, because of their standardized form and use in commerce, benefit from special rules regarding the passing of title. The title to chattels is generally very secure. A thief acquires no title to chattels, and so a third party who buys a stolen car in good faith is liable to the original owner for its value despite being a pure innocent.[14] However someone who in good faith gives good value for a negotiable instrument like a cheque takes good title even if he buys it from one who has no valid title, like a thief.

[11] See D. R. Harris 1961.

[12] See Goode 1987, 449–51 for the distinction between bills of lading to ascertained goods, which essentially do confer ownership in the chattels, and those to a specified proportion of a total cargo, which do not.

[13] 'The identification of the right to possess a bill or note and the right to sue thereon corresponds to the double nature of a negotiable instrument as a chose in action and a chattel and is produced by the 'reification' of the debt claim under the instrument or its"merger" into the paper embodying it': Z. Chafee, 'Rights in Overdue Paper', 31 *Harvard Law Review*, 1104 at 1109 (1918), cited in Zeigel et al. 1987, 643–4.

[14] For the exceptions to this rule, which is embodied in the latin phrase *nemo dat quod non habet*, see Bell 1989, ch. 21.

Money is a different kind of property again. Money was originally only coins which had their own intrinsic value, being made of precious metal. Because, however, they were used as currency, i.e. as a universal medium of exchange and store of value expressed in units of account like the £ sterling, essentially the same rule applied to the passing of title in money as later applied to negotiable instruments. This characteriztic is often expressed by the phrase 'money has no earmark'. In other words, if someone gave good value for money, unless the actual coins he took could be specifically identified, he took good title to them even from a thief. Thus Mann describes money, originally coins but later banknotes as well, as 'negotiable chattels'.[15] Paper money was a later invention, and essentially consists of a negotiable instrument which serves as currency. Now, of course, most coins are not intrinsically valued for their metal content, and for that reason may be regarded as essentially the same as paper money, that is as metallic negotiable instruments denominated in reference to a particular unit of account and serving as currency.[16]

Intellectual property rights, as we shall see, are considered by some to fall into the category of choses in action, but if so they are atypical because they are not rights *in personam* at all. Patents, copyright, trade marks, industrial designs, and so on are rights to monopolies. A patent for an invention entitles the patent-holder to the exclusive working of the invention, and so the scope of the monopoly is determined in reference to the scope of the invention, that is, the novel advance on the prior state of the art.[17] Any one else who works the invention is liable for infringement. As monopolies, these rights clearly correlate to duties *in rem*, since everyone has a duty not to do what the monopoly reserves to the right-holder.[18]

[15] Mann 1992, 10.

[16] Ibid. 19–28.

[17] For the history of the patent monopoly and other, now defunct monopolies to produce certain goods, see Fox 1947, pt. I.

[18] Goodwill, if it were really property, would fall under the classification of monopoly. '[T]he goodwill of a business . . . is merely the right to go on using the old name, coupled with the expectation that custom will still follow the name'(Pollock, 1894, at 319), i.e. even if the business is sold to another. It thus constitutes a monopoly over the use of a name which is obviously of commercial value. Thus on the sale of the assets of a business, the buyer typically 'buys' the goodwill as well, which in fact constitutes a contractual term forbidding the seller to trade under the former name. In this way, the buyer, who wishes to carry on using the business's assets in the same way, 'buys the business', not just the business's property. Thus the 'assignment' of goodwill amounts to nothing more than the contractual restraint on a previous owner's freedom to trade. Lawson and Rudden (1982, 33) state that while 'no third party can be restrained from trading in such a way as to reduce the value of the goodwill', '[y]et as a marketable object goodwill must be considered property'. I disagree. There is no conceivable right *in rem* here, for the marketable asset is a creation purely of contract, raising no rights or duties in any others besides the contracting parties. It amounts to a negative contract of employment, in which the previous owner is restrained from acting in a particular way. Goodwill as property exists only because there are some general duties protecting it, viz. the legal monopolies that the use and registration of trade names and trade marks confers.

Finally, we must consider funds. Funds do not exist as a species of property right as do the others, but exist as a kind of second order property right in the property of others. The character of funds, however, goes some way to explaining the proprietary character of many choses in action, such as shares, interests in trusts, and even, as we shall see, debts. A fund itself is nothing more than a property or group of properties defined as a set. It is held by one or more persons, call them Os, to manage or hold for another or others, call them As. The Os must keep the fund separate from the rest of their property and, usually, they may exchange the individual component properties of the fund for new ones.[19] Thus defining the property as a fluctuating set and keeping it separate allows one to keep account of various substitutions, so that the fund may change its component parts while maintaining its identity. The As for whom the fund is held do not, strictly speaking, have any rights to any of the individual component properties of the fund. They only have an interest in the fund itself via their rights against the Os, who actually own the fund. It is the personal legal relation between the As and the Os which determines the rights of the As to the fund properties, so the interests of the As are in this sense choses in action, rights *in personam* against the Os. The most common examples of these rights are shares in companies and beneficiary interests in trust funds. The shareholder has no property rights against the various properties of the company. The company is the legal person which owns them. The shareholders have rights to proportionate shares of any dividends which may be declared, to proportionate shares of the division of the company's assets if it is wound up, and to a proportionate number of votes to elect the directors of the company. The beneficiary under a trust or cestui que trust (pronounced *settee key trust*[20]) has rights against the trustee, who is the legal owner of the trust property, to manage the trust fund and to distribute the benefits of the trust property, either as capital or income, in accordance with the law of trusts and the directions of the settlor of the trust (the one who set up the trust by making the trustee the legal owner of the property) which are usually written down in a trust instrument.

There is another kind of second order property right which is akin to an interest in a fund, but it is instead an interest in a specific, non-substitutable piece of property, sometimes rendered as a *jus in re aliena*, a right in the property of another. They are common in respect of land. One may have a right of way across the land of another, called an easement. An easement only exists as an attachment to another piece of land, that is, one can only own an easement over Blackacre as a function of owning Whiteacre, a

Since these have already been mentioned, there is no need to distinguish a different category of goodwill, especially one whose character is entirely contractual, and thus not of property.

[19] See Goode 1976 pt. I, 384–6, 1976 pt. II, 529–30.

[20] The term is French; medieval English lawyers argued their cases in Norman French, and a number of terms of art in English law derive from this usage. Their pronunciation is peculiar.

neighbouring property. So easements cannot be sold separately from Whiteacre. In this way they constitute a kind of accretion to the property right that an owner has in Whiteacre. One may have the right to take property from someone else's land, cut timber for instance. This is called a 'profit à prendre'. Profits, by contrast with easements, can exist *in gross*, meaning that they can be transferred as property rights on their own unattached to the ownership of any land. Perhaps the most common interest in the property of another, however, is the security interest, which can apply to all kinds of property. This is essentially a right to possess or to sell the property of another if that person fails to meet a personal obligation, usually the repayment of a debt. The most obvious example is the mortgage of land.

If the exclusion thesis is correct, the *in rem* character of property must apply to all of these objects of property. In order to see how, we must first take on board another elemental conceptual feature of property, which I have elaborated as the separability thesis.

The Separability Thesis, or the 'Thinghood' of Objects of Property

The 'separability' thesis may be expressed as follows:

> Only those 'things' in the world which are contingently associated with any particular owner may be objects of property; as a function of the nature of this contingency, in theory nothing of normative consequence beyond the fact that the ownership has changed occurs when an object of property is alienated to another.

This thesis embodies two propositions. The first, that some idea of contingent association or 'separability' informs our understanding of what things can be property, is neither novel nor particularly controversial. While some persons would wish to treat every aspect of value that a person can, in the loosest sense of the word, 'possess', as a kind of property, this is neither the general view nor one to be recommended. There is no good reason why we should hold that our talents, our personalities, our eyesight, or our friendships are property. What makes it difficult to regard these examples as property is not that we cannot exploit them in some way, though *exploiting* one's friendships or personality has an immoral connotation about it. Nor is it the case that we cannot *exclude* others from them; some like our talents or our personalities are essentially exclusive anyway, though we can deny other persons the benefit of our talents, or the personal intercourse which might reveal our personalities; we can prevent others interfering with our eyes, and thus our eyesight, and we can protect our friendships, and other social relationships, such as business partnerships or marriages, by avoiding the company of those who might pose a danger to them. The difficulty lies in treating these things as separable from us in any straightforward way. We do not trade our talents, give away our personalities, licence our friendships to others, or pay taxes with our eyesight.

This first aspect of the separability thesis may perhaps be captured by saying that we are 'entitled' to our rights generally, but as MacCormick says, we have 'title' to our property:

> Some fact or event must obtain or occur whereby *this* person has a right to . . . *this* thing . . . since things (as distinct from limbs and bodily organs, which become things in law only on being severed from a living body) do not have necessary links with particular persons, it follows that a person can have a legal right *to* this or that thing as against some other person only if he or she has some title which in law confers that right to that thing.[21]

A necessary criterion of treating something as property, therefore, is that it is only contingently ours; we must somehow show why it is ours because it might well not have been; nothing similar need be said about those things with 'necessary links with particular persons', like our talents, our personalities, our friendships, or our eyesight. Of course many rights which are not property rights would be counted as property rights on this simple 'contingency test'. Rights arising under contracts, or rights that arise on the violation of a tort, say to damages, are contingent as well, since one has no necessary contractual rights or rights to damages. What distinguishes a property right is not just that they are only contingently ours, *but that they might just as well be someone else's*.

This aspect of contingency is embodied in the second proposition of the separability thesis. The contingency of our connection to particular items of property is such that, in theory, there is nothing special about *my* ownership of a particular car—the relationship the next owner will have to it is essentially identical. 'In theory' is there to point out that it is of course true that we may become emotionally or otherwise 'attached' to specific pieces of property, but while these attachments may have moral or political significance, or even legal significance in a secondary way,[22] these attachments are utterly irrelevant if, or to the extent that, the object is treated as property. The converse proposition is that, to the extent that an individual personal relationship is the legally recognized essence of the relationship between a person and the putative object of property, that relationship fails to be a property relationship. This, too, might seem straightforward in respect of material objects, but recall the chose in action, a property right founded on a right *in personam*. One might well expect that the *personal* relationship between the debtor and his creditor is very much the essence of this legal relationship, and so it cannot be property. We will see how it is.

[21] MacCormick 1990, para. 1100.

[22] e.g. family homes are subject to special provisions of the law of bankruptcy; see *Insolvency Act 1986*, s. 336; *Re Citro* [1991] Ch. 142.

It is not uncommon to identify the separability of property with the power to transfer, and so it is worthwhile dwelling for a moment on the insufficiency of 'transferability' to do the conceptual job the separability thesis does. Munzer, for example, *relies on* transferability to distinguish between property rights that one has in one's body from other so-called 'body rights', which he dubs 'personal rights'.[23] 'Personal rights are body rights that protect interests or choices other than the choice to transfer. Property rights are body rights that protect the choice to transfer.'[24] Perhaps the choice to transfer provides a useful criterion (amongst others) for distinguishing property in the context of rights to one's own body, but in general it does a poor job in picking out property rights. Separability is a conceptual criterion of property which defines the objects of property and gives rise to transferability. To be conceived of as an object of property a thing must first be considered as separable and distinct from any person who might hold it, and is for that reason rightly regarded as alienable. This is not a conceptual criterion of things themselves, but of the relations that obtain between people and everything else. Some of these relations are ones which rely upon a clear distinction between the person and the thing, and in some of these cases the thing is a legal right, like a right to the payment of a debt, or to be paid the balance in one's bank account; these are cases of property rights. In others, the relation itself partakes of some of the qualities of the person who stands at one end of the relation; my personality is bound up with my body, and so my relation to my body is similarly very personal; so are my personal relations to my friends, and my personal rights under most kinds of contract. This distinction is not well captured by asking whether the person has a right protecting a choice to 'transfer the thing', especially since, as we have seen, 'transferring property' is so often treated as analogous to 'conferring value on' or 'creating a benefit for' another, so that one must, at least at the outset, treat one's labour as one's property, even though one's career or employment provides, particularly these days, an almost vital constituent of one's identity.

Indeed, it is worth pointing out again here that it is not inconceivable that one might own untransferable property. As I mentioned at the end of the last chapter, if the government suddenly placed a ban on the transfer of houses their owners would not, necessarily, suddenly be without property. It would all depend on why the ban was imposed. While it makes sense to ask, as a kind of test of something's property status whether it is transferable, a negative answer is not determinative. It makes sense because, being separable, there is no obvious reason why there should be a ban on transfer, and such bans are atypical and require explanation. But untransferable property is not inconceivable. What makes it impossible to conceive of certain rights as property rights, such as the right not to be murdered and a great many other rights which are not without distortion called body rights, such as the

[23] Munzer 1990, 44–56. [24] Ibid. 48–9.

right to assemble or the right to marry or to make binding agreements, is that one can not conceive of how such rights could be *separated* from one—they are the constitutive rights that being a person entails having. We simply do not stand in relation to them as we stand in relation to our property.

The case of certain rights *in personam*, such as rights under certain contracts and licences are especially illustrative. A contract of employment is not freely alienable because both the employer and the employee consider an essential part of the contract that the work is to be done by the latter himself for the former himself. The personal aspect of the contractual right and obligation is not separable from the person who has it; the labour involved is an aspect of the employee's personal experience, the act of an agent, not some free-standing 'thing' which can be stripped away from him. The freely alienable taxi licence is not like the licence to practise medicine, since the capacity to do the latter is something which is intimately connected to the person holding it, to his history in terms of education and qualifications, and to his intelligence and skill, none of which can be separated from him.

To move beyond treating separability as mere transferability, we must return to the two senses of our separability from our property. In the first sense, it refers to the loss or destruction of a person's relationship to it. In the case of a right to property, its loss or destruction works no constitutive change in the owner; his identity or personality is not necessarily implicated in his relationship to the thing. Secondly, we also think of separability in terms of alienation *to* others, principally in terms of exchanges or gifts, but also in terms of paying money for fines or court judgments or in taxes. On this second view separability is not conceived of as the disappearance of the right while the owner remains intact, but as the continuing identity of the right through transfers. The first sense emphasizes the independent identity of the owner, the second the independent identity of 'owning this thing'. Thus we can ask two questions to plumb the nature of this separability: 'is the owner still the same person if he no longer has this thing because it is taken away from him or destroyed?' and 'does a different person who takes on the relationship to the thing stand in essentially the same position as the first person?'

The second question is the one which we should use, since it is easy to show that the first does not identify property. For example, I would be the same person if I lost one of my limbs, or if my relationship to a friend was severed because that friend died, but my relationships to my limbs and my friends are not property relationships. I am not, of course, saying that I might not change, perhaps for the worse, because of the loss of a leg or because my best friend died. These and other events in my life affect me, and thus will shape my personality to some extent, but I do not undergo a constitutive change in my character on the very occurrence of these events, and so, in this respect, losing my limbs and losing my friend is no different from losing a wristwatch or selling my house. The first question fails to differentiate them. Nevertheless, the reason these events have a power to change me is because of the significantly personal ways I stand in relation to my body and to my friends. In order to assess the personal quality of those relationships, we need to assess the difference between my relationships to my body and my friends and the relationships *others* have to those same things. That requires the use of the second question.

While this second question clearly allows us to answer that an owner's relationship to objects like apples, or to land, is property, since we all stand to these objects in essentially the same way, intangible property like choses in action and intellectual property, and rights in or to our own bodies and the bodies of others, as in slavery, provide the most thought-provoking problems, so they will be discussed in turn.

The problem with choses in action is that the objects of the rights are not just there in the world: they arise as a result of personal dealings between people, and it is natural not to think of either of the parties to such special relationships as substitutable by other people *per se*. Debts, while undoubtedly property, are close to the line because they are just barely things which permit the substitution of one right-holder for another while maintaining roughly the same character. From the debtor's perspective, the assignment of a debt can appear fundamentally to alter the whole debtor–creditor relationship, since a creditor may choose or not choose to enforce a debt, mercilessly or otherwise. Indeed, one commentator has pointed out that the debts of individuals became generally assignable only after imprisonment for debt was abolished, thus removing one extremely personality-rich element of the relationship.[25] Choses in action illustrate one type of connection which limits what things can be property, viz. the connection of a personal relationship, that is one in which it fundamentally matters who the personalities to the relationship are, as in a contract of employment.

A nice discussion of various ways of looking at intangible property was conducted in the *Law Quarterly Review* at the end of the last century.[26] The debate focused on the question of what was a chose in action, and the character of the argument was framed by Blackstone's division[27] of all personal property into two classes: choses in possession, that is material objects where ownership constituted the actual enjoyment of the things through their possession, and choses in action, where the owner had only a 'bare right to occupy the thing in question: the possession whereof may, however, be recovered by a suit or action at law from whence the thing so recoverable is called a thing or *chose in action*'.[28]

[25] Bailey 1931–2, 549–50.

[26] Elphinstone 1893 kicked it off, and Williams 1894, Sweet 1984 and 1895, Pollock 1894, and Brodhurst 1895 joined in.

[27] Bl.Comm. 389.

[28] Bl.Comm. 396.

In the most basic sense, choses in action are any right to take legal proceedings which may result in the award of property.[29] But the interesting question is which of these rights count as those particular 'choses in action' that are understood to be property rights. The authors made reference to various rules of law whose application turned on whether or not something was personal property.

For example, in execution of a judgment of the court, a sheriff could only seize the defendant's personal property in possession, and so any other property the defendant had must lie in action. This test, obviously, distinguished choses in possession from choses in action, not choses in action from rights in action which were not property at all, but it led Elphinstone to write that the interest a bailor has in his goods in the possession of a bailee was a chose in action, since the sheriff could not seize them.[30]

Other tests focused on which rights of action fell into what the law considered to be someone's personal property in particular cases. Were they, like other personal property, forfeited to the Crown for outlawry or on commission of a felony? Rights in action founded on contract or for torts wherein the damage was to goods were, for the damages were seen to be certain, but not rights in action for damages 'wholly' uncertain, e.g. for trespass.[31] Did they fall into the debtor's personal estate in bankruptcy? Rights in action to damages for tortious injuries to property did, but those to damages for tortious injuries to the person or reputation were too personal, and therefore did not.[32] Could they be taken so as to found the act of the crime of larceny, i.e. theft of chattels?[33] At common law, upon marriage a wife's property became her husband's, and so one might ask whether specific rights of actions became his or remained hers upon marriage.[34] Was the right assignable? This appears to have turned, first, on whether the object of the right were certain, or uncertain, as in the uncertain amount of damages that would be obtained in an action for tortious damage to the person,[35] secondly on the ground that particular rights, such as contractual rights as well as rights in action for personal injury damages were too personal,[36] and thirdly, on the public policy ground of prohibiting maintenance, i.e. the keeping alive of legal actions afforded by allowing a plaintiff to sell his action.[37]

[29] As Williams 1894, 145 points out, the term 'chose in action' was in use before any general term 'property' was in use, and so the character of a chose in action could, originally at least, hardly turn on whether or not the right counted as property. See also Sweet 1894, 315, who says of Blackstone's definition of choses in action as a species of property 'is so incomplete as to be almost worthless'.

[30] Elphinstone 1893, 313. This view was refined by Williams, who pointed out that a sheriff was entitled to seize bailed goods the debtor was entitled to retake at will. Williams 1894, at 153.

[31] See Williams 1894, 148.

[32] Ibid. 145–6.

[33] Sweet 1894, 312–313.

[34] Williams 1894, 153; Sweet 1894, 313.

[35] Elphinstone 1893, 315; Williams 1894, 147–51.

[36] Williams 1894, 151; Sweet 1894, 306, 313–14.

[37] Elphinstone 1893, 315; Williams 1894, 147–51; Sweet argues that this was especially the case as regards real actions to recover land, for the view was that peaceable 'terre-tenants'

The authors' attentions to these various rules show, if anyone needed convincing, how the 'separability' aspect of property should not be reduced to transferability. It might, for example, be a better test of the property status of our right to our kidneys to ask, not whether we may sell them, but whether they can be removed and sold by our trustee in bankruptcy to pay our debts.

Underlying these rules which inform us about the status of particular rights in action under the positive law of property in English law are more basic considerations about the nature of the object of property in these problematic rights. In particular, the certainty or definability of the object and whether it is 'too personal' seem prominent. Clearly the idea that a right *in personam* against another may be 'too personal' to be property accords with the general claim of the separability thesis, but with a little elaboration we can see that the 'uncertainty' criterion, and the policy against maintenance may as well.

We must look at why these rights are uncertain. Brodhurst argues that in respect of choses in action, the 'thing' in action is the property which the prosecution of the right allows us to gain possession of.[38] This is partly right. The holder of a chose in action does not have an actual property right in any specific property of the one against whom he holds it, but he is meant to have a notional value which can be conceived of as specific property. And to the extent that one can only conceive of a right in property as a right to some fairly certain measure of value, then a right in action to a wholly uncertain amount fails to qualify. With respect, however, the uncertainty of value argument is a weak one. Many rights in action which are clearly property, in particular debt instruments such as bonds and shares in companies, fluctuate in value so much that if this test were universally applied much of what we regard as property would not be property. Of the contributors to the debate, Pollock's contribution was the most theoretically abstract, and he argued, concerning 'exclusive rights, [which] though not merely personal, are only remotely connected with any tangible thing', that

> These rights can be and are regarded in law as having distinct and measurable values, and whatever has such value is a thing, though not a bodily and sensible thing. These benefits can be part of a man's inheritance or goods, of his 'estate and effects', to use the largest term known to our law; they are capable of transmission and, for the most part, of voluntary alienation. We must recognize as things, in fact, all objects of exchange and commerce which are recognized by the usage of mankind.[39]

In view of what he says in the last sentence one presumes that the qualification of 'distinct and measurable' he places on value in the first would not

ought not be disturbed by litigants who had bought up old rights of actions in the days before there were effective statutes of limitations: Sweet 1894, 306–11.

[38] Brodhurst 1895, 67–9.

[39] Pollock 1894, 319.

exclude the uncertain fluctuating values of things like bonds or shares. It is submitted that what makes some uncertain and fluctuating values the proper objects of property is again whether there is too personal an element, and this is perhaps raised by the concern with assigning rights of action in tort for damages for personal injury or reputation. It is not the uncertainty of the damages that might be won, but the fact that a plaintiff in such a case remains a participant even after assignment. Unlike in an action for damage to property or breach of contract, the plaintiff's participation in the suit as injured party whose damages are to be assessed does not allow one to regard the plaintiff as simply assigning his rights away. He remains thoroughly personally involved until the case is decided, that is, until the chose in action is prosecuted to a conclusion or settled. But by the same token, this way of looking at the matter casts new light on the issue of uncertainty. The real problem of uncertain objects of property cannot be mere uncertainty of value, for as we know many kinds of property like shares and bonds fluctuate in value, at times wildly, yet are still property. But the 'too personal' rights of action, like the right to damages for injury to the person, are uncertain in a different way: there is an uncertainty of calculation or determination of value. The value of a share fluctuates with the economic health of the underlying business, but it is easy to calculate the 'share' of the value of the business which the share represents; it is a simple fraction of its total value. In this the fluctuation of the value of the shareholder's property is no different from the fluctuation in market value of any chattel he might own. In the case of personal rights of action, however, the uncertainty of value is of a completely different kind; it is not the shifting appraisal of the market of the worth of something, it is the unpredictable calculation of the fruits of litigation in which the plaintiff must play a central part. Of course a market for personal injury claims might develop so that such uncertainty could be tamed, presenting a purchaser with an investment opportunity framed with a credible risk/return forecast; that would depend on developing techniques for predicting the results of personal injury and defamation actions, which might to our late twentieth-century minds appear much more plausible than to these early twentieth-century writers.

These authors' views on intellectual property are similarly stimulating: not one of them embraces the idiotic fiction that intellectual property constitutes property in ideas (patents) or expressions (copyright). They see it for what it is, a certain class of rights to monopolies. Elphinstone doubts that intellectual property rights are choses in action, for they are not rights *in personam*, but rights against the whole world; until someone violates the right, there is no right in action, whereas in the case of a debt its very existence depends upon such a right.[40] Sweet regards intellectual property as incorporeal property, but not truly choses in action for 'their essential quality

[40] Elphinstone 1894, 314.

is that they are permanent property—not necessarily perpetual, but wholly different from such transient things as debts and other rights of action'; however, if one must choose to treat them as either choses in possession or choses in action, Sweet prefers the latter alternative, at least in the context of bankruptcy.[41] Brodhurst goes so far as to treat them as choses in possession on the basis that the benefit that one receives by having copyright is not secured by action; one enjoys the benefit of it simply by having it, by one's 'constructive possession' of it: if one's copyright is infringed, one then obtains a right in action for what amounts to a trespass.[42] Each of them is in his own way right.

Intellectual property rights are akin to choses in action because they are abstract legal rights, with no direct connection to any thing, tangible or intangible. But they are not claims to receive some share or amount of the property of others, as choses in action typically are. They are rights directly to a practice of exclusion, as directly as are property rights in chattels or land, correlating to duties *in rem* by which all subjects of the legal system have a negative duty not to do something. The duty is not one to refrain from interfering with material objects, but to refrain from working an invention or copying an original work or from representing one's business or its products by a certain name or symbol.

While patents are not property rights in ideas,[43] nor copyrights property rights in expressions,[44] nor again trade marks property rights in symbols or words, in general it does no harm to speak of rights in ideas, or in manuscripts, or in marks, any more than it does to refer to one's rights in one's labour. And in the same way that labour forms part of one's life experience, the development of an idea or the creation of an artistic work can never be separated from the inventor or artist; it remains the inventor's or artist's forever. The light bulb is Edison's invention whoever makes use of it, and *Bleak House* is Dickens's whoever reads it. Whatever rights the inventor or the artist has, when we start speaking of property rights in ideas and artistic works, things begin to lose sense. A true property right in an idea or an expression would constitute a right of exclusion from that idea or that expression itself. Subjects of the law would have a duty not to read about or understand an invention or take in the expression in a book or a painting (a funny notion since patents are published when granted, and a copyright is a right exclusively to disseminate a work). Intellectual property rights are monopolies *defined* in terms of ideas and expressions and symbols.

Treating property in patents and copyrights as property rights in monopolies that are defined in terms of ideas and expressions, rather than as

[41] Sweet 1894, 315–16.

[42] Brodhurst 1895, 69–75.

[43] On the history of the patent monopoly, see Fox 1947, pt. I; Coulter 1991.

[44] An excellent, but very long discussion of the common law protection of literary works can be found in *Millar* v. *Taylor* (1769) 4 Burr. 2303.

property rights in the ideas and expressions themselves, may appear to be a slippery slope which would lead to all property rights being defined as rights to monopolies of some kind. As we have seen, the right to a piece of land is not completely exclusive. Passers-by may gain value by looking at one's garden. Why, then, do we not say that the landowner has a monopoly on various uses defined in reference to the land, of course, but no direct property right in the land itself? Neither the land owner nor the patent holder has a complete right to all facets of use or value that the thing, the land or the idea, provides. The difference, however, lies in the characterization of the landowner's and patent-holder's respective use-rights. The landowner's use-rights are essentially indefinable, comprising every possible use of land. One cannot draw up an exhaustive list of them, and this is true even if others like the passer-by may gain some value from the land. The exact opposite is true of the patent-holder's use-rights. The patent is an exclusive right to a particular use of the invention or idea, that is, working it to produce goods for sale in the market. But this is only one of a limitless number of ways in which an idea may be 'used'; one can study it, use it to illustrate scientific principles, use it as the basis for further inventive endeavours, and so on. That the market use of the idea is often the most valuable use in economic terms (though clearly not always, and probably rarely as a proportion of the patents that are actually granted), that does not alter the fact that it is one use only. A patent is like the 'lease' to extract oil mentioned at the end of the last chapter; in the same way that the lease was not really a property right in the land, the patent is not a property right in the idea or invention.

An actual right that may be close to a true right to an idea is the right of the State to its official secrets, which might be regarded as a property right to certain information, since the law imposes a general duty on everyone to exclude themselves from it.[45] The problem with treating this as property is not its exclusionary structure, but the separability aspect. It is not clear that the State's exclusionary right to information might just as well be someone else's, such that any individual legal subject might enjoy the same kind of right. The State has a number of monopolies, like that on violence, which are justified in reference to its special position, and it would seem likely that this kind of truly exclusionary monopoly on information is similarly justified (if it is justified), for example by the claim that it is necessary to maintain security.

So far I have been elaborating the separability thesis with examples of real kinds of property, choses in action and intellectual property. Nowhere, how-

[45] Rights of persons, in particular companies, to their confidential information do not count as property rights, for this information is protected directly not by the legal imposition of duties *in rem* but by contracts between the person or company which holds the information and other individuals, typically their employees. The only duties *in rem* in tort law or criminal law which assist are not directly aimed at the protection of confidential information, but at prohibiting persons from interfering with the land or chattels of the confidential information holder. Cf. A. S. Weinrib, 1988.

ever, does the conceptual impossibility of separating a particular thing from the person who has it remove that thing from the realm of property more clearly than in the case of rights to our bodies. The analogy of property to the relation one has with one's body is grounded on the fact that both involve exclusive use. One has the right of exclusive determination of what one will do with one's body (subject of course to the same basic prohibitions against violence and other recognized moral norms), as one does in respect of those things which are one's property. The distinction between the two is that an owner is not necessarily connected to, but is separable from, the things he holds as property. Furthermore, as was mentioned in discussing abandonment, the relationship of property dictates the absolute control of the owner over the thing (to the extent humanly possible, of course), and the corresponding absence of any 'control' of the thing over the owner. This entails that the owner can rid himself of a thing that he holds as property. This is not the case with our bodies. We are stuck in, or to, but certainly with, them.

The case of body parts[46] is particularly illustrative of the influence of circumstances on the application of the separability criterion, because the extent to which we regard our body parts as separable from us is a matter of intention, social convention, and technology, even though our body parts are clearly material objects in the world, and so like other chattels are obvious candidates for objects of property. As MacCormick points out, the connection of our bodily parts with our bodies shows why they are not generally regarded as our property, even though they are clearly protected by duties of non-interference and even though our rights to them are 'alienable', given that we can waive a right to assault, releasing others from these duties, say, to let a surgeon do a biopsy. Until quite recently, technology did not prompt us to consider doing without them, much less passing them around. We did not therefore regard our connection to them as contingent: they could not just as well be someone else's body parts. One does not normally regard one's kidneys as property, *unless* one is actually considering selling them or giving them away or otherwise getting rid of them. In those contexts, they *are* conceived as property. If one is attacked and stabbed in the kidney, one may, having formed an intention to sell a kidney, regard the attack not only as an attack upon oneself but as a destruction of property. Nowadays, however, it would not be the least bit legally absurd were X to bring an action for conversion (for the wrongful interference with a chattel) against the assaulter who took or destroyed X's kidney.[47] But not having formed any intention of this kind, one does not conceive of the attack as a tort or crime affecting property. Social convention also affects the conception of what parts of our body are separable from us. Imagine a society in which a man's

[46] For an excellent discussion of the justifications for and against permitting a market in body parts, see Munzer 1994.

[47] See *Moore* v. *The Regents of the University of California*, 479 (1990) 793 P2d.

hair was considered to be essential to his physical strength or sanity. Cutting a man's hair might be regarded along the same lines as doing a frontal lobotomy. It would count as an attack upon his personality, on himself, not as an attack on part of his worldly goods. The role of technology is obvious. To the extent that the removal of an organ causes death, such an organ cannot be regarded as property. Consider the idea of selling one's brain. If, however, science proves capable of disconnecting an organ so that one remains essentially the same person, as is the case with a kidney, we can regard such an organ as a contingent material possession, and therefore one's property.

The issue of having property in a dead body raises similar issues.[48] Clearly, during one's life one cannot treat one's body as one's property, because one cannot do without it. So the idea of its being included in 'the rest and residue of my estate' is out of the question, because it was not the property of the testator. Yet a corpse has no necessary attachment to any living human. So it can be as much the subject of a property right as anything else. But is it still attached to a self? We generally act as if it is. We speak in respect of a dead person as still having a possessive relationship to his body, as in 'his body was recovered from the Thames'. In other words, we treat a corpse in a way which shows respect for the person who was the living body, not as the last remains of his physical material but as the last remains of his self. The relationship of a person to his body in life continues to affect deeply our treatment of his body, even after death.

Our labour, the work of our body and mind, is protected by various duties on all others, such as the duty not to commit assault or murder. We can release others from their duty not to assault us. Furthermore, we can conceive of our labour as being separable from us in some respect: we can labour for others. But the 'separability' criterion seems weakly instantiated by labour because labour is constituted by our intentional actions which form part of our life history, and therefore our identity. A contract of employment employs the whole person, and secures the employee's human participation in some co-operative project; it does not merely extract some resource from the employee. 'Property' only applies to our labour metaphorically, or under a stipulated definition of property used by some economists.[49] 'Selling' our labour is a metaphor for doing something for payment; it is not the same thing as actually transferring something for payment, as is the case with property.[50]

The fact that our criterion of separability is conceptual, of course, gives us free rein to imagine other property systems with different objects of property. One can, for example, imagine a property right not to be murdered.

[48] See Mathews 1983.
[49] e.g. Demsetz 1967, 348–9; Posner 1981, 109–11.
[50] Cf. Harris 1996, 68–73.

Imagine a society in which only nobles had the legal right not to be murdered, and where everyone else had to rely on the morality of their fellows or on self-defence. Now say some down-at-heel nobles discovered that they could legally sell their rights not to be murdered, and did so. Then we would have an example of a separable and exclusive right not to be murdered, i.e. a property right not to be murdered. But while this is a case of *imaginable* property, it violates the concept of property we actually have in terms of the role the it plays for us. We do not have a property right not to be murdered because *our* legal right not to be murdered is not justified by a title, purchased or not. Our legal right not to be murdered is based upon considerations about the universal status of persons. A person is conceived as having the right simply by being a living human. Such a right cannot be conceived as separable any more than a person's life can be. One cannot separate one's life from oneself, abandon it, give it away, or sell it, because one *is* one's life or, at least, whatever one is one is not the same thing without it. Similarly, we could conceive of all our contractual rights and obligations as freely alienable, involving no personal bonds, perhaps in the way that feudal offices were conceived,[51] but we do not. That we can imagine circumstances in which they would be so does not make them so. For us, these are all 'personality-rich' relationships: while we can notionally regard the object of the right, the contractual relation, the protection of one's life or body, one's talents or capabilities as 'things', they are not the right kind of things for property given the way we understand them.

Similar considerations go toward characterizing slavery as the ownership of persons and the circumstances which make that possible. The notion of property involved in true chattel slavery, in which the slave is regarded as essentially non-human, a sophisticated animal which is controlled by the whip, is utterly different from what might be called 'status' or 'contractual' or 'chose in action' slavery, in which the slave is regarded as a subject of the law, who is conceived to have legal duties compliance with which is a matter of his responsibility.

In true chattel slavery, the slave-owner owns the slave as he does a tame animal. The slave-owner extracts value from the body of the slave by acting on it, applying external stimuli of various kinds (stick or carrot, as appropriate, though as history illustrates, mostly stick). What distinguishes this kind of slavery from status slavery is that the slave is not regarded as a responsible human agent with duties under the law. He has no duties—he just provides value more or less adequately, as does a cow, a car, or a vein of ore. On this view of slavery, the slave is harvested, usually for the energy of his labour, but also possibly for his material parts if need be.

Under status slavery the slave is himself a subject of the law—he may or may not have rights (even very minimal ones), but he certainly has *duties*.

[51] See Megarry and Wade 1984, 815–16.

Principally, his duty is to do the bidding of his owner. The important feature of this definition of slavery is that the slave is treated as a responsible human agent. In this circumstance, what is the owner's property? Essentially, it is a very extensive right to the services of the slave. The owner is the legally intended beneficiary of the slave's duty to do the bidding of his owner, whoever his owner is. Thus, as a right to a service, to the performance of a duty *in personam*, the ownership of a slave is akin to the ownership of a chose in action. On the other hand, unlike the case of a debt, such a right does not lie wholly 'in action', for the slave-owner typically has a number of self-help measures, like corporal punishment, which may work to bring the slave to the performance of his duties. Yet the difference between this and chattel slavery remains, for the attentions of the slave-owner here are not merely means to harvesting the slave as an object, but are intended to make the slave do himself what by rights he must. Defining slavery in this way is to make it directly comparable to the right to the service of an employee. Various differentiating factors can be mentioned: the remedies available to the employer are much less extensive and onerous than those available to the slave-owner; generally, it is not the case that the slave negotiated his way into the arrangement. But the most important distinguishing factor is the *reason* which underlies legal recognition of these different arrangements: the law of contracts legally recognizes that (notionally equal) individuals can create binding agreements, whereas the law of slavery recognizes that one class of persons (slave-owners) should be able to reap the entire practical value of the existence of another class of persons (slaves).

It is not clear whether chattel slavery and status slavery can be coherently combined, or the extent to which they might overlap in effect. It is not clear, for instance, whether a status slave could have a duty to do the slave-owner's bidding so extensive that it could include a duty to render up parts of his body on request, or take his own life. Taking one's own life, for example, would extinguish the slave's status as a legal subject, which is the foundation of his slavery.

On the views expressed above, if a relationship is a property relationship, there must be an owner and there must be something owned, and these two cannot be the same things. Furthermore, if one stands in the relationship of owner to a thing, then it must be possible for someone else to own it as well. Does it make no sense, i.e. does it violate the logic of property rights, to say 'I own myself'? If this means 'I have the right to determine what I will do', it makes formal sense as a property statement, because that right is clearly one which another person, i.e. a slave-owner, might have. On this definition of 'owning oneself', one might own oneself or one might not. On the other hand, if the statement means something like 'I am intimately connected to my life experiences and my personality' or 'regardless of how they beat me, I still have to exercise my will to act and, in that sense, remain in possession of myself' then it is nonsense as a literal statement of property rights. (Whether it is a salient metaphor in context is a different question.) Such a statement is not contradictable: on this meaning of the statement it is impossible not to 'own oneself'. That does violate the logic of property and, therefore, one cannot literally have property rights in one's life experiences or one's personality or one's will. A statement that *X* owns *Y* is always a statement of fact, not a statement of a conceptual truth.

This suggests that, given our common sense beliefs about personality, we cannot literally say that we own our entire bodies, as wholes. Neither can we own all of our intentional actions, since our actions, as life experiences, are similarly necessary for our sense of who we are. But this raises the conundrum: if I can't own my body, how can someone else (chattel slavery)? If I can't own the right to determine how I shall act, (assuming that having this right, if I have it, profoundly shapes our life and thus the person we are and become over time) how can someone else (status slavery)? The answer that follows from the above discussion is this: there are certain things which people may generally be able to own, but which one person cannot. The slave-owner can own my body, or own a right to all my actions. He can trade or give away those property rights to other persons who will become my new owners, and it does not in any way affect the foundation of *his or their* personalities. But I cannot be the owner of my body or actions since they are inextricably tied to *my* personality. This is no different from the impossibility of holding a debt against oneself. The one person who cannot hold my legal obligation to pay him a certain sum is me. Clearly, to the extent that someone else owns my body or my actions, I cannot be treated as fully human under the law, for my personality is not a matter of my own determination. So although a slave-owner owns a slave, he cannot own another 'person', for slavery reduces the slave below the status of person. Even the status slave is less than fully human under the law—while he is regarded as a responsible 'human' agent in that he has duties, his humanity is reduced to such an extent that he does not really count as an individual with personality.

This draws together our understanding of chattel slavery and status slavery: to the extent that we regard both our right to our bodies and our right to determine how to act as essential for our humanity, if that right is held by someone else our humanity is reduced. On either definition of slavery, therefore, a person loses the status of an individual with personality, even if under status slavery one is not reduced to an animate object. Indeed, one might well decide that status slavery is simply incoherent: on one hand, it relies upon the slave's humanity in imposing duties on him, yet on the other, by that very imposition (the duties are so overwhelming) it takes away his humanity. In other words, the legal model of status slavery is incompatible with the reality of the situation: it treats the slave both as a person and not as a person at the same time.

I have explored all of these examples to show that what determines the things that can be treated as property, i.e. their 'separability' or 'thinghood', is a conceptual criterion: for a thing to be held as property, we must not conceive of it as an aspect of ourselves or our ongoing personality-rich relationships to others. The key is not alienability, or at least 'transferring' the value of the thing, for clearly we can deal with our body parts, our friendships, our ability to work, and our civil rights in ways which benefit others; such dealings do not constitute the transfer of property. Furthermore, as the example of the ban on the transfer of houses shows, this does not mean that for a person to hold a thing as property that person must be able to give the thing away or sell it. Neither does it mean that a person must be able to, as of right, abandon a thing or destroy it. Yet to mention again the connected point from the last chapter, an absolute or very restrictive ban on separating oneself from a thing may in the right circumstances alter the character of one's rights to a thing. A right to an estate which one was bound to maintain, and which one could neither transfer nor abandon nor destroy, would not be a right to property in the conventional sense. At some level of restriction, the rightful possessor or occupier of a thing simply does not consider it 'his property': it might take on the character of a part of his very existence, as perhaps family seats might have done.

The beginning of wisdom here is to realize that there is not a world of 'things' out there all ready to be appropriated as property.[52] 'Thing' here is a term of art which restricts the application of property to those items in the world which are contingently related to us, and this contingency will change given the surrounding circumstances, including our personal, cultural, and technological circumstances. On the other hand, the law of property is not, in general, concerned with how personally one might become emotionally attached to particular pieces of property. While Margaret Radin has emphasized how our personal and cultural circumstances can lead to particular items of property, like wedding rings,[53] becoming 'constitutive' of their owner's identity, simply because a particular owner's relationship with an item of property is idiosyncratically personal does not mean it is not property—my attachment to my house or wedding ring does not remove it from the realm of property; that would only occur if the circumstances had so changed that in general all pieces of jewellery of this kind, whoever held them, the jeweller, a wife or husband, an executor of a will, and so on, regarded these as constitutive of their identities. This is not to say, of course, that we should not deal with property in different ways in different circumstances, bearing certain considerations in mind; the point

[52] That is, a world of things out there which naturally fall to be treated as property. Cf. Pollock 1894.

[53] Radin 1993, 35–71.

is that whatever we do as regards the expropriation of family homes, or the treatment of a bankrupt's wedding ring, we will be working within a legal framework in which these items are still property, and therefore subject, prima facie, to all the usual property norms.

6

The Duty of Non-interference and Ownership

The separability thesis and the exclusion thesis are joint conceptual foundations for our understanding of property. The duty to respect property by not interfering with it should not involve the duty-ower in any personal dealings with the owner in order to respect his ownership, and this is made possible because the relation is mediated via the things the owner owns which, as separable things, exist in their own right and can therefore themselves be the object of duties *in rem*.

The duty of non-interference with respect to most kinds of property is quite straightforward. The duty can, broadly speaking, prohibit two classes of interference: specific interference with the owner's own use and the unlicensed use of the property by a non-owner which to some extent dispossesses the owner; both clearly interfere with the owner's determination of how his property is to be used. Unauthorized handling, occupation, consumption, destruction, dispossession, and keeping property from its true owner are all comprised in 'non-interference'. Each of these prohibitions does not apply to all things that are property. An apple can be handled, consumed, destroyed, and taken, and in the sense of taking we can dispossess the owner of it, but we cannot occupy an apple in any meaningful sense. Land can be occupied, but not, save in the case of land next to the sea, totally destroyed, although fixtures, like buildings, walls and so on, which are regarded in law as part of the land, can be and, though it cannot be taken, an owner can be removed or excluded from the occupation of his land. An owner cannot be dispossessed of his copyright or patent (though he can be defrauded of it), though clearly these monopolies can be interfered with by unauthorized copying and working. When, however we consider choses in action, it appears that the idea of a general duty of any kind, which would correspond to the property right in its classical formulation of a right *in rem*, has no meaning.

Consider a debt, a purely intangible right to the payment of a certain sum. While a debt can be stolen, because its owner, the creditor, can be defrauded of it,[1] a debt cannot be destroyed, or damaged, or taken, or otherwise inter-

[1] See Penner 1996, 809–10. That appears, at least, to be the law according to the Privy Council in *Chan Man-sin* v. *AG for Hong Kong* [1988] 1 All ER 1. There is however, an unresolved technical problem, in that even though he is being defrauded the creditor intentionally assigns title to the debt and should, strictly speaking, pass title to the defrauder. In theft, only possession of the property passes, not title.

fered with in any way which an impersonal duty *in rem* seems well placed to prohibit. The reason is obvious. A debt is an abstract personal right. It has no obvious presence or existence in the world, not even a negative presence like a monopoly in the market place, with which any person might interfere.

Figuring out how a sensible duty of non-interference does protect choses in action is the key to understanding how they are property, but this task is complicated by the fact that common law jurisdictions recognize two separate kinds of ownership of rights in action, choses in action properly so called, which are rights in action recognized by the courts of common law, which may therefore be rather confusingly called *legal* choses in action, and *choses in equity*, or equitable interests, rights recognized originally by a different court, the Court of Chancery, also called a court of Equity. They differ in significant ways, so they will be dealt with in turn.

Legal Choses in Action

Choses in action, for example, company shares, bank balances, and debts, are a special kind of property in which the owner is conceived of as holding a piece of the total worth of a company, or money in a bank, or a certain sum of the debtor's wealth, in other words, some determinable share of the things owned by the entity or person against whom the chose is held, *even though this is technically not the case in law*. One has no legal right to any existing share of an operating company's wealth. A bank balance is simply a legal right to demand a certain sum; it is not truly 'money in the bank' that one owns. A creditor has no rights in the property of his debtor.

Even though a debt may be 'stolen', and a chose in action embodied in a negotiable instrument, being a chattel as well, may be stolen literally, the general duty of non-interference with property does not directly shape the nature of the chose-holder's right. The protection is indirect, as it protects what, for want of a better term, I will call the 'wherewithal'[2] of the entity or person against which the chose is held, which term I stipulate to cover all the property held by those entities or persons which provide the assets from which the chose may be satisfied, such as the company's or the bank's assets, or the property of an individual debtor. That wherewithal is what is protected from depredation by the general duty of non-interference.[3]

Choses in action, therefore, are rights in respect of the property of other legal owners which the law is happy to allow their holders to treat as 'things'

[2] 'Wherewithal' is comparable to the Roman and civilian term 'patrimonium' which indicated all the property in someone's estate; in some modern civil law systems, this term might now be more inclusive, covering all the rights of an individual. See Samuel 1994, 527–8.

[3] And creditors can, of course, act on this. If, for example, I lend money to you as a car-dealer, protecting myself by taking a charge over your stock-in-trade, I may insist as a term of the contract that you insure the cars against theft or negligent damage.

in their own right, i.e. property in their own right. It is not *because* they are alienable that they are things. Rather, it is because they are things that they are alienable. The criterion of 'thinghood' or separability applies to these rights in such a way that they partake of the duty of non-interference in an indirect way.

How so? While these rights are technically rights *in personam* to certain performances, the performances all involve the transfer of certain sums of money, or sums of money which may readily be made certain as and when the time comes for their transfer, as when a dividend is declared or a debt payment falls due. They are, in a sense, like 'money in the bank', in that the entire quality of the relationship between the right-holder and the one whose wherewithal provides the sum is reduced, in a sense, from a personal one to one in which the personalities of the parties to the relationship determine nothing of its nature. Thus the impersonality of the relationship *in personam* fulfils the 'separability' criterion, allowing the right to appear as if it reaches right through the debtor or the bank or the company to the property it legally holds. It is this property, the property of the debtor or company or bank, which benefits directly from the general duty *in rem* of non-interference. Thus the proprietary character of the chose in action is indirect because the chose in action correlated to the general duty *in rem* only through means of a fiction, i.e. that the chose-holder has a right to a determinate portion of another's property. Now, this is not to deny in the least that the 'personal' qualities of the one against whom the chose is held matters; the investment expertise of a bank or the quality of the management of a company or the profligacy of a debtor has an obvious bearing on the question of whether the chose will be honoured. These factors clearly go to determining the *value* of these rights. But this is precisely the trick that is turned by making these rights property rights. By removing these considerations about property to the realm of valuation, the right itself is stripped down to a right to a 'thing', a piece of the wherewithal of another, the value of which fluctuates with the value of that wherewithal just as the value of any other piece of property may fluctuate. In this case, of course, the fluctuations are to a greater or lesser extent determined by the personal behaviour of the corporate directors, or the debtor, and so on.[4] Unlike a contract of employment, the quality of the personal performances of the parties is not the essence of the legal relationship itself, and thus of the rights and duties it defines. Choses in action are therefore things in relation to other kinds of rights between persons which arise because of the contingent, voluntary obligations that arise between persons. Within the realm of personal rela-

[4] For two very interesting views on the possibility that value itself can be reified so as to form the object of property, which incidentally suggest that civilian law may have paid much more attention to these theoretical details than the common law world has, see Rudden 1994 and Mincke 1993.

tions, or rights and duties *in personam*, certain of these are thing-like, in manifesting a reduction in their 'personality-richness', in the same way that the connection of material objects to people is personality-poor by comparison to the connection people have to their *actions,* attributes, and body parts. Again, this is reflected by the extent to which the general duty *in rem* protects any particular right *in personam*. Consider a standard contract of employment. My employer's right *in personam* to my work is a purely personal right; it has nothing to do with how much property I have. Thus it does not benefit at all from the general duty *in rem* which protects my wherewithal. In contrast my right *in personam* to my salary payment as it falls due, while a personal right against my employer, is also a legal debt which I own; whether I get paid depends very much on the state of my employer's wherewithal, and I appreciate very much that it, and thus indirectly my right to be paid, is protected by the general duty *in rem*.

My submission about the proprietary character of choses in action, then, is that *to the extent* that we regard choses in action, these rights *in personam,* as property rights, we do so because of their relative 'personality poverty' in relation to other rights *in personam*. What makes these problematic property rights is the fact that while the relationship is humming along and parties are meeting their obligations, when banks are honouring their depositors' balances, dividends are paid, and debt payments are made on schedule, these rights fulfil very much the role of property that money does. When things go awry, however, when holders are apt to launch shareholder suits or actions against their debtors, the rights revert, in a sense, to their *in personam* origins.

To understand how choses in action are still property rights despite this possibility, we must careful assess certain fixed views about the relationships between rights and remedies. There is a clear sense in which it is right to say that where there is a right there is a remedy, a statement often rendered in the latin *ubi ius ibi remedium*, which is this: if an individual has no remedial rights in a legal system through which he can vindicate a right that he supposedly has, that right is not recognized by the system. From this it follows that the creditor or shareholder has no straightforward property right in the general wherewithal or particular fund[5] the independent component properties of which are protected by general duties *in rem*, for that creditor or shareholder cannot bring an action for damages against someone who wrongfully interferes with the property. However it is false to say that despite this lack of a direct remedy, the system of rules is not geared to protect the proprietary character of these rights, that is as rights to a particular fund held by an owner, or to his general wherewithal. The background rules of bankruptcy attach these rights to the actual property if things go badly wrong, i.e. if the rights can no longer be honoured as intended. The

[5] For a discussion of the common law's recognition of funds, see Goode 1976, pt. I, 384–6.

rights of the creditor become rights to an actual share of the debtor's wherewithal, such as remains, which is held by the trustee in bankruptcy or liquidator of a company, and the trustee in bankruptcy or liquidator must pursue claims for any interferences with the property, specifically to benefit the creditors.

These last two paragraphs present us with something of a paradox. The chose in action is most like property, like 'money in the bank', a certifiable asset, when the right is largely underpinned by remedial rights *in personam*, such as the right to sue a company for one's correct share of dividend, or a bank for failing to honour the value of one's bank balance. It is in these circumstances, when the remedy *in personam* is useful, i.e. when the debtor or bank or company is solvent, that the proprietary remedies to sue anyone who interferes with the wherewithal are left to these legal owners of the property. The right is least like 'money' in the bank, that is a fairly certain economic value, and most like a claim founded on a personal relationship with a wastrel creditor or badly managed company when things have gone badly wrong and the creditor or shareholder has various rights or claims which are much more clearly proprietary.

But this is less of a paradox than it appears. When things are going smoothly, the creditor or shareholder or bank depositor can be least involved. It involves no personal pursuit of economic value, akin to employment. The creditor or shareholder or bank depositor simply has a legal right to money. The more impersonal, the more it is like property. When things go wrong, one's asset suddenly becomes more personally demanding, in that now one has to do something, find a lawyer, participate in a legal action and so on. These rights begin to look more like rights to services under a contract of employment, in which one is susceptible to the failings of one's employees; the 'performance' of the debtor, the company, or the bank now largely shapes the benefit of the right, such as it is. Therefore the character of a chose in action in not particularly shaped by the fact that the remedial rights when things are running smoothly are personal but are proprietary when things go badly wrong.

Thus, as second order property rights, that is, rights to property through the ownership of another, choses in action are thus rightly regarded as special or compromised forms of property just to the extent that the personal quality of the relationship is capable of reasserting itself, so that the right does not appear to be just a right to a share of some property, but rather a right that a specific individual or a group of individuals like a board of directors, with all the faults and failings they may have, perform services to a particular standard.

Choses in Equity and Equitable Ownership

All of the above can be applied with greater force to the case of choses in equity, although these appear even more like property. Indeed, the rights of cestuis que trust are such that they are regarded as owners almost on the footing of legal owners themselves. In order to understand this, however, recourse must be had to the jurisdictional division in the English legal system which gave rise to the present structure of the law of trusts. The law of trusts can be regarded as setting up a second, complete, law of property in the same legal system.

This situation arose as the product of the work of two distinct legal jurisdictions, the common law and what became known as 'equity'. The common law was administered in the King's courts which dealt with the 'common' law of England, i.e that law which applied universally, as opposed to the local law administered by the courts of individual manors. Early on, however, the chief minister of the Crown at the time, the Chancellor, an ecclesiastic who felt able to concern himself with men's immortal souls, and thus their consciences, began to entertain suits by disappointed litigants complaining of decisions by the common law courts. He would, exercising his personal authority, order the winners of an action at common law not to act upon their legal rights if in good conscience they ought not to do so, in effect overturning the decisions of the common law judges. In time this quasi-legal function of the Chancellor led to the development of a separate court, the Court of Chancery, which in theory gave decisions based on the flexible 'maxims of equity' in contrast to the rigid application of the rules of common law, although this is a caricature. The jurisdiction of these separate branches of judge-made law was unified by statute at the end of the nineteenth century, and since that time both law and equity are applied by one system of courts. The extent to which the separate systems of rules of common law and equity have 'fused' remains controversial.

One of the most important creations of equity was the law of trusts. In general, equity worked to amend or supplement rules of law over the breadth of private common law, but the trust was special, for this device of property law was recognized only by the court of Equity and so the branch of law attending to trusts was shaped entirely by it. Indeed, the rules of Equity which concern trusts and trusteeship make up the largest part of any law school course on equity, and many courses abandon the other matter entirely, concerning themselves solely with what one great scholar, Maitland, considered the greatest contribution England made to legal science, the trust.

A trust exists when a particular fund of property is held by a legal owner 'on trust' for a cestui que trust or beneficiary, which means roughly the following: the legal owner has all the legal powers to deal with the trust property, but he must do so entirely for the benefit of the cestui, who is said to have the benefit or enjoyment of the property. In this way equity devised a kind of 'co-ownership', where all the trouble of managing the property and distributing the benefits of it in all sorts of ways can be laid at the door of one person, the trustee holding the legal powers, while the cestuis have nothing to do but receive benefits according to the terms of the trust.

The common law was and is absolutely blind to the existence of trusts. It regards the trustee as the full legal owner of the property. It is only Equity which recognized and recognizes the duties the trustee has to distribute the benefits of the property to the cestuis.

Although this, in a sense, is a more complicated picture than that of legal choses in action, the structure is essentially equivalent. The cestuis have no direct ownership of the trust fund; they have rights *in personam* against the trustee that he carry out the terms of the trust so that the benefits of the trust property are distributed to them accordingly. Thus the cestui's interest is a chose in equity, a right in that branch of judge made law called Equity, to sue the trustee for the property distribution of income or capital or whatever that the trust instrument obliges the trustee to pass his way from the trust fund.

However, there are two features in particular of the cestui's chose in equity which distinguish it from the legal chose in action. First, the cestui's rights typically arise as a result of a gift, whereas someone who has a legal chose in action normally acquires that right through a contract, by purchasing shares or entering a contract which gives rise to a debt. As a result, the cestui does not typically define the trust agreement which defines the terms of his rights against the trustee, the legal owner of the property. They are determined by the settlor, that is, the person who transferred the property to the trustee to set up the trust in the first place. While any particular trustee must agree to take on a trust, the general principle of Equity is that a trust shall not fail for want of a trustee; some trustee will be found to carry out the trust. Thus trusts are typically unilateral acts of a settlor to create a structured gift for one or more cestuis que trust. Secondly, and partly in virtue of the foregoing, trust property is always held in a fund kept separate from the rest of the trustee's property, and the trustee is not able to borrow from the fund or use the fund for his own purposes. This is quite opposite to the general case of the legal chose in action; the money lent to a debtor or paid to a company for the issue of shares or the money deposited in the bank is used by the recipient in all sorts of ways, and dealt with as an accretion to his total wherewithal, out of which, the debt, or bank balance, or dividends, must be paid.

Having said this, it is clear that the cestui's interest is even more like property than is a legal chose in action, for two reasons. The first is that, because the trust property is kept separate from the trustee's other property and because the trustee is not able to use it for any of his own purposes, the cestui benefits much more directly from the general duties *in rem* not to interfere with the property of others. In particular, his rights are tied to the fate of the actual property in a way that the legal chose in action holder's are not. If the trust property disappears, is destroyed or stolen for example, the cestui's rights disappear as well (to the extent that remedies for tortious destruction or conversion cannot be pursued by the trustee, where for example, a thief cannot be found): the trustee is not bound to honour his duties to distribute property which is gone. This is not the case with a debt, for example. If the debtor's property is stolen, this may affect the likelihood that the creditor will be paid, but his right remains intact. Legally, the debtor retains his duty to pay the debt. The second reason has to do with the fact that trusts are traditionally gifts, like family trusts set up to look after dependants. From the perspective of the settlor, the trust is a device for making a structured gift, by which he may, for example, give the income of the trust property to one person for a time, reserving the capital value for someone else. The choses in equity the cestuis receive are their rights to this structured gift. The trustee is not a person with whom they have any personal relationship of any substance—he is the personification of the trust agreement, and it is that which really settles how the gift is to work. He is like a human instrument. There can hardly be any doubt, then, that on the criteria we have applied to legal choses in action that choses in equity, the beneficial interests under a trust, are property rights. Not only is the cestui a much more direct beneficiary of the general duty *in rem* not to interfere with the trust property, the cestui is clearly the prime beneficiary, since according to Equity, at least, the trustee is not regarded as himself benefiting from that duty at all, since he has no recognized interest in the trust property.

The more vexed question is whether the cestuis can rightly regard their relationship to the trust property itself as ownership. In other words, can we say that the cestuis' rights *in personam* that the trustee administer the trust according to its terms are so secure that they really own the trust property itself? In order to answer this, we must pay close attention to the scope of the duties which correlate to the cestui's rights. The question is who is bound by those rights, and in what ways.

Harris lays out the nature of the problem in respect of choses in equity, i.e. equitable interests, in land in this passage; it is somewhat complicated, but the reader should not be concerned with the actual definition of 'overriding interests' or the character of particular registration mechanisms:

> Students of land law are introduced, usually at an early stage in their studies, to a well known dichotomy. A claim to some use or enjoyment of land avails either only against a particular proprietor, or against all comers to the land. In the former case it is a personal right; in the latter case it is an 'interest in land'. If it does fall into the

latter category, some qualification needs to be introduced into 'all comers', depending on other subclassifications of interests in land. It may be legal or equitable; it may or may not be registrable as a land charge; and (where the title to the land itself is registered) it may or may not be an 'overriding interest'. If merely equitable, the interest [may be enforced against all persons who acquire the legal title to the land or any other interest in it] *except* the bona fide purchaser of a legal estate for value without notice and those claiming through him. If it is registrable as a land charge but has not been registered, it binds all save the purchaser of a legal estate for money or money's worth (or sometimes, all except a purchaser of any interest in the land). If it is not an overriding interest nor protected on the registered title, it binds all except, in the case of registered dispositions, a registered transferee for valuable consideration; and, in the case of unregistered dispositions, all except a purchaser of a legal estate. These subclassifications qualify the range of protection. They are, however, all posterior to the initial dichotomy. If the claim is an interest in land, it binds all (with, perhaps, an excepted category). If it is not an interest in land, it can only bind a single obligor.[6]

So we have the following breakdown of possible rights in respect of land; first there is the basic dichotomy between personal rights against a specific proprietor, and proprietary interests in land. The latter are either legal, equitable, or protected by registration under a statutory scheme. These divisions can, in turn, be differentiated by the extent of the sphere of those subsequent takers of the property who will be bound by the right-holder's interest. If the right is an interest in land, the right-holder's interest binds all the world, but as we see there are various exceptions to this general rule if the interest is equitable, or subject to registration.

The general thrust of this view is that we are to judge whether an equitable interest in trust property is an interest in the property itself by deciding whether, if the trust property be wrongly transferred out of the trust fund to a third party who has no intention of holding it as a trustee, that third party must respect the equitable 'title' of the cestui. In other words, is he bound by the trust? If the class of third parties, these subsequent takers of the trust property who are bound by the cestui's equitable interest amounts to every possible subsequent taker, then we can say with a clear conscience that the duties protecting the cestui's interest are truly general duties *in rem*, since in that case all the world must treat the property as trust property. In that case, the cestui would own the trust property itself or, rather, would be a co-owner of the trust property to the extent of his interest in it. (Remember, there may be more that one cestui, and their particular interests are like co-ownership shares in the property determined by the terms of the trust.) Unfortunately, the cestui's rights do not bind all the world. They bind every one except the *bona fide* purchaser for value (i.e. someone who in good faith buys the property) without notice that the transfer is in breach of trust, and those people who are transferees from him (i.e. once the trust over the property is

[6] Harris 1987, 180.

defeated by a the good faith buyer, it cannot be revived—it is gone forever). So the question is, do the cestui's rights bind a class large enough to say that there is a *general* duty to respect the cestui's interest in the trust property? How big a hole does the exception for good faith buyers blow in the net catching subsequent takers of the property?

This question has given rise to a longstanding controversy, which remains pretty much unresolved.[7] The opinion I shall offer here is that it is incorrect to treat the cestui's interest as ownership of the trust property *per se*, though it is admitted that this is a matter of judgement about which reasonable people may differ. What is more important is to consider the factors that shape the judgement.

The first factor to consider is the way in which the class of subsequent takers who are bound by the cestui's interest is conceived. If we say that 'everyone *except*' is bound, then we adopt the position that the duty to respect the cestui's right is *general*, but subject to an exception. However it is just as reasonable, and indeed better reflects the history of the way the court of Equity developed its rules on the matter,[8] to say that only the trustee, *and those that take from him in circumstances in which they must in good conscience adopt the* in personam *duty of the trustee to the cestui*, are bound by the trust.[9] The historical process of identifying those subsequent takers of the property who would be bound by the trust, viz. those who took with actual knowledge of the trust, then the heirs of a trustee, then those who took by way of gift, and so on, can be plausibly explained as a series of determinations of who is bound in conscience by the trust, which enlarged the class of legal owners of the property who were bound bit by bit. Conceptually, the binding of the successor in title was conceived of as his acquiring the duty *in personam* to the holder of the interest when he acquired title to the legal estate. The list of categories of persons who are bound may be quite long, and so appear to be almost as large as 'all the world', especially if the rule about who is bound is more easily stated as 'everyone but'. But to the extent that we conceive of the subsequent taker's susceptibility to the cestui's rights as a matter of adopting the trustee's personal duties, because of some unconscionable dealings or his personal relationship to the trustee, then the cestui's right in the trust property is not a property interest in the trust property itself; rather, his property in his equitable interest itself is just very well protected, for unlike a plain legal debt, the duty-ower's breach can result in another duty-ower filling his shoes.

As I have emphasized, however, the institution of property is a normative practice, and so practical matters are ignored at our peril. Even if the extension of the trustee's duties to a class of takers is regarded as the shifting of a

[7] See Waters 1967 for a summary.
[8] See Simpson 1986, 177–81; Burn 1994, 57–8.
[9] Burn recognizes that either formulation is coherent: Burn 1994, 58–9.

personal obligation, this tells us nothing in practical terms about the actual size and significance of the classes of those who are bound by the trust and those who are not. For example the equitable rules on what counted as 'notice' of an equitable interest in the case of land were such as to catch many wholly innocent buyers of land. In other words, if the 'personal' obligation of the trustee is shifted almost willy-nilly to any subsequent taker, then the personal nature of the adoption of the obligation may diminish to the vanishing point. In that case, while personal in conception, in practice the cestui's interest is a property right in the trust property itself. This view is strengthened even more in the case of land by the fact that many equitable interests may be registered or protected on registers. In effect, the registration of equitable interests is sufficient to make them bind all subsequent takers.

Land, however, may be a special case. With respect to equitable interests in other kinds of trust property, especially property like shares which regularly circulate in commerce, the list of subsequent takers subject to taking on the trustee's obligations may be a tiny percentage of the class that might regularly be expected to buy the trust property from a fraudulent or careless trustee who sells it in breach of trust. In this case, the cestui is very much more like the owner of a legal chose in action. That is, if the obligor, the trustee, is a rogue or a wastrel or an incompetent the powers of Equity to extend the trust obligation to others may be of little practical use. Thus our conclusion must, unfortunately, be that the cestui's ownership of the trust property itself will vary with respect to the kind of property in question. This is, perhaps, somewhat unsatisfying, but if I am right about the dependence of our idea of property on the relationship of an owner to general duties *in rem* not to interfere with the property of others, then I am unable to see that more can be said. Indeed, the fact that the status of equitable ownership has proved controversial supports this explanation, by which attributing the term 'ownership' to a cestui's right in trust property is a matter of judgement, which will be very much influenced by the way that particular rules work in practice.

It is worthwhile re-iterating here two points. First, no similar controversy arises in the case of legal choses in action. No one believes that a creditor, for example, has any recognized property interests whatsoever in the property of his debtor. Secondly, none of the previous discussion affects in any way our conclusion that the cestui que trust owns his chose in equity, i.e. the right to his proper distribution of property from the trust, any more than we doubt that a legal chose in action like a share, i.e. the right to dividends and so on, is the property of the person who holds it.

Having examined the most difficult kinds of property, which raise complicated matters about distinguishing property and personal rights, we are now in a position to look once again at the way that different branches of law interact. Contract will be the subject of the next two chapters, but here we can examine the way that the law of wrongs and property are related.

Property and the Law of Wrongs

Focusing as I do on the general duty *in rem* to define the character of property norms, it is obvious that the law of property in a sense depends on the law of wrongs. It does so in two important ways. It defines the contours of the right to property, and it determines, in part, who has property rights.

Through the various actions that the civil law of tort and the criminal law provide, the limit of property rights is set. For example, one does not have the right of exclusive use in land to the extent that passers-by have a duty in law not to look at the property. Neither, for example, is it a trespass if a plane flies over one's land at a reasonable height, nor is it a violation of copyright to reproduce short passages from a book. Because rights correlate with duties, the shape of a right is determined by the shape of the correlative duties. Remember, however, that a right is not defined only by the ambit of its correlative duties, but by the interest which justifies it, that is, the reason for having the right–duty relationship recognized in the legal system in the first place. So while the law of wrongs sets the boundaries of property rights by its various duties[10] and in this sense defines it, the right itself and these actions are also shaped by the interest in exclusively determining the disposition of things. For example, because the interest includes the interest in the social use of property, the law of tort recognizes that the owner of land may confer a licence on a person to enter his land. Such a person cannot be a trespasser so long as the licence exists.

There is, however a wrinkle in this explanation. Many actions in the common law of tort are based on 'strict liability', which is to say that the defendant is liable for interfering with the plaintiff's rights regardless of whether he was at fault, for example negligent, in doing so. For example, one is liable under the common law action of conversion for interference with someone's goods even if one innocently bought them from a thief who stole them from that person. The liability is 'strict' because in order to succeed in his action for damages all the true owner must do is show that one took possession of the goods, not that one did so knowingly or recklessly or negligently. Since however, ought implies can, one is liable to the true owner even though we may doubt that one can have a true duty not to do something unintentionally.[11] Thus we must modify our characterization of property rights to a certain extent, again taking the interest in property into account. The interest in property, in particular in security of possession, is given such

[10] For a general discussion of the various actions in tort for the protection of property, see B. S. Markesinis and S. F. Deakin, *Tort Law* (3rd edn., Oxford, Clarendon Press, 1994), ch. 5; W. V. H. Rogers, *Winfield and Jolowicz on Tort* (14th edn., London, Sweet & Maxwell, 1994), chs. 13, 17. For an excellent discussion of the basis of personal property actions see Goode 1976, pt. I. For the criminal law of interferences with property, see Smith 1993.

[11] There is of course, no difficulty with a duty not negligently to interfere with the goods of others, for an agent can act so as to take care.

weight that property rights are not defined only in terms of duties *in rem*, but in terms of *liabilities in rem*. The law confers remedial rights on the owner to pursue actions for damages for interference with his goods, however that interference came about, against whoever has interfered. These liabilities therefore shape the protection of property and thus property rights by extending the circumstances in which property rights can be vindicated. This is one of the circumstances where the definition of the owner's rights is extended to encompass the benefit of this rule-imposed liability on innocent defendants. There is nothing to confuse us here so long as we keep the normative relations clear. Liabilities correlate to powers or rules in a legal system. The owner here has no power to make the innocent defendant liable; the rules of law do that. However, it is nonetheless in his interest that the liability is imposed. The interest of the property-owner in the security of his possession prevails over the interest of the innocent receiver in the security of his receipt.

Samuel appears to regard strict liability for conversion as giving a 'property' flavour to the tort, so much so that strict liability may be regarded as constituting the essence of the distinction between proprietary tortious actions and actions which vindicate obligations.[12] But we should realize that things might justifiably be otherwise, for this is a case of two innocent parties, the owner whose goods have been stolen and the innocent buyer from the thief (who is, of course, himself liable, but who has usually disappeared or has no money, so the owner has scant chance of recovery against him). It is not necessarily the case that this difficult situation need be decided in the owner's favour for there to be property. The main rule is that the primary obligation not to interfere applies to everyone, and as a natural consequence of that the owner's correlative right *in rem* should entitle him to follow his property into the hands of a third party for, as we have seen, his right is in respect of the *res*, the thing, and the duty is conceived as a duty towards it. But the determination of the dispute between the owner and the third party need not depend on strict liability, any more than it need do in the case of an action against the first interferer, e.g. a thief. If there is any fault on the part of the third party in his receipt or use of the property, or if a thief just gave it to him, then we have no difficulty in insisting that the original owner ought to prevail. But the right to property would still be vindicated by requiring the two innocent parties to share the loss; and the right to property would not disappear if the law were keen to insist upon security of good-faith receipt so that the owner should bear the loss. In these cases, property rights are weakened from one perspective, since the remedies following the interference with title are weakened. Nevertheless, providing a defence for the innocent buyer does not overturn the character of the right. Conversely, from the perspective of the good faith purchaser, his property rights are

[12] Samuel 1994, 529–31.

strengthened. Remember, the specific right to this piece of property is a crystallization of the general contingent right to acquire property by various means. The interest in 'security of receipt' is itself a property interest. It is an interest in the effectiveness of the general contingent right to property, that is that the rules by which it is crystallized into specific rights to particular pieces of property are effective and just. The special rules of title which apply to negotiable instruments and money are realizations of this aspect of the interest in the exclusive use of things, in particular to the fairness of the rules governing the power to transfer. So while it is correct to consider the impact of remedial rules when we define the contour of property rights, it is worthwhile pointing out that their effect is most consequential in difficult third-party situations, where both parties to the dispute have legitimate interests in property. Thus, *pace* Samuel, strict liability is not necessarily the hallmark of a property action in tort; rather it suggests that in a particular sort of context the law favours the property interest in security of possession over the property interest in security of receipt. Other actions in tort which are just as proprietary, in that they remedy interferences with property, do not favour the owner's interest in the same way. In general, the owner's right to freedom from interference with his property that causes damage, but which does not interfere with his possession, is protected by an action for negligence; the liability for property damage is not strict.

The other way in which the law of wrongs, specifically the civil law of tort, shapes the law of property is by providing one definition of the owner. The owner is that person whose rights are protected by the general duties *in rem* not to interfere with property *and* who is given remedial rights to bring an action for damages against those who breach this duty. So, for example, if the occupation of a mere licensee of land is interfered with, but the licensee cannot sue the person doing the interfering himself but rather has to rely on his licensor to sue, then the licensee is not, by this criterion, an owner. If, on the other hand, as is the case with a bailee of goods, the licensee does have the right to sue someone who interferes with his possession, he is an owner. If the licensee of a patent may himself sue an infringer, he is an owner, while if he has to rely on the original patentee to sue on his behalf, he is not. On this definition of ownership, an owner is a person with property rights which are attended by remedial rights. (This definition is not the only one, and we will look at others further on.)

According to this definition, it is the distribution of remedial rights, not their character or substance, which determines ownership. Whether a property-holder can only get damages for theft or interference with his property, or whether he can get the return of the thing itself, does not determine whether he is an owner or not. What determines that is whether he has any remedy at all, not its specific character. If we recall what the separability thesis and the exclusion thesis tell us, we see that if the character of one's property rights were to be derived from the character of whatever remedies the right-holder may have, we are led into intractable problems of defining not only ownership, but property itself. For example, if it were a necessary criterion that a property-owner could get back what he had lost through interference, then much property in the common law, such as chattels, interferences with which are generally remedied only by awards of damages, could not be property. Furthermore, property in intangibles such as patents could not be property under any legal system, for one cannot 'get back' a period of effective monopoly once it has been infringed.

The importance of this definition of ownership is that it assists our characterization of those second-order property rights, choses in action like debts and interests in funds. If someone interferes with the debtor's wherewithal, or with the property in a trust, or with the assets of the company, the holder of the chose in action or equitable interest is not, in general, able to sue the interferer in his own right; the debtor or company or trustee must do so. In other words, the second-order interest the right-holder has in the property of the owner is reflected again in this aspect of the personal relationship between the two. The owner of the chose in action is not an owner of the properties in the funds or wherewithal against which the chose is held; rather, the legal requirement or contractual obligation on the owner of this property to sue is an aspect of the personal obligation. Simple debtors, in general, are not obliged by the terms of the debt to sue; the creditor relies on the debtor's own willingness to do so. Directors of companies are not required by the terms of the share relationship to do so, but must treat the decision to pursue litigation as a business decision to be made in the best interests of the company. Most stringently, trustees are obliged by the law of trusts to act in the best interests of beneficiaries and for no other reason, and this must control their decision to pursue litigation. This test of ownership emphasizes that the property held by the holder of a chose in action is property in a personal relationship which reflects an interest in things, not property in those things themselves.

Given this interaction between the law of tort and the law of property, is it possible to keep them separate?[13] As Samuel says, 'once one says that the law of tort is about 'interests' [like property interests] one is in effect saying that what was once the *object* of an aspect of legal science (the law of tort) has now *become* the science'.[14] But it is possible to distinguish the two so long as we do not replace the interest underlying one branch of law with that of another. Tort remains separate from property because the interest underlying tort law is an interest in not being harmed. Now, if the law of wrongs

[13] It seems easier to distinguish the criminal law as a general category since it not only protects different legal interests, it serves an interest of its own, i.e. the interest of the state in punishing those who maliciously violate its rules.

[14] Samuel 1994, 527, italics mine.

makes any sense at all there must be some content to the notion of harm which transcends every specific tort the system recognizes. This is not to say, however, that the appearance of property in tort law is no more complicated than the fact that, in so far as property is a legally recognized interest that can be harmed, it will put in an appearance in that branch of law dealing with harms, because the harm–tort equation is not a necessary one. We normally regard the harm or wrong caused by a breach of contract as a matter of contract law. So it is not clear that the notion of harm or wrong alone works to distinguish tort law in an obviously principled way. Of course, one can certainly conceive of a breach of contract as a civil wrong, as the violation of a valid interest recognized by law. Consider the view of Coval et al.:

> Property law determines which means an individual agent has rights of non-interference with; contract law determines which means each individual has rights of non-interference with when individuals have acted jointly in the creation of the means; and tort law determines what constitutes an interference in means.

On this view, both property and contract define legal interests, while tort sets the limits of protection to them. I think this is somewhat difficult to defend, since the nature of things themselves, whether material resources or something intangible like a monopoly, does not define the scope of what counts as an interference with them, and our rights to property, the 'means' which property law determines, can extend only so far as we have correlative duties. But if it turns out impossible to maintain that the law of tort can be explained as serving a general conception of an interest in not being harmed,[15] then the upshot is that tort becomes fragmented, with its various parts associating with those interests those parts protect. This danger, however, is not one which shakes the independence of the law of property. The danger is not that property collapses into the law of tort, but rather that the property torts fall into the law of property, the same way that breach of contract now resides in the law of contract, not the law of tort.

Ownership and Possession

I would now like to discuss a couple of concepts the true nature of which is raised by the description of property that I have given: ownership and possession. These concepts have a complicated status and meaning in the common law, which has drawn much scholarly attention.[16] It is beyond the scope of what I am trying to do in this book to decide, for example, whether common law 'possession' is applied on the basis of a host of different factors,[17] or

[15] Although see Samuel 1994, 529–30.

[16] Maitland 1885 and 1886, Rose 1985, Lawson and Rudden 1982, ch. V, 41–53, Turner 1941.

[17] D. R.Harris, 1961.

whether there is a concept of ownership which does any work.[18] What is apposite here is an explanation of these concepts which is aided by the definition of property as the right of exclusive use.

'Ownership' simply describes the situation that obtains when a person has a property right in something. An 'owner' is one who has property rights. While this is roughly right, complications arise which will be the focus of the discussion below. Possession, on the other hand, has no such clarity even at the outset. Possession refers to a situation of fact which describes the control that a person may have over an object and, obviously, as one can imagine, the law has done its best to describe this control, proffering all kinds of tests to establish when someone has possession of something. To complicate matters further, this control is related to ownership, since the corresponding duties *in rem* can be treated as duties not to interfere with this control, and so it matters not only what a person does to establish whether he has possession, but who he is. In other words, possession is the opposite side of the coin to actual non-interference, and ownership or property rights are the opposite side of the coin to the general duties *in rem* not to interfere. Although possession is a matter of fact, one can count on legal systems to deem certain circumstances to constitute possession in order to reflect the interests of owners. For example, because people who own land are not required to remain upon it at all times, and may go away for extended periods, the law may hold that the most minimal acts in respect of the land constitute possession by the owner, while on the other hand, the same minimal acts would not count as possession by a non-owner.[19] This legal stipulation of what counts as possession may make the relationship of possession which an owner has over the object of property in question appear as abstract as the purely normative relationship of ownership. The two, however, must be kept distinct.

No one can do anything to interfere with a person's ownership of an item of property, since that is a normative relationship. A person can only do things which interfere with a person's possession. Interference is factual, and alters a person's factual relationship to an item of property. The only thing that can alter a person's ownership of his property are rules of law or the exercise of legal powers. This is not a profound point, but one that must ever be borne in mind. My right to bodily security remains even if I am under attack. My interest in bodily security, the reason I have the right and there is a corresponding duty not to attack me, remains, and this reason applies to my attacker throughout the assault. While in general no confusion results from saying that my attacker is interfering with my rights, or attacking my right to bodily security, we should bear in mind the confusion this may cause.

My main interest in considering possession at all is to explore how this

[18] Harris 1986; Buckland and McNair 1965, 71–90 (by F. H. Lawson).

[19] See Burn 1994, 893–7.

matter of fact contributes to applying the norms of property. In particular, how does (factual) possession count as a reason for (normative) ownership? How does possession (including legally deemed 'possession') draw the application of legal rules, or constitute the exercise of legal powers, which then alter the ownership of the thing in question. As we have seen, facts or acts having nothing to do with possession may do so. The commission of a felony once operated to shift the ownership of the felon's property to the Crown; the exercise of various legal powers, like the court's declaration of personal bankruptcy or the owner's sale of the property, do not depend on any change of possession. But in English law, particularly in respect of the ownership of land, possession has played an important role in the concept of ownership. Possession itself is regarded as a ground for property rights, and this can be framed by saying that possession is a good root of title. This allows the possibility of relative titles, since more than one person may have shown sufficient possession in the course of time to establish a title. The system does, of course, have rules to establish the better title, and this is generally the person who can show an earlier possession sufficient to confer title. What this means, of course, is that the legal system may, in the abstract, recognize more than one title to the same piece of property. I say 'in the abstract', for it is clear that these different title-holders do not have equal rights in the property for the time being. Not only does the actual possessor benefit for the time being from the general duties *in rem* which protect his use of the property, but even his rights *vis-à-vis* his title itself may be superior to those of other title-holders. For example, at common law, only the person seised of land, i.e. the person regarded by the law as presently in possession of a freehold estate in the land, could transfer title by sale, since only he could put someone else in the same position. The person who might be able to prove better title and regain seisin (possession which conferred these rights) had only a right of action or a right of re-entry, and this was originally inalienable.[20] Thus only the title of the person seised of the land could be transferred.

Thus with regard to material things, the common law notion of ownership relies doubly on the concept of possession. Not only does ownership equate with a right to possession, correlating with the general duties *in rem* not to interfere with property, but one owes one's title, directly or indirectly,[21] to the fact that one has taken advantage of these general duties *in rem* by occupying or taking hold of the property. In other words, one becomes an owner by purporting to be an owner, by acting as if the duties *in rem*, in so far as they protect this item of property, protect one's own possession, rather than anyone else's.

Now this appears to many as a problematic and unsophisticated concept

[20] See Maitland 1886.

[21] i.e., through a chain of successors in title or transferees of someone who grounds his title in possession.

of ownership. It is problematic because, while the factual possession of land or chattels is at least possible, one cannot obviously possess a chose in action or intangible property like a patent or copyright. Indeed the division in personal property between choses in possession and choses in action may be regarded as an artifact of this unsatisfactory state of affairs. One might, therefore conclude, that we need at least two kinds of ownership to encompass all the property in the legal system, one conceptually linked to possession, and one not. That would be a pretty awful state of affairs, but fortunately it does not obtain.

It does not because this difference in the basis upon which a right to property may be acquired (i.e. in the case of some kinds of property, like land and chattels, by taking possession, while in the case of other kinds, like copyright, obviously not) does not entail a difference in the concept of ownership. Showing why is assisted by making reference to the purported lack of sophistication of a concept of ownership closely tied to possession, so we can discuss that at the same time. Referring to the rules of the common law by which only the title of the person who also had seisin of the land could alienate his title, Maitland characterizes this lack of sophistication:

> [O]wnership, mere ownership, is inalienable, intransmissable; neither by the act of the party nor by act of the law will it pass from one man to another. The true explanation of [this] will I believe be found . . . in what I shall venture to describe as a legal incapacity, an inability to conceive that mere rights can be transferred or can pass from person to person. Things can be transferred; that is obvious; the transfer is visible to the eye; but how rights? you have not your rights in your hand or your pocket, nor can you put them into the hand of another nor lead him into them and bid him walk about within their metes and bounds. 'But,' says the accomplished jurist, 'this is plain nonsense; when a gift is made of a corporeal thing, of a sword or a hide of land, rights are transferred; if at the same time there is a change of possession, that is another matter; whether a gift can be made without such a change of possession, the law of the land will decide; but every gift is a transfer of ownership, and ownership is a right or a bundle of rights; if gift be possible, transfer of rights is possible.'[22]

With respect, this is a caricature of the un-accomplished jurist or layman, and is untenable. While I can see the physical transfer of a chattel with my eye, I cannot see a gift of a chattel with my eye, even when legal transfer depends upon transfer of possession. The mere transfer of possession has never been regarded as transfer of ownership; physical delivery must always be accompanied by an intention to part with *ownership*; that intention is not only invisible to the naked eye, but is inconceivable absent the recognition of that abstract relation in law. Indeed, if this view were carried to its logical

[22] Maitland 1886, 489. For similar distinctions between an abstract and a 'corporeal' notion of property, see Samuel 1994, 529–36, Goode 1976, pt. I, 378 (comparing common law ownership to the abstract ownership contemplated by equity).

conclusion, then whether we called it ownership or not, the titleholder could have no rights whatsoever to anything out of his possession, for such rights are wholly intangible abstractions of the legal system. Maitland would have to provide a corresponding visual manifestation of these rights to make sense of them, such as a show of righteous indignation on the dispossessed owner's face as he does battle with his dispossessor. Thus even the unsophisticated must recognize abstractions, not just the scenes before their eyes, to understand property of any kind. And, conversely, the accomplished jurist used to abstractions is vulnerable himself. 'The transfer of rights' is not merely abstract, it is a metaphor with very dubious, if not untenable, foundations. The only thing that is clear when I give property to you is that you now stand in the equivalent normative position *vis-à-vis* the thing I gave you to the one I just did. Your rights are equivalent to mine. Whether we treat this as your assuming my rights, or as the extinction of my rights and the simultaneous creation of equivalent rights in you is of little moment. There is merit in each view. In favour of the former, the rights are the same in the sense that they correlate to essentially the same set of duties *in rem*; but in favour of the latter view, the rights are clearly different, in that our rights do not exist in virtue of the same sets of facts; my title to the rights depended on, let us say, some previous transfer, while yours depended on my transfer to you. Our general but contingent right *in rem* to property is crystallized as a special right to this property on different facts. On the latter view, the 'transfer' of rights is untenable as an abstraction. Rather, an equivalent (but not identical) normative situation is *created* for you when I exercise my power to give you the property.

The belittling characterization of the common law concept of ownership depends on the same misapprehension of the role of abstraction, by mistaking the way factual possession underpins ownership. We must distinguish between facts conferring title and facts upon whose continuing existence title depends. A system in which ownership depended on continuing factual possession might reasonably be characterized as having a deficient concept of ownership. Title derived in that way would restrict the right to the use of a thing to those uses which counted as possessory. In other words, 'ownership' would merely be a right not to be interfered with so long as one maintained a certain, positive, engagement with the thing. But this does not characterize the common law. Title in the common law does not depend on any continuing state of possession,[23] but on acts of taking possession, which facts create

[23] The title of an adverse possessor is not extinguished when he leaves possession, so is not dependent on any continuance of possession; he retains a better title than a subsequent adverse possessor despite losing his possession. The right of the paper owner to bring an action, however, does depend on a continuing adverse possession, and so may only lapse if there is a continuous adverse possession; in this way, the ultimate superiority of the adverse possessor's title does depend upon the continuance of possession by someone other than the paper owner.

new titles, that is, new abstract rights, which remain until they are extinguished. At common law one cannot even extinguish one's title by abandonment, i.e. by relinquishing possession. Only by lapse of time, and only where the original owner has the opportunity to vindicate his title against someone else who creates a new title by possessing the thing, can an owner's rights be lost.[24]

Once we observe a normative practice of dealing with things, the participants are dealing with abstractions, since such a practice depends on norms like rules and rights, which are abstract. Little is to be gained by trying to measure which system is 'more abstract', whatever *that* means. The level of abstraction required to deal with particular things as property turns on the nature of the things themselves. Material things are not abstract, but our categorization of them, and our treating them as quantities of *x* or numbers of *y* is. Rights are abstract, and property rights in the rights of others are abstractions concerning other abstractions. Land is not abstract, but a legal estate, that is 'time in the land' or a period of use of the land, is. The concept of possession merely serves to indicate one sort of facts upon which changes in the normative situation as regards property rights in material things occur.

A similar idea about the abstract character of ownership gives rise to a claim about the purported irrelevance of ownership in the common law. It is common to draw a distinction between the law of property in roman law and civil law systems and that of the common law by saying that the former systems emphasize ownership, while the common law emphasizes possession.[25] The common law emphasizes possession at the expense of ownership, apparently, (1) by protecting the right to possess, as opposed to ownership *per se*; and (2) by recognizing a number of relative titles rather than a single, absolute relationship of ownership in the face of which all other claims to ownership must fall. I should say, rather, that the common law has a notion of ownership which, linked to possession but not overcome by it, accurately reflects the character of the practice of property and the nature of the rights to which it pertains. If the practice of property is rightly conceived primarily from the protection the law provides by instituting a general, easy to follow, duty *in rem* requiring non-interference with things, then title is a function of the way that a person moves from one of the multitude owing the duty in respect of a particular thing to being a person who takes advantage of it. These transitions, like sales or court orders or inheritance have, until the creation of modern property registration systems, been largely inaccessible or invisible to the vast majority of duty-owers. One's title, therefore, is a matter of history which may be distinctly private. It is easy to conceive of absolute, that is, non-relative rights *in personam* which only concern the parties to the transaction creating them, whether contractual rights or the

[24] Regarding chattels, see Hudson 1984; regarding land, see Burn 1994, 893–7.

[25] Although see Buckland and McNair 1965, 71–90 (by F. H. Lawson).

right to sue someone in tort for an infraction; only the parties to the transaction are possible right-holders. It may turn out that, on the facts, they have no legal relationship—the contract may be void, or the injury not actionable—but there is no question that a third party might have the rights instead. Similarly, rights to things like bodily security can be regarded as absolute, since everyone has their own. No one has relatively better title to these rights. But any item of property is in principle accessible by any one at all, and does not wear its ownership on its face and, in particular, it does not wear the history of the transactions concerning it on its face. Like contractual rights or rights arising from torts, the legal relationship of ownership will depend on documents and human memory,[26] but in the case of land in particular, which lasts forever and may see various changes in occupation, documented and remembered facts may not only work to support or deny one claim of ownership but may do so in respect of several claims. The common law properly recognizes the uncertainty of this history, and thus the reality of this practice, by abjuring the abstraction of absolute title and embracing the abstraction of relative title. Note that this does not mean that the law has no concept of best title, even if in any one dispute between a plaintiff and defendant the law will consider only the relative merits of their two titles. It does: the best title is the one supported by the earliest provable possession. Secondly, it follows from this concept of relative or multiple titles, that the protection of the right to possession is a sensible way of protecting ownership, since this is in essence nothing more than the protection of the relative title holder when he is in charge of the property.[27]

We should therefore regard the claim that ownership is less realized in the common law as stipulative at best. No less normative force is accorded to property rights in the common law. The common law differs by having a different concept of ownership, not less of one.

There is, finally, one more issue concerning ownership: given that A and B both have rights in a thing, what criteria identify one of them as the owner? Honoré argues convincingly that neither enumerating the 'rights' of either party, nor viewing the rights of the owner as less 'restricted', nor taking the holding of a particular incident as the criterion successfully solves the problem.[28] He continues: '[a]t first sight a hopeful avenue of inquiry is to ask what happens on the determination of the various interests in the thing under consideration. This brings us to a further standard incident of ownership, viz. its residuary character.'[29] Honoré points out that 'it is a characteristic of

[26] Pottage 1994.

[27] Which is not to say that protection of the right to possession may not be excessive in some circumstances, generating multiple rights of recovery, as in the case of the interference with bailed goods, where both the bailor and the bailee may sue the convertor. See Markesinis and Deakin, above, n. 10 at 404–10.

[28] Honoré 1987, 176–9.

[29] Ibid. 177.

ownership that an owner has a residuary right in the thing owned',[30] i.e. that on the determination of an interest less than full ownership,

> rights, including liberties, analogous to the rights formerly vested in the holder of the interest, vest in or are exercisable by someone else. That person may be said to acquire the corresponding rights. Of course the corresponding rights are not identical with those formerly vested in the holder of the interest. The easement holder had a right to exclude the owner; now the owner has a right to exclude the easement holder. The latter right is not identical with, but corresponds to the former.[31]

It is clear that residuarity is a function of property defined as the right of exclusive use. 'Residuarity' describes the return of property to the grantor following a licence, that is the relaxing of the rules of exclusion on the part of the grantor in favour of the grantee, which can be on any terms, for a term of years, for a life, for particular uses, for consideration, etc. Residuarity thus follows from the institution of property whenever the social use of property is permitted.

It would seem to follow from this that in cases where different interests are held in the same piece of property by different persons, for example where A holds the freehold and B holds a lease in Blackacre, that if one wished to identify the owner, one would choose the ultimate residuary, here A, for the lesser rights arise from his grant. Honoré thinks not. His argument appears to be that actual cases in the law belie taking residuarity to be determinative in his way. For example, an 'owner's' rights may be acquired by the State should the owner's rights lapse. Similarly, feudal lords had the right of escheat over their tenants' land, the right to repossess a tenant's interest should the tenant die without heirs. Honoré asks the same rhetorical question in both cases: is such a right one to acquire ownership, or is it a mere expectancy? By posing this question but not answering it he indicates that he does not think an answer is determinative of the issue: the test of ultimate residuarity leads to the State being the true owner of all the land. He concludes that it is a necessary condition of his ownership that the extinction of other interests in the property inure to the owner's benefit, but that this is not a sufficient condition.[32] 'In the end, it turns out that residuarity is merely one of the standard incidents of ownership, important no doubt, but not entitled to any special status.'[33]

Campbell convincingly argues otherwise.[34] The State should not be regarded as the ultimate residuary because its right to the property is dependent on the occurrence of a contingency which will not necessarily happen; its right is not conditional the way the right of an owner of the land to the reversion when the term of a leasehold expires is, because the leasehold is

[30] Ibid. 178.
[31] Ibid. 178.
[32] Ibid. 179.
[33] Ibid. 178.
[34] Campbell 1992, 92–4

certain to expire. The difference in the positions of the holders of such rights is that 'most legal systems allow conditional rights to vest only when the contingency upon which their coming into force depends is one which is bound to occur, sooner or later'.[35] Since the lapse of ownership due to intestacy without heirs or abandonment, the events upon which the State takes, is not bound ever to occur, it is not correct to treat the State as the ultimate residuary.

The correct perspective on residuarity is from the point of view of the *creation* of lesser interests, not their termination. Determining who is the owner of something is to determine who may create lesser titles in a thing. These lesser interests which ultimately expire do not spring up from nowhere, after all. It *follows* from the fact that the owner or his predecessor created these lesser interests that the 'corresponding rights' will vest in him when they come to an end, for they are created out of *his* right to exclusive use. From this perspective it does not really matter whether the State is the ultimate residuary or not, since the State has no right to create lesser titles in the property of its subjects; if it wants to do that it must buy the property like anyone else or expropriate it, and thus make itself the owner.[36]

Once again then, the right of exclusive use proves a useful tool for getting to the bottom of a sticky problem, here elaborating a definition of 'owner' which coincides with our standard usage and normal intuitions.

Now that I have vindicated a concept of ownership in respect of which possession has a significant role to play in terms of the creation, extinction, and transfer of ownership, we can scotch one silliness whose persistence I can only attribute to the fun of astonishing laymen or undergraduates in law. That is the view that in English law, no one but the Crown owns land. Consider this statement, for example:

> It is a common, but erroneous, belief that individual people own land in this country. . . . [Following the Norman Conquest in 1066] [t]he King, by virtue of conquest, regarded the whole of England as belonging to him. This remains the case today, so that it is still true to say that all land in England and Wales, technically speaking, is owned by the Crown.'[37]

Whether such a view is even 'technically speaking' correct is doubtful;[38] the technical point is better put, 'all land is *held* of the Crown'.[39] It is true that immediately after the Conquest, the right to hold land was not property. Such rights were not freely alienable, not inheritable, nor could they be left

[35] Ibid. 94.

[36] The State may of course pass general legislation creating rights in property, such as legislation creating rights for tenants against their landlords, but when the State does this it is not exercising any powers of ownership.

[37] M. Thompson, *Land Law* (London, Sweet & Maxwell, 1995), 7.

[38] Simpson 1986, 47–8; see also Pollock and Maitland 1968, 4–6.

[39] Simpson 1986, 1.

by will; all manner of services were attached to them; and they were extensively personal in that they were intended to reflect personal bonds of loyalty. Such, I am afraid, is the nature of feudalism. Indeed, in legal terms one can define feudalism as that state of affairs in which there is no property in land, but rather that rights to land are specifically intended to reflect an individual's status in the political, economic, and legal[40] order. How land became property as the feudal regime governing land-holding waned is itself interesting,[41] but one need not detail that history to upset the view that the subjects of English law do not own land. As we have seen, the Queen or the Crown is, nowadays at least, not the ultimate residuary at law, even technically speaking, and therefore is in no way a beneficiary of the general duties *in rem*. But although that is decisive as regards the question of ownership, it is interesting to explore a concept of owning land *as* holding of the Crown. Such a concept incorporates into the theory of ownership of land the fact that land has special political significance. Land is not only property, it is territory, the extent of the jurisdiction of the State. Owning land depends on political sovereignty in a much more direct way than does the ownership of chattels, for the ability to maintain one's rights to land depends on whether the State is able to hold its territory against invaders from without or rebels from within. In this way, all land that is owned is *held* of the State, and the residual influence of the common law tenurial system allows the theory of property in land in England to incorporate this important truth. Far from obviating 'ownership' in the common law, the theory that all land is held of the Crown defines landownership in an unusually accurate way.

The Definition of Property

It is appropriate to conclude this part of the book with a revised definition of the right of exclusive use: It is

the right to determine the use or disposition of a separable thing (i.e. *a thing whose contingent association with any particular person is essentially impersonal and so imports nothing of normative consequence), in so far as that can be achieved or aided by others excluding themselves from it, and includes the rights to abandon it, to share it, to license it to others (either exclusively or not), and to give it to others in its entirety.*

I have devised this definition in light of the exclusion thesis and the separability thesis, but the underlying strategy has been to isolate those norms which most closely characterize the practice of dealing with things that we recognize as property.

[40] They reflect the legal order because, *inter alia*, right to land also conferred legal jurisdiction, i.e. to run a court of law dealing with local legal issues.

[41] See, e.g., Simpson 1986, ch. III; Barton 1976.

7

Property and Contract I: The Power to Sell and the Influence of Markets

I have argued that the power to transfer property is part and parcel of the right of exclusive use, but that the power to sell property or otherwise dispose of it by contract is not. In other words, I have argued that the power to sell is really a hybrid 'power', in which the power to make contracts includes the power to make contracts concerning the power to dispose of property. In some contracts of sale, these powers are kept quite distinct. In England, for example, the sale of a house is distinctly separated into the stages of contract and conveyance (transfer). In the first stage the parties exercise their powers to make contracts, and only in the second does the seller exercise his power to transfer, being so obliged by the contract. By contrast under the sale of goods law, title passes under the contract either when the contract is formed or at any other time the contract specifies. No separate act of delivery is essential.[1]

In this Chapter I would like to discuss two aspects of the interaction between contract and property. The first has to do with the power of sale and the nature of contracts. One fallacious way of claiming that the power to sell is a hybrid power, i.e. not wholly comprised within the right of exclusive use is to claim that selling property always involves obligations. The buyer has the obligation to transfer his property (his money), and the seller has the obligation to transfer his goods. Thus the power to sell necessarily is a power to create legal obligations, not only to transfer property. This is a very traditional understanding of the categories of rights and laws. As I mentioned in Chapter 3, contract and tort are generally regarded as together forming the law of obligations. Nevertheless, this argument is fallacious, because not all contracts create obligations. This is a fairly controversial statement, and will take some spelling out. The reason I do so here is simply that, having made the controversial claims I have about the nature of property, it would be dangerous to draw false support from a distinction framed in traditional terms. In brief, what I shall argue is that the power to sell is a hybrid power to make *bargain agreements* about the transfer of property, the exercise of which in many cases does *not* create obligations.

[1] Nevertheless, the power to transfer property and the power to enter contracts are distinguishable. See Watts 1995, 52–3, for a discussion of the different criteria which apply for the effective exercise of the power to transfer property and the effective creation of a binding contractual obligation.

The second aspect of the relationship between contract and property is the influence of the market on the recognition of different forms of property, in particular money. My claim that property and contract are conceptually distinct looks untenable if the very existence of certain kinds of property depends on the existence of a market. Here I want to argue that none of the kinds of property we generally observe are conceptual creatures of markets. Rather, they are conceptual creatures of economies, and economies do not have to be based on contractual exchanges.

The Power to Sell

Theorists typically assume that contracts must give rise to executory obligations, i.e. obligations to do something in the future even if in the very near future, without explaining quite why. It appears to be one of the founding dogmas of contract law that all contracts involve futurity, and this undoubtedly has something to do with the extensive influence, if not the tenacious grip, that the theory of promising has exercised on the theory of contract.[2] This passage from Llewellyn is a good example:

> Contract in the strict sense is the specifically legal machinery appropriate when [an exchange] economy moves into the phase of credit—meaning or connoting thereby future dealings in general; in which the mutual reliance of two dealers on their respective promises comes of course into major importance.[3]

Similarly, Atiyah says '[w]hile 'exchange'—simultaneous exchange—may exist in a pre-legal or non-legal world, contract is crucially different from mere exchange. Contract involves futurity and the concept of obligation.'[4]

Both of these views clearly contemplate the possibility of an analysis of at least some exchanges which does not rely on notions of future obligations, yet at the same time they deny that such exchanges could count as contracts. Atiyah makes the point elsewhere in a different way, specifically doubting whether a promissory analysis would be appropriate in all cases:

> The fact is that much social co-operation can take place without promising, so long as there is a sufficient degree of trust. For example, voluntary exchanges can be made, either simultaneously, or by one person trusting another, 'giving' credit to the other. Logically, it has been argued that even a simultaneous exchange may imply a promise, but that may well be to read into a relationship of trust or confidence ideas derived from a different cultural tradition.[5]

In this passage, we can discern two alternative bases for applying a non-executory analysis of contracts: the first relies upon the simultaneity of the

[2] See Atiyah 1981; Fried 1981; cf. Raz 1982; for a sceptical view, see Craswell 1989.
[3] Llewellyn 1931, 717; Posner 1986, 79–80, also favours this view.
[4] Atiyah 1986, 1.
[5] Atiyah 1981, 135.

exchange; the second relies upon an unexplored notion of trust as the 'giving of credit'.

The latter basis is so problematic as to be useless. It clearly implies the creation of some kind of executory obligation on the debtor to meet his obligations under the exchange. While we may happily take Atiyah's point that a simple equation of this with our notion of promising may be somewhat culturally imperialistic, it is difficult to make sense of a credit relationship which did not involve executory obligations, even if we did not want to regard these obligations as strictly promissory. There is no potential in this approach for avoiding an executory analysis.

The first basis, however, is clear. If an exchange is simultaneous or, rather, instantaneous, in that the passing of property from each party to the other occurs in the same instant, there is clearly no basis for imputing any executory obligations. Before the exchange, there are none, and a moment later, following the exchange there are none. I take it that no one will doubt the conceptual possibility of an instantaneous exchange, rare though these exchanges may be in practice. We can all imagine a situation in which there is very little trust regarding whether someone would complete an exchange after he had received his own benefit. Picture two children trading prized objects, each of them simultaneously releasing one and grasping the other. Nevertheless, trades of this kind would certainly constitute exchanges, exchanges that are essentially equivalent to trades or sales generally. This suggests that any analysis of contracts which could incorporate instantaneous exchanges would be preferable to one which excludes them by definitional fiat, as the executory analysis must. Pointing out that very few contracts are actually instantaneous in the necessary way is not an answer to the conceptual issue they raise, and exploring how they work will lead to a more broadly-based analysis of contract than the executory one. We can begin by comparing the difference between an executory contract and an instantaneous one, what I shall call a 'simple exchange', with the difference between a promise and a gift.

A promise is binding, that is, the duty to perform it arises, when it is communicated. The normative consequences of a gift, i.e. the passing of property, arise not on the basis of any communication however, but rather *when the gift is made*, that is, when the transaction is carried out. Similarly, obligations arise on the basis of communications in the case of executory contracts, whereas obligations arise when performance takes place in the case of a simple exchange.

The obligations that arise in the case of promises or executory contracts are obvious: the parties must do what they said they would. In the case of gifts or simple exchanges, the rights and duties involved are those of ownership. When a gift is made, the former owner now has the general duty *in rem* not to interfere, and the new owner is released from that duty and is now the beneficiary of it. The same goes for the case of simple exchanges, except that each party will become a new owner of one thing and a former owner of the one he exchanged for it.

Promises and executory agreements normally rest upon spoken or written communications, while gifts and simple exchanges often depend upon a prior understanding of actions, such as the action of placing goods on the cashier's counter in a shop. They are nevertheless equally 'intentional', in the sense that they are equally intentional acts, even if standard transactions are more dependent upon conventions of behaviour. The parties in both cases understand what is going on. Indeed, we only make sense of the conduct, regarding a simple exchange as *that* rather than as two coincidental gifts, when we understand what the parties think they are doing, and the same goes for distinguishing an executory contract from coincidental gratuitous promises.

The analysis is that in the case of gifts and exchanges the actual transfer of property is determinative of a change in the normative situation. That is not, however, to treat the mere physical act, the transfer *of possession* of property, as determinative. A gift of a chattel does not occur whenever possession of the chattel is transferred. Merely putting someone in possession of something does not transfer title. A gift by delivery only occurs when the donee is put into possession with the intention that property will pass. Likewise, a transactional analysis of simple exchanges does not do away with the relevance of intention. Yet, while they are intentional, transactions like gifts or simple exchanges need not be understood as depending upon the creation of some attenuated kind of obligation. When I give someone a gift, I do not have impliedly to promise not to take it back in order to make it effective; after I give it, I am in no better position than anyone else who is not the owner to make a claim on it, and so any promise I would make is superfluous, if not positively misleading in its implication.

Transactions like gifts or simple exchanges or, for example, the exercise of a legal power like the power to make someone a knight, rearrange or create rights and duties[6] *which achieve at once the intended normative result*. Promises and executory agreements rearrange or create rights and duties *whose future fulfilment, and only that, will generate the intended normative result*. When I simultaneously pass my coins over the counter and take away my chocolate bar there is nothing further to be done, since the ultimate goal of exchanging this property for that is achieved. If I contract to build you a wall, however, though we have new rights the minute the contract is made, these are not rights we remain content with: what you want is the wall, not merely the right that I build you one. The completed wall is the intended

[6] I mention the 'rearrangement' of rights to cover the view that property rights pass from one owner to the other in the same way that title can be regarded as 'passing'. It does not matter to the analysis whether one regards the exchange of property rights in this way or as the extinguishing of the old owner's property right simultaneously with the creation of a new property right in the new owner.

result. The distinction between executory contracts and simple exchanges is as natural as a distinction between a present and future tense. Sometimes we agree to exchange property right now, and sometimes for certain work to be undertaken or property to be delivered in the future.

This is not to deny the obvious similarities between the two, the most obvious being the element of trust. An executory analysis looks capable of explaining all contracts partly because executory obligations involve trust, generating as they do legitimate expectations and reliance, and so, apparently, do all contracts, even simple exchanges. *Caveat emptor* or not, there is at least one representation that A makes when he trades or sells me his lawn mower upon which I am entitled to rely, i.e. about which I am supposed to be able to trust him: that he has title to the thing (or authority to sell it). Similarly, if A agrees to mow the lawn next Thursday for £5, we are entitled to trust that he will do it, barring unforeseen circumstances. 'Trust' may be a bit nebulous here, but it is clear that we are getting at A's integrity or reliability, which A invites us to believe he actually possesses so that either contract may go forward. But the reliance is essentially different in the two cases. The duty not to misrepresent the facts is a duty to make one's statements conform to reality. The duty to keep one's promises or agreements is a duty to ensure that (future) reality will conform to one's statements. The first is a duty about what one ought to say; the second about what one ought to do.[7]

This distinction provides a structural distinction between simple exchanges and executory contracts, since the former only involve representations, while the latter typically involve both. If A says the lawn mower runs before selling it to me, and it does not, there is no future act of his which can alter the misrepresentation (which is not to say that there cannot be any remedy for misrepresentation). This is equally true of representations about the future. If A says the lawn mower will run for a year barring abnormal use, and it does not, again, while the representation is about the future, it is about a future reality about which A can do nothing. His representation is a prediction about future performance on which he invites us to rely. It is not about what A will do, but about what the facts indicate to him the machine will. Executory contracts involve both representations and executory obligations. When I hire A to build me a wall, A both undertakes to build it and makes representations that he knows how to build a wall, that he will be able to secure the raw materials, and so on. If it is useful to distinguish between executory obligations and representations about the future in order to understand executory contracts, *a fortiori* we must not confuse them if we want to understand simple exchanges, since these do not involve executory obligations at all, but only representations. Though all contracts involve

[7] The point is well made by Craswell 1989, 502.

trust, depending as they do on either representations or executory obligations or both, they do so in different ways.

The analysis so far is intuitively grounded in the idea that simple exchanges are instantaneous, so until now we have avoided the conceptual issues which arise when one party performs before the other. Turning our attention to the analysis of the formation of contracts in terms of offer and acceptance reveals how a non-executory analysis can be extended beyond the simultaneous simple exchange.

The standard analysis of contract formation in terms of offer and acceptance applies both to executory contracts and to simple exchanges, but the analysis applies differently. In both cases the law essentially takes a 'last-act' analysis. What concludes an executory contract is acceptance of an offer; if the 'acceptance' is conditional on the modification of the offer, it is not an acceptance but constitutes a counter-offer, and is therefore not the last act in the formation of an agreement. In the case of simple exchanges, the notion of the 'last act' is interpreted to account for the way in which the actual passage of property, not the fulfillment of contractual obligations, satisfies the contractual agreement. In the case of simple exchanges of property, the representations surrounding the transaction set the terms of the agreement but none of these statements counts as an offer or an acceptance.

It is clear that the point of advertising and displaying and pricing goods is to represent many of the terms upon which goods will be exchanged. And making those representations themselves may entail duties, such as a duty not to advertise falsely. But in simple exchanges of property, neither invitations to treat nor any verbal 'offer' to enter the transaction are well conceived as contract-forming offers because, it is submitted, the basis of the agreement is the fact of the transaction itself, in the same way that the basis of the transfer of title in the gift of a chattel is the actual, factual delivery of possession. It is the reciprocal passing of property which gives rise to the creation or rearrangement of the rights and duties of the parties, i.e. to the normative consequences of the contract.

On this analysis, both offer and acceptance are constituted not by communications of intentions, but by performance according to the terms of the contract previously established by the preceding representations, which terms are often understood as a matter of convention. Thus, the performance of the party who acts first *is* his offer, while the performance of the party who acts second *is* his acceptance. In this way the contract is formed the moment it is completed, and vice versa. This is not as strange as it may appear at first glance. In English law we are all accustomed to analysing unilateral contracts as those in which performance constitutes acceptance of the offer. The standard example is the typical 'reward' case: in law, I make an offer when I post a notice saying I will pay £50 for the return of my lost dog, and your bringing me the dog is both your acceptance of the offer *and* the performance of your side of the contract. A simple exchange of property is one in which *both* the offer and the acceptance are constituted by performance. The crucial feature is that the agreement itself and its normative consequences arise simultaneously; the agreement itself does not exist until it is completed. It does not exist prior to completion, because the last act of completion, the acceptance of the offer, is the concluding performance under the contract. It therefore encompasses the case of the simultaneous exchange, but does not dependent on *simultaneity* to work.

On this view, the 'offer' I make when I place the chocolate bar on the counter is as much an invitation to treat as the shop's display of goods on the shelf. It marks my willingness to trade on the terms announced by the shop. But it is my proffering of the money which constitutes my offer, and the cashier's acceptance of that money, and his providing me with my change if necessary, that constitutes acceptance. Since I am already in possession of the chocolate bar, I need not be put into possession of it by the cashier, but nothing turns on that. If I were buying a packet of cigarettes, the cashier's taking the cigarettes from the shelf and handing them to me might be the last act of the transaction, and so might constitute acceptance. Thus it is the taking of the money for the goods, in whatever sequence that occurs, that makes the contract, and the law's characteristic 'last-act' analysis of contract formation applies here as well as it does in the case of executory agreements. Thus, for example, should the cashier not be able to complete the transaction by giving change for my £5 note, no contract is formed since only the last act of performance serves as acceptance completing the contract. Untypically for this book, in this case I do wish to bring this analysis in somewhat close contact with the common law. I do this because dealing with the analysis of contracts is somewhat off my patch in this work, and so I would like to verify the plausibility of this view, by looking somewhat more closely than usual at the state of the law. In the obvious analogous case where it is clear that obligations arise by virtue of an actual transaction, the case of gift, the law does look to the completion of the transaction, the delivery, before recognizing the transfer of title.[8] What about sales?

What the law appears to do is to identify the point at which the transaction is actually under way. I place my goods on the counter and the cashier indicates assent by ringing up the price. Rather than directing its mind to the point when the transaction gets under way, the law might just as well have paid attention to the completion of the transaction, i.e. my paying my money and receiving my change. Unfortunately, however, because it is generally assumed the law regards as the 'last act' the point at which the transaction

[8] Despite Equity's unwillingness to perfect gifts imperfect at law there are exceptions; a donor who has done all he is obliged to do to effect a transfer will be regarded as having transferred property in equity, as in, for example, *Re Rose* [1952] Ch. 499. See Hayton 1991, 217 ff.

begins, one *can* regard offers as conditional promises even in the case of simple trades or sales, however unsatisfactory this seems. One can say that when I place the chocolate bar goods on the counter, not immediately proffering my money, the cashier accepts my offer *as a conditional promise* to pay, as soon as he rings up the price. On this view the transactional analysis would rarely apply, since so few transaction are *really* instantaneous. There is a moment or two when I have an obligation to pay the purchase price some reasonably short time in the future. But this, it is submitted, is not a justifiable interpretation of the way in which such a transaction is generally regarded, nor is it plain what the law on this point is. While it appears well established that displays of goods or advertisements are regarded as invitations to treat, rather than offers, so that no contract is formed until, at the very least, a cashier 'accepts' the 'offer to purchase' which the customer makes when he brings the goods to the cashier,[9] it is not clear at what point the contract is actually concluded. In the leading case, *Pharmaceutical Society of GB* v. *Boots Cash Chemists*,[10] Somervell LJ says, 'having got the [articles] which they wish to buy, [customers] . . . come up to the assistant saying, "I want this". The assistant in 999 times out of 1,000 says "That is all right", *and the money passes and the transaction is completed*.'[11] This analysis, in referring to the passing of money and the completion of the transaction, does not clearly indicate at which point the contract is formed. The attention to the passing of money and the completion of the transaction provides logical room for holding that the sale is not legally enforceable until the transaction is completed. Somervell LJ also says, 'the contract is not completed until, the customer having indicated the articles which he needs, the shopkeeper, or someone on his behalf, accepts that offer',[12] but nowhere in the case is it explicitly stated what constitutes that acceptance. Birkett LJ, quoting Goddard LCJ's decision at first instance, states that 'there is no sale until the buyer's offer to buy is accepted by the *acceptance of the price*',[13] but that, in the normal course of events, could mean accepting the money for the goods as justifiably as it could mean the ringing up of the price, or an oral 'I accept'.[14] All of the judges emphasize that the offer and acceptance analysis should be shaped to reflect the reasonable expectations of the parties, hold-

[9] See Treitel 1991, 12–13.
[10] [1953] 1 QB 401.
[11] Ibid. 405–6, italics mine.
[12] Ibid. 406.
[13] Ibid. 407.
[14] An opposite view may of course be taken, one which would extend the notion of offer to a point well prior the one adopted by the Court of Appeal in *Boots*. The U.S. case of *Lefkowitz* v. *Great Minneapolis Surplus Stores* 251 Minn. 188 (1957) is often cited in this regard. There the court held that an advertisement advertising the sale of fur coats worth $100 for $1 on a first come, first served basis was an offer, which was accepted by the plaintiff whose attempt to purchase was refused on two occasions although he was the first person in the store. The result in this case is better explained as a misuse of contract law, in which the notion of offer has been extended in order to ensure that the would-be purchaser had a remedy against a trader whose pre-contractual representations capriciously engendered detrimental reliance.

ing that the view by which the mere placing of goods in one's basket as one moves through the aisles of the store would constitute the completion of the sale would be highly unreasonable and impractical. Taking the requirement of reasonableness and practicality seriously, however, favours the transactional analysis. If it turns out that the prospective purchaser has not enough money to pay for the goods or decides that he has picked up the wrong product or even simply decides he does not want to go through with it, the practical and reasonable view, it is submitted, is that the transaction is not completed and he should be able to withdraw. Similarly, if a shopkeeper, after ringing up the purchase, finds he cannot give change, or notices a defect in the product which he is unwilling or unable to remedy, he as well should be able to withdraw. Refusing to complete the transaction here is like refusing to sign a contract that has been prepared and the other party has signed. Refusing to sign may be inconvenient for one or both parties, and perhaps a duty to compensate the other party for expenses incurred in reliance may in some cases be justifiable. But there is no contract.

The manifest difficulty in distinguishing invitations to treat from offers, and what exactly constitutes offer and acceptance in a wide variety of commercial circumstances involving tickets and vending machines,[15] does not fortify one in the belief that the executory analysis of contract formation in all cases is either necessary or efficacious. It is not implausible to assert that a transactional analysis more genuinely reflects the layman's understanding of many common, relatively simple contracts. The essence of the transactional analysis is that only actual performance rearranges the rights and duties of the parties in the way that is intended by the contract. Until the time when all required performances are carried out, the duties one party has to another are not to make misrepresentations, nor to cause undue reliance, and perhaps to compensate for detrimental reliance if the expected performance is not carried out.[16] A technical property question arises in respect of the passing of property which constitutes an offer. This is technical, because nothing as regards the theory of contract is at stake, yet it is important for claims made where one party does not accept a transactional

[15] See Treitel 1991, 14; McKendrick 1990, 27–8.

[16] It is worth pointing out that although this analysis may appear to be similar to Atiyah's well-know reliance-based approach to contractual liability, the transactional analysis of contracts is actually completely different. Atiyah's approach develops a new analysis of *executory contracts*, i.e. those contracts in which obligations are undertaken to do something in the future, or rather, it analyses the basis for holding that someone is bound by a representation to do something in the future. As the quotations from Atiyah in the text show, Atiyah does not believe that the modern law of contract can countenance a non-executory analysis. See Atiyah 1981, chs. 5, 6, 7. This 'reliance' theory of promising is one basis upon which someone like Atiyah might claim to assimilate the law of contract and the law of tort into one law of obligations, in which a plaintiff's claim for a remedy is always a matter of the defendant's defeating his reasonable reliance, and where a promise itself amounts to a (usually) conclusive admission that the reliance is legitimate. See especially Atiyah 1981, 143–8, 173–6, and 184–99; Raz 1982.

offer and yet is in possession of the offeror's property. Has title passed, or not? If it has not, i.e. if title passes only on completion of the contract, then the offeror may simply demand the return of the property, or take it back if that is possible. If property does pass on the offer and the contract is not completed by a performance constituting acceptance, the offeror's claim would lie in restitution for the return of value transferred, the value of the offeree's unjust enrichment. In most of the cases where the transactional analysis is apposite, i.e. in the case of shop sales, there is unlikely to be much of a problem. The buyer can always just pass back the goods, which would satisfy the claim conceived either way, and a buyer is unlikely to care whether he is returned the actual notes and coins he paid over as long as he receives the right amount.

My argument here is not, of course, that the transactional analysis should be globally applied to all contracts, effecting an universal ousting of the traditional executory analysis of contracts. The law of contract must accommodate both analyses, depending on the circumstances of the contract. Both analyses approach the issue of contract formation in the same terms; they differ only in what constitutes offer and acceptance. In this way we have a unified approach to contract formation while at the same time recognizing the true diversity in contracts which can be formed. The distinction between executory and transactional contracts that has been drawn here reflects not only a concern with the validity of different theories of contract; it reflects, as one would expect, a genuine difference in what these two kinds of contract generally achieve, and thus a genuine difference in the way they serve the meaningful goals of the parties to them.

The suitability of applying the transactional analysis to relatively simple exchanges like sales reflects the general practical interest in initiating exchanges with ease, while at the same time only regarding the exchanges as binding when they are complete. The transactional analysis leaves many possibilities of avoiding carrying through to completion where the failure to carry through raises little chance of detrimental reliance, and where the reasons for not completing are common and sensible: the buyer does not have as much money in his wallet as he thought, or his credit card has expired, or the cashier cannot give change, or the product is faulty and there is not another in the shop or the buyer has no time to wait while a replacement is fetched. The recognition of transactional agreements might in part be a historical artifact of the expense of litigation. That is, treating a half-completed sales transaction as entailing the creation of obligations to complete may not be realistic given the relatively exorbitant cost of actually pursuing such rights in court. Nevertheless if this attitude to the situation is genuinely and generally accepted as just, the law would not be wrong to adopt it. One can, of course, imply all sorts of escape routes covering contingencies of the kind mentioned, and others, in order to insist that the executory analysis still applies; one could say, for example, that my offer to buy the chocolate bar is conditional on my having 26p in my pocket. It is submitted, however, that that is a complicated and unnecessary way of trying to accommodate these agreements into a law of contract and, again, it fails to accommodate instantaneous simple exchanges at all.

I would go further. I would claim that simple exchanges of property are the paradigm case of the bargain agreement between strangers. The simple exchanges of property they permit generally involve little in the way of any kind of ongoing relationship, and the value of the transaction to each of the parties is typically purely a matter of the consumer surplus gained by trading one thing for another. The analysis recognizes these agreements as for all intents and purposes momentary market interactions, of major consequence in aggregate terms, but relatively trivial considered individually. Forcing them into the executory mould necessarily requires the identification of executory obligations the enforcement of which no one would realistically regard as justified.

Executory contracts, on the other hand, are suitable for the attainment of much more extensive and complicated goals. They are generally suited for co-operatively ensuring results which are intended to come about some time in the future, for contracts for the provision of services or complex transactions for the exchange or supply of property. They can therefore enable complicated market dealings, but may also serve to establish relationships which, while commercial, may acquire the attributes of joint projects, establishing constitutive obligations.

The distinction raises two functions of contracts concerning property, which must be kept separate. The most important one, and the only one in the case of simple exchanges, is to serve as a historical justification for the passing of title. I have title to the chocolate bar I bought because of the agreement I made to exchange money for it with the store's agent. The law regards agreements as significant normative events, one of whose functions is to justify the exercise of a power to transfer property. Thus the power to make binding agreements legitimates the titles of those who have received under them. The former owner can not now deny the justice of his intentional transfer, i.e. the exercise of his power to transfer his property, claiming restitution or restoration of the property. The second function occurs only in executory contracts; contracts can also create rights *ad rem*, rights concerning the property of others which arise because of the obligations they have undertaken, in this case, obligations undertaken by contract.

All of this goes to show that the better view of contract is that it is the law governing the power to rearrange or create rights, duties, and powers by agreement. It is not merely a power to create obligations. As such, the power to sell is the legal power to create an agreement concerning the exercise of the power to transfer property, that agreement becoming a legally recognized fact the terms of which manifest the character of the transfer. As such, we see the right to sell as very much a creature of contract, but not because it creates obligations.

The Influence of the Market

My claim that contract and property must be strictly distinguished appears to deny the manifest truth that some property owes its very existence to the institution of contract, that is property which exists only given that there is a market.[17] Consider money: money, to name a significant item of property, exists only in virtue of the market since money's dual nature is as a store of value and *a medium of exchange*. And isn't it the case that property rights, like patents or copyrights, depend upon the existence of markets: what value would such monopolies have other than the value of exploiting them in a market?

In the first place my argument is not, of course, that no property exists because we have markets; the use of property as money in particular clearly bears this kind of causal relationship with contract, and this is true of patents and copyrights as well. Rather, my claim is that these kinds of property rights are not conceptual creatures of contract, such that outside the realm of markets their nature is indiscernible or inexplicable.

The reason for saying so is this: various kinds of property exist because of the fact that our economy is structured in such a way that we treat the benefits of some personal obligations, that is, some rights *in personam*, like debts as property rights. Treating these rights in that way, however, does not depend upon their status as rights *in personam* arising by virtue of contracts. Exactly equal rights can arise in gift and command economies. The particular structural feature of our economies which permits us to do so does not have to do with the reason these obligations exist, but because we treat some obligations *per se*, that is, rights to *future* property benefits secured through personal obligations, as a form of property in its own right. Let me explain.

A person can benefit another by giving him property now, or by promising to give him property in the future. Similarly, an authority can benefit someone in either way as well. The right to a future delivery of property is a valuable thing to have, and to the extent that it can be regarded as an essentially impersonal right to the delivery of property, as we have seen, that right may be regarded as property itself. Thus the owner of this right to future property can give it away. Or an authority which has such a right may rely upon it to make other commands transferring value, for it knows that it represent economic power. The advantage to an economy which recognizes such rights is obvious, for it allows people to bring future values, which they

[17] J. W. Harris was the first to raise this point with me.

do not presently have but expect to have, into the economy by creating rights *in personam* to an amount of this future value. So, for example, they can exchange property they will earn through their labour, for a house to live in right now.

But hold on, the reader might urge; where does this notion of exchange come in? Does that not imply an immediate return to the concept of a market economy, i.e. one based on contract? It does not, in fact, and the best way of explaining why is to look at one category of property which one might reasonably think is unavoidably dependent on the existence of markets, that is, money.

Money can be defined as a store of value and a universal medium of exchange expressed in or denominated in reference to units of account.[18] Now, of course, nothing is distinctive about money in so far as it is a store of value. Any property that does not waste away, and can be used in a valuable way in the future can serve that function. Neither does its expression in terms of a unit of account make it special.[19] Any kind of fungible property which is easily measured and whose supply relative to other things of value remains fairly constant is suitable for that purpose. What apparently makes money special, and wedded to markets, is the linking of these characteristics with its function as a *medium of exchange*. For if we speak of exchange, do we not necessarily speak of those bargain agreements in which money serves as a universal means of payment?

Yes and no. True, if we are speaking of a total economy which comprises a market economy, money does necessarily serve as a means of exchange in bargains. But it is not true that the only cases of exchange in which money can be used are bargain exchanges. We must not be mystified by the word 'exchange'. Typically, we often treat the term to specify bargains in which both sides transfer property, as when I buy a chocolate bar. But 'exchange' has a broader scope of application than this, and it is in this broader sense, unconnected to the reasons which motivate the exchange, that money serves its function.

At the launderette I exchange a £5 note for coins. I have exchanged one form of property for another. But is this a bargain exchange? Clearly not. I do not negotiate with the attendant to get the coins at the best price. There is no competition between lauderettes on the basis of who will give more 20p coins for a £1 coin. I am merely exchanging one form of property for another which is more useful to me at the time.

This of course also happens in the context of contractual exchanges. For

[18] See Mann 1992, 8–30. It is also true that nowadays only money issued by a sovereign State counts as money in the law, though this was not always the case: ibid. 14–23.

[19] The abstractness of the unit of account which attends money issued by sovereign States following the general legal trend away from obligations on issuing banks to convert paper currency into quantities of precious metal is interesting in its own right, but does not detract from the general point: see Mann 1992, 43–64.

example, when I go to a casino and exchange cash or a cheque for gambling chips, this is clearly an exchange of one kind of property for another. It clearly facilitates the primary contract that I and the casino will enter into, i.e. the gambling contract, since it is more convenient to gamble with chips than with cash or cheques. Nevertheless, neither party is gaining any advantage by that mere swap of cash for chips. In the context, the parties regard the two kinds of property as exactly equivalent in value. It is like exchanging one kind of money for another. While it is true that the casino has the legal obligation to re-exchange my chips at the end of my gambling session for cash or a cheque once more, and this obligation arises from the contract I have with the casino, this is a mere collateral obligation which facilitates the true contractual purpose, that is, to gamble. This exchange itself does not partake of any bargaining or negotiation in which the parties look to their own individual interests to secure a personal advantage. Similarly, the chose in action represented by my bank balance that I receive from the bank when I deposit cash is not a bargain transaction. The contract between me and the bank is to offer me this straightforward equal value for equal value exchange service, to make my economic affairs more convenient *in consideration of*, not the profit they can make by negotiating a favourable rate of exchange with me, but the interest they earn while my money is in their hands, and the increasingly many charges that attend my use of this facility. Of course, the value of £50 cash in hand may differ from the value of my £50 bank balance because the bank may fail. But this does not change the character of the exchange. If a bank fails, it is unable to meet its obligation to provide this exchange facility, and therefore my bank balance may become worthless, as it depends on this facility. But this is an all-or-nothing state of affairs. If the bank looks to be in difficulty, a run on the bank may push it over the edge. But until that happens, the bank has no legal right to discount the value of my balance in view of its shaky position. In other words, the bank has no right to turn this non-bargain exchange into a bargain exchange. (Whether, as a large depositor, it is in my interest to start bargaining rather than relying upon strict rights that may become worthless is a different matter.)

Thus money is useful as an economic tool not only as a store of value which can be used in bargains, but as a store of value to be cashed in for different but equally valuable property later on. It is this cashing-in function, this convenient exchangeability function, that makes something money. As such, money can play a role in all types of economy, not just a market one.

Understanding this deepens our understanding of different kinds of economy. A command economy could very reasonably make use of money, as present rights to future transfers of property (when cashed in), denominated in units of value. It could shift these rights from one person to the next in the same way as it could any other kind of property. But money becomes particularly useful in a command economy when the power to command economic transactions is decentralized. Command economies need not operate so that every economic transaction is directly commanded by one central authority. They can operate by giving various actors the power to command transactions. This decentralizes the power of command, but does not change its character. A command economy is one in which the terms of all economic transactions are set by an authority, not one in which every transaction is itself commanded by a single commanding authority. In decentralized command economies, the decentralized power of command may be framed in terms of general rules, giving various actors various rights to cash in their money for other forms of property. Therefore, within the command economy itself, goods are not distributed because people give property to each other; neither do transactions in which the goal is to negotiate oneself into a better economic position take place,[20] so that competitive markets form. Rather, a system of authoritative exchange rules operates, and one could hardly deny the value of money in such an economy.

Similarly, a gift economy is not one in which each transaction is itself a gift; when B cashes in A's promise to pay £10, A is not making a gift. B might have been given the right to cash in the promise by C, who might have been given it by D, who was himself the object of the original promise. But, again, it is hard to deny that such an economy could benefit from the institution of money.

Thus money appears to present a problem, but that is only because money indicates a *way* in which a form of property is regularly employed which at first glance seems to depend upon contractual exchanges. Obviously, money's use as currency is not a conceptual feature of the particular kind of property we use as money, whether a chattel or a chose in action and so on, except in so far as we apply rules of title making it negotiable. 'Real' money, like gold or silver coins, is nothing more than a particular chattel whose properties are such that it serves admirably as a store of value and a medium of exchange. Banknotes are a particular kind of promissory note, i.e a promise to pay a certain sum, which also perform these functions well.

It is worth re-emphasizing that, while money, as property which serves as currency, is not a creature of contract or markets, to say this is not to say that the use of money in contractual transactions is the same as its use in gifts or in command transactions. These transactions manifest different ways of exploiting the practice of property. The point I am making is that the general forms of property are available for each kind of transaction, and in that way are independent of any one sort of economy. By the same token monopolies on the use of inventions or the sole right to copy are not only comprehensible

[20] I am not denying that, when an individual in a command economy has the power to to command particular exchanges, such as 5 units of currency for a loaf of bread, that his choice to do so does not reflect his consumer surplus in having the bread. What I am denying is that, under such an economy this consumer surplus is 'given its head', so to speak, so that prices (the terms of the exchange) are dictated by aggregate supply and demand.

against the background of a market. Even in a gift or command economy such rights could exist, and they would shape the gratuitous transactions that people could make, or form the subject of economic commands. Even if there was no market in artworks, for example, an artist would still regard the sole right to copy a valuable entitlement.

Neither would I deny that the law of contract has played a significant role in the particular shape of different kinds of property we see in the law. True, the power to grant a non-owner the right to use one's land, under various restrictions, time limits, and so on is what permits an owner to create a lease, and any lease can be gratuitous or created by command. But the law of contract has clearly shaped the development of the legal nature of the lease since leases are typically bought and sold, not granted gratuitously. But by the same token, it would be equally as foolish to deny how the legal appreciation of gratuitous transactions has shaped other rights of property law, such as strict settlements[21] and trusts.

The point, however, can be more generally made. When considering the character of a right to see if it is a property right, we must always consider whether it can form the subject of a gift or a transfer by operation of law or authoritative command,[22] not only whether it can may be the object of a contract.[23]

[21] See e.g. Burn 1994, ch. 4.

[22] See also the tests of personal property employed by those involved in the *Law Quarterly Review* dispute over the nature of a chose in action, Ch. 5.

[23] For example, Wade 1948 claims that, contrary to general legal opinion, there is no reason to believe that a landowner may not create an irrevocable licence, and the irrevocable quality of the licence should not turn on the remedies available to the licensee if the licence is wrongfully withdrawn, in particular specific performance. But his description of the nature of a licence is obscured by the fact that he only considers licences granted by contract. Wade reviews a case, *Vaughan* v. *Hampson* (1873) 33 LT 15, in which the court treated a gratuitous licence as wrongfully revoked and therefore awarded the ejected licensee damages for assault. Although the case does employ a distorted notion of an interest in land, Wade treats this case only as a variation on the view, in his opinion bad, that only grants of a well-recognized interest in land, such as an easement, create irrevocable rights in respect of land: ibid. 66–7. He must regard the case in this way since he has already decided that the only other possible way of creating irrevocable rights is by contract: ibid. 60 ff. But surely it is the strongest possible support for his position that a gratuitous licence can be conferred on terms which make it irrevocable, for that would show that the owner of property has the power to create irrevocable obligations even though there is no possibility of specific enforcement in equity, since equity will not assist a volunteer.

8

Property and Contract II: Hegel's Idea of Property

Hegel's discussion of property in *The Philosophy of Right* is an extremely interesting and original account of the nature of property that has been variously interpreted.[1] All of these interpretations try to make sense of, and can therefore all be placed under the general rubric of, a 'personality' theory of property, and it is that sort of theory which will be explored in this Chapter. As I shall portray it, a personality theory of property is one which explains property as a relation between persons and things which is essentially determined by the nature of persons and things, specifically by the fact that persons have wills and things do not.

The position I shall argue here is that some version of Hegel's theory must be correct, that is, that some theory of property which takes the difference between persons, which have personality, and things, which do not, as the essence of the idea of property must be right. But I shall argue that Hegel's description of that relation is flawed and leads to a flawed understanding of property. The reason is the all too familiar one of entwining the analysis of property with the analysis of contract.

In a manœuvre remarkable for its lack of explanation, Hegel associates property with contract to show that property as an idea is perfected by contract, and that contract is dependent on property. In doing so Hegel mistakenly elides two aspects of autonomy which are perfectly distinguishable.

The Structure of **The Philosophy of Right**

The Philosophy of Right is divided into three parts, Abstract Right, Morality, and Ethical Life, and his discussion of property is found in the first. The third part, Ethical Life, is much the largest part of the book and depicts the step-by-step progress of the Idea of Right as it becomes fully instantiated in actual human society (and thus actual human history) through the forms of Family, Civil Society, and the State.

For Hegel, Right, i.e. what is right, is only understood when one understands certain stages of development of the will and human consciousness, and each stage carries a corresponding concept of right.[2] Very roughly,

[1] See e.g. Radin 1993, 35–71; Brudner 1991; Stillman 1989; Hughes 1988.
[2] Hegel 1942, para. 33.

Abstract Right corresponds to a stage of consciousness consisting of the most bare and abstract form of personality, which is essentially characterized by the ability to choose freely, to act as an agent capable of originating action. Understanding the nature of this stage of consciousness is all that is necessary to understand property, contract, civil wrongs, and the criminal law. This stage of consciousness characterizes the legal subject in private law, and here right appears to consciousness as the priority of formal rights over the good. The second stage, Morality, corresponds to a consciousness which is no longer mere personality, but which regards itself as a subject, an existential being with a determinate history and various needs, interests, desires, and projects.[3] At this stage, individual self-determination or living the good life or, simply, 'the good' is the appearance of right and characterizes what ought to be. Finally, in Ethical Life, these two stages of consciousness, these 'moments' in the Idea of Right, are transcended as conflicting elements and reunited in a harmonious way. At this stage, Right appears as it actually is, in a society in which individual self-determination is the goal of society, and society the goal of individual self-determination.

One aspect of this complex depiction of the nature of right is how this final overcoming and preservation of 'right' in Abstract Right and 'good' in Morality affects those particular institutions which are characterized by one of these mere appearances of what is right.[4] Once the nature of society reflects the true idea of Right in Ethical Life, does Abstract Right, and thus private law, or Morality, and thus the ethics of leading the good life, have any residual force and, if so, to what extent? This is a matter which I shall not explore here. It may be that the flaws I detect in Hegel's treatment of property in Abstract Right are of little consequence set against the whole picture of the work, particularly if the moment of Abstract Right is substantially transcended in Ethical Life. Nevertheless, proceeding on the hardly radical assumption that what comes first provides a foundation for what comes later, the clarity, rigour, and basic sense of the characterization of property in Abstract Right may be legitimately assessed on its own.

One cautionary point: brilliant or not, Hegel's treatment of property and the entire field of private and criminal law is really very brief. It is a testament to the importance and originality of his thought that such a short treatment has been so fruitfully examined. Nevertheless, this brevity may account in part for what in many ways is a regrettable disregard of the alternative courses which, from the same starting point, his dialectic might have followed. The following criticisms, therefore, are primarily directed to the flaws in the characterization of one small part of a global theory; they do not necessarily threaten the overall tenor or approach of *The Philosophy of Right*.

[3] Ibid., paras. 105, 106.

[4] This question is extensively treated in Brudner 1989 and 1991; E. J. Weinrib 1989; Taylor 1979; and Pelczynski 1971.

The Will and the Idea of Right in The Philosophy of Right

The subject-matter of the philosophical science of right is the Idea of right, i.e. the concept of right together with the actualization of that concept.[5]

The basis of right is, in general, mind; its precise place and point of origin is the will. The will is free, so that freedom is both the substance of right and its goal, while the system of right is the realm of freedom made actual, the world of mind brought forth out of itself like a second nature.[6]

Hegel frames the matter of what is right as a matter of an aspect of human consciousness (mind), the (free) will, finding its existence or becoming actual in the real world. 'Idea'[7] is for Hegel what we grasp when we understand something, say beauty, not merely as an abstract concept but as a phenomenon in the real world.[8] In the case of right, the phenomenon is the 'system of right', or the realm of freedom in human affairs, and it must be understood in terms of the concept of the free will.

Hegel characterizes the will as the unity of two 'moments', one universal and one particular.[9] Since the free will can withdraw from any particular purpose or need or impulse, it can isolate itself from the world, standing back from any particular inclination as it considers it or dismisses it. From this perspective it has no determinate character but the mere possibility of willing, and as such is universal.[10] On the other hand, the will also has the nature of identifying with particular inclination, and viewed from this perspective the will has a particular character, the character of actually willing a particular thing at a particular time.[11] These two 'moments' of the will are unified to form the free will. Both moments are essential, and only in relation to each other does the freedom of the will exist, for it is the internal relation of potentiality to actuality, and the universal to the particular, which characterizes it.

According to Hegel the free will has a number of forms, which are determined in the way the will abstracts from any particular inclination, and in the way it makes itself determinate.[12] The most important distinction is between the form of the will when it is merely free *in itself*, and when it is also free *for itself*.[13] The will is free *in itself* whenever it self-consciously chooses: in this case the will displays its essential features, its ability to withdraw from any particular inclination, and its ability to choose any particular one. Being true to character, then, the will is free *in itself*. The will is free *for itself*, on the other hand, when it not only acts true to character by self-consciously making

[5] Hegel 1942, para. 1.
[6] Ibid., para. 4.
[7] I follow Knox in capitalizing Idea when the word has this significance.
[8] Hegel 1942, translator's footnote (#2) to para. 1.
[9] Ibid., paras. 5, 6, 7.
[10] Ibid., paras. 5, 7R.
[11] Ibid., paras. 6, 7R.
[12] Ibid., paras. 8–32, especially 30, 30R.
[13] Ibid., paras. 21, 21R, 27.

choices, but also judges its choices with the will itself as the ultimate purpose in mind. When the will acts in this way, it finds its purpose in itself; it makes the will itself the ultimate goal of exercising the will. In other terms, when the purpose of free choices is freedom itself, then the will is free *for itself*.

The importance of this for *The Philosophy of Right* cannot be overstated. According to Hegel, the philosophical inquiry of right is the inquiry into the way that the will *for itself* is manifest in actual human relations. Right concerns the way that persons, who can make free choices, can make freedom the goal of those choices. On this view freedom is clearly not simply an instrumental capacity for achieving some ends, but *is* the end. It should be pointed out that Hegel's concept of freedom is complex, and involves the entire set of social relations, from law to morality to the institutions of society like the family and the State. His description of the will that is free *for itself* is not vacuous; taking freedom as an end does not mean that the goal of free choice is choosing *per se*; the will free *for itself* can only be understood in terms of the actual human situation, which will involve relations with things and with other people. Freedom is situated in human society.

Free will unfolds as an Idea only as various social relations of differing complexity are examined. These actual relations which show the effects of persons making free choices are the material which must be studied in order to understand the nature of the right. 'An *existent* of any sort embodying the free will, this is what right is. Right is therefore by definition freedom as Idea.'[14] For this reason, understanding right is not only a matter of theorizing on the basis of some fundamental concept of the free will, but involves looking at actual social relations over the course of history and treating these forms of life seriously as manifestations of free will.

> The determinations of the concept in the course of its development are from one point of view themselves concepts, but from another point of view they take the form of existents, since the concept is in essence Idea. The series of concepts which this development yields is therefore at the same time a series of shapes of experience, and philosophic science must treat them accordingly.[15]

For Hegel, the simplest of those relations are embodied in the law, specifically in property, contract, and civil and criminal wrong.

Abstract Right and Property

At the stage of Abstract Right, the form the will takes is 'personality'.[16] This is a description of self-consciousness in which the will has itself, an ego, as the ultimate purpose or rationale underlying all its determinate aims. The

[14] Ibid., para. 29. [15] Ibid., para. 32. [16] Ibid., paras. 34–9.

external world is directly confronted as an alien, threatening other. This consciousness constitutes the capacity for rights. Opposed to the external world, self-consciousness identifies with its 'negative' capacity at this stage. It is the self-consciousness of one who understands freedom as freedom *from* the external world in its ability to choose. Therefore, the form of right which reflects this consciousness is essentially negative, i.e. protective of the will's pure capacity of withdrawal from any determinate feature of the real world, not positive in the sense of binding the will to move in particular ways in the real world. Hence, the imperative of right at this stage, 'Be a person and respect others as persons',[17] can be elaborated only in the negative form of a prohibition: '"[d]o not infringe personality and what personality entails." The result is that there are only prohibitions in the sphere of right, and the positive form of any command in this sphere is based in the last resort, if we examine its ultimate content, on prohibition.'[18] At this stage, self-consciousness seeks to overcome the alien external world by taking charge of it in some way. The relation of the will to things, to others, and ultimately to itself through these external relations, governs the content of Abstract Right. Hegel sets it out as follows:

> Right is in the first place the immediate embodiment which freedom gives itself in an immediate way, i.e. (a) possession, which is *property*-ownership. Freedom is here the freedom of the abstract will in general, or *eo ipso*, the freedom of a single person related only to himself. (b) A person by distinguishing himself from himself relates himself to another person, and it is only as owners that these two persons really exist for each other. Their implicit identity is realized through the transference of property from one to the other in conformity with a common will and without detriment to the rights of the other. This is *contract*. (c) The will which is differentiated not in the sense of (b) as being contrasted with another person, but in the sense of (a) as related to itself, is as a particular will at variance with and opposed to itself as an absolute will. This opposition is wrongdoing and *crime*.[19]

Property is the relation of personality to the external sphere of things, understood in terms of the free will. The essential elements of this relation are (1) the free will of persons, (b) the absence of wills in things, and (c) the substantive end of consciousness at this stage, which is to appropriate all things.[20] Hegel explains the last element as the will's destiny to become determinate:

> A person must translate his freedom into an external sphere in order to exist as an Idea. Personality is the first, still wholly abstract, determination of the absolute and infinite will, and therefore this sphere distinct from the person, the sphere capable of embodying his freedom, is likewise determined as what is immediately different and separable from him.[21]
>
> A person has as his substantive end the right of putting his will into any and every

[17] Ibid., para. 36. [18] Ibid., para. 38. [19] Ibid., para. 40 (italics original).
[20] Ibid., paras. 41–4. [21] Ibid., para. 41.

thing and thereby making it his, because it has no such end in itself and derives its destiny and soul from his will. This is the absolute right of appropriation which man has over all 'things'.[22]

Having a free will, a person has the absolute right to appropriate any thing which has no will itself. This explains the principle that a thing belongs to the first person who appropriates it, since his will is then embodied in the possession of the thing. The next prospective appropriator is not confronted by a will-less thing, but a thing already filled with the will of another, in the sense that it has become a manifestation of that other's existence as a free will.[23]

Of course, appropriating something is not the same thing as merely desiring to have it. As an embodiment of will, it must reflect the will of the appropriator. Hegel describes, in order of satisfactoriness, different modes of appropriation: taking possession by occupation, forming a thing, marking it, using it, and, finally, alienating it. My taking possession of a thing by holding or occupying it is 'subjective, temporary, and restricted in scope'.[24] It is unsatisfactory because it is precarious, lasting only as long as possession itself. My forming something is thus superior, for the change in the character of the thing can be permanent, and reflects my will whether or not I am in physical association with it.[25] Marking something as mine is superior to forming it in the sense that it directly and unambiguously represents my will, but is unsatisfactory because it is only a representation of my will, and is thus a very slight determination of my will.[26]

Use is much better. When I use a thing my will is 'externally realized' in it: my changing, destruction, or consumption of a thing both reveals a determinate movement of my will and displays the thing used as having no will of its own.[27] Use is a particularly powerful manifestation of the will when it is apparent that I use a renewable resource in a way which will sustain my using it indefinitely.[28] Nonetheless, use is a temporal manifestation of will; the right to property lapses where no use is made of a thing, for then the will is effectively utterly withdrawn from it, and so property can be acquired by prescription.[29]

Alienation of property follows from the fact that as a willing being, I can withdraw my will from any thing which is separable from me.

The reason I can alienate my property is that it is mine only in so far as I put my will into it. Hence I may abandon (*derelinquere*) as a *res nullius* anything that I have or yield it to the will of another and so into his possession, provided always that the thing in question is a thing external by nature.[30]

The interesting part of alienation is not abandonment, but alienation to another. This aspect of alienation provides a natural progression, according

[22] Ibid., para. 44.
[23] Ibid., para. 50.
[24] Ibid., para. 55.
[25] Ibid., para. 56.
[26] Ibid., para. 58.
[27] Ibid., para. 59.
[28] Ibid., para. 60.
[29] Ibid., para. 64.
[30] Ibid., para. 65.

to Hegel, into the right of contract, and here is where I think he goes astray.

Up to this point, all of what Hegel says accords with my analysis of the right of exclusive use. However here, at the transition from property to contract, the congruence falls apart. I have argued that the essence of the right to property is the right to have things treated in line with a social practice in which we do not interfere with things that are not our own, and which is institutionalized in the normative system through those general duties *in rem* I have so often mentioned. Hegel, however, gives short shrift to this characterisation of the way other persons, other 'determinate wills' in his words, recognize the property of others. Hegel argues that the perfection of property occurs in contract, in which persons recognize each other as owners in a more direct way than by simply not interfering with each other's property.

This view leads to the obliteration of anything but a formal distinction between rights *in rem* and rights *in personam*. But it also renders Hegel incapable of appreciating how essential it is to distinguish the interests people have *in things* from all other interests, or interests *per se*. Furthermore, he does slight justice to contract itself with his insistence that a contract is always a case of mutual alienation of property. In all of this, Hegel entangles property with contract. Since Hegel is only able to assimilate property with contract because of the way he characterizes things, it is appropriate to start with that.

Hegel's Idea of Things

As we have seen, according to Hegel the signal characteristic of a thing is that it is something that exists without a free will, and therefore can be possessed as property by a person.

Hegel describes a thing as 'that whose determinate character lies in its pure externality', or as 'inherent externality'.[31] This 'externality' is in relation to the 'internality' of personality. The question is whether Hegel, on this model of externality and internality, conceives of everything not internal as being 'external' in character for the purpose of property rights. Unfortunately, it seem that he does.[32]

Hegel writes:

> Mental aptitudes, erudition, artistic skill, even things ecclesiastical (like sermons, masses, prayers, consecrations of votive objects), inventions and so forth, *become subjects of contract, brought onto a parity, through being bought and sold, with things recognized as things*. . . . We may hesitate to call such abilities, attainments, aptitudes, &c., 'things', for while possession of these may be the subject of business dealings and contracts, as if they were things, there is also something inward and

[31] Ibid., para. 42R. [32] See Brudner 1991, 20, n. 45.

mental about it. . . . Attainments, erudition, talents, and so forth, are, of course, owned by free mind and are something internal and not external to it, but even so, by expressing them it may embody them in something external and alienate them . . . and in this way they are put into the category of things. Therefore they are not immediate at the start but only acquire this character through the mediation of mind which reduces its inner possessions to immediacy and externality.[33]

This passage is confusing. It suggests two ways in which things internal can become external for the purposes of property. The first is by the very act of making them the subject of a contract, bringing them onto a parity with what are normally recognized as things. Secondly, the passage presents as an elaboration of this contractual externalization (business dealings, etc.) a completely different and independent ground for externalization, viz. embodiment in something already external. Hegel has already dealt with forming a thing, and thereby impressing one's personality on it. It seems obvious that such impressions into material things, such expressions, should be alienable as such, i.e. as material things, since it is obvious one can withdraw one's will from them. The question is whether the mere *expression* of an internal thing by making it the subject of a contract is sufficient to render it external and therefore subject to being treated as property.

It is plain that Hegel believes that some internal things cannot be so treated, under any circumstance. Treating something as a thing for the purpose of property requires that one be able to withdraw one's will from it, and this cannot be done in terms of the substantive characteristics of one's self consciousness, one's universal freedom of will, one's ethical life, or one's religion. The will cannot be sensibly withdrawn from these things, so they cannot be property. For this reason they are also imprescriptable.[34] On the other hand, persons *can* withdraw their will from their own bodies, and maim themselves, or even take their own lives.[35] This does not mean that it is ever right *for others* to treat *my* body as a thing,[36] for my body is the manifestion of myself *to others*. So even where the will can be withdrawn from something, it does not entail that that thing can be coherently regarded as a thing for the purpose of property.

With respect to the products of one's abilities, Hegel argues:

Single products of my particular physical and mental skill and of my power to act I can alienate to someone else and I can give him the use of my abilities for a restricted period, because, on the strength of this restriction, my abilities acquire an external relation to the totality and universality of my being. By alienating the whole of my time, as crystallized in my work, and everything I produced, I would be making into another's property the substance of my being, my universal activity and actuality, my personality.[37]

[33] Hegel 1942, para. 43R.
[34] Ibid., paras. 65, 66, 66R.
[35] Ibid., para. 47.
[36] Ibid., paras. 48, 48R.
[37] Ibid., para. 67.

This paragraph and the remark that follows it seem to be directed to pointing out that the very idea of *using* one's own powers only makes sense if one is not utterly committed to their completely determined use; in other words, a determinate will is not a will but a thing if its entire course of action is determined by another. Unless there is a quantitative restriction on the alienation, one has alienated one's entire personality, and thus has tried to alienate oneself as a thing. Yet externalization here seems to mean little more than the fact that one's work can be coherently conceived apart from the person himself, i.e. that we can distinguish a person's labour from that person himself in a way that we cannot distinguish a person from his personality.

If everything that can merely be conceived apart from the person himself *qua* personality is a thing for the purpose of property (save for the special case of a person's body), why should the expression of these things as the subjects of contracts be particularly relevant? These passages occur before Hegel actually discusses contract in its own right, so he may simply be preparing the reader for his view that contractual rights are things as much as material goods, binding together property with contract. Indeed, before the section on property, in the course of attacking the Roman Law and Kantian distinctions between types of rights, e.g. between *ius ad personam* and *ius ad rem*, Hegel makes the following revealing statement:

> To be sure, it is only a person who is required to execute the covenants of a contract, just as it is also only a person who acquires the right to their execution. But a right of this sort cannot for this reason be called a 'personal' right; rights of whatever sort belong to a person alone. Objectively considered, a right arising from a contract is never a right over a person, but only a right over something external to a person or something which he can alienate, always a right over a thing.[38]

This paragraph shows that Hegel makes the opposite mistake to the one Hohfeld made.[39] He similarly reasons that rights *in rem* and rights *in personam* are only formally different, but rather than conclude with Hohfeld that all rights *in rem* are just bundles of rights *in personam*, Hegel concludes that all rights *in personam* are really rights *in rem*, property rights in things. By equating 'something external to personality' with 'thing', Hegel supposes that the right to have someone carry out a duty founded on a contingent relationship with the right-holder, i.e. to perform under a contract, is to be conceived on the same footing as a right to property. Hegel completely disregards the distinction between duties *in rem* and *in personam*, and to be consistent must hold that contractual rights manifest a relationship no more personal than the relationship between a householder and all the other subjects of the law who respect his right of property and do not trespass. On this view, the paradigm or characteristic position regarding the alienability

[38] Ibid., para. 40R. [39] Ch.2 above, at 23.

of contractual rights should be that they are alienable, which is clearly not the position at law.

But though this is Hegel's view, it still does not explain how contractual dealings are significant in making various actions (labour) or skills or abilities into things for the purpose of property. Just because something is the subject of an agreement does not obviously suggest that it is being conceived of in some special way that serves to externalize what is previously internal. The point cannot be that, since contracts take at least two people, and they must agree on the subject matter, externalization is necessarily achieved in contract because at least two people must have a meeting of minds or joint conceptualization of the thing in question. It is the expression and communication of the internal thing which does that, not the fact that the context is a contractual one. Making a contract respecting something 'internal' *rests* on this ability to conceive of the thing and express the conception. It does not account for it.

In truth, contract is essential for Hegel's explanation of things because in his view contractual exchange is the true basis of property: only when exchange is related to property is the idea of property fully understood. Because he dismisses anything like the *in rem/in personam* distinction he is able absolutely to overlook the basic rights and duties *in rem* regarding non-interference with the property of others, however fundamental they are. Until he gets to contract, Hegel deals with the right to property simply as a relation between an owner and a thing, even though his theory entails that others have a duty of non-interference because of the presence of the owner's will in his property. The instances where Hegel mentions the basic right that others not interfere with one's property are remarkably few. In paragraph 48, in discussing property in one's body he explains why others are not to treat one's body as an appropriable thing, nor why they may not do it violence. He justifies the rule of first possession in paragraph 50, and in paragraph 51 speaks of the recognizability for others that possession of property must show. Nowhere does Hegel discuss the nature of this recognition of the owner as right-holder by those who comply with the duty not to intefere with his property, and therefore it seems plausible when he makes his transition to contract to treat the recognition of the opposite party in an exchange as the first instance of the recognition of another as an owner. We cannot say we weren't warned: in the passage from the introduction quoted above Hegel says: '[r]ight is in the first place the immediate embodiment which freedom gives itself in an immediate way, i.e. (a) possession, which is *property*-ownership. Freedom is here the freedom of the abstract will in general or, *eo ipso*, the *freedom of a single person related only to himself*.'[40]

But a concept of property in which the *recognizability* of the person's occupation of things matters so much cannot make sense without some

[40] Hegel 1942, para. 40 (italics mine).

content being given to the relation *between persons*. In his passage entitled 'Transition from Property to Contract' Hegel does not regard the right that others not interfere with one's property as a matter of the recognition of rights at all; he seems to reduce property to a matter of an individual person's own recognition of externality via his ownership of things, as if no interpersonal recognition at all were required for a person to hold something as property. The passage in full is as follows:

> Existence as determinate being is in essence being for another. One aspect of property is that it is an existent as an external thing, and in this respect property exists for other external things and is connected with their necessity and contingency. But it is also an existent as an embodiment of the will, and from this point of view the 'other' for which it exists can only be the will of another person. This relation of will to will is the true and proper ground in which freedom is existent.—The sphere of contract is made up of this mediation whereby I hold property not merely by means of a thing and my subjective will, but by means of another person's will as well and so hold it in virtue of my participation in a common will.[41]

This is an astounding position to take, for not only does it render the concept of property indistinguishable from contract, but it makes no sense of alienation by exchange. It is simply a matter of conceptual priority that, before two persons can exchange what they own, their ownership of the things to be exchanged must be recognized; the prospective traders must recognize that each other's property must not be interfered with as a matter of right. If that were not the case, there would be no basis for the exchange.

In any case, given that this is Hegel's view, it is now apparent why contracting makes the internal external, creating things as property. Only in contract does the true recognition of the right to property exist. It is also apparent now why contractual dealings are significant for understanding how skills, abilities, etc. can be treated as things. Since only in contract is property truly manifest, contract brings into existence things which are the truest examples of property. As Brudner states, according to Hegel, '[w]e understand property when we relate 'things' to a conception of being that reveals them as true or real only as owned'.[42] So if it is only in contract that property-ownership as a form of right is made full or complete, then 'things' alienated via contract, i.e. contractual rights, are the highest example of things that can be treated as property.[43] Says Hegel: '[c]ontract brings into existence the property whose external side, its side as an existent, is no longer a mere "thing" but contains the moment of a will (and consequently the will of a

[41] Ibid., para. 71 (ref. to another para. omitted).

[42] Brudner 1991, 18.

[43] As we have seen, this is implied very early on. At Hegel 1942, 43R, the remark to the third para. of Property, he states, '[b]ut it is not until we come to deal with alienation that we need begin to speak of the *transition* of such mental property [mental aptitudes, erudition, etc.] into the external world where it falls under the category of property in the legal sense.'

second person also.)'[44] It is beyond the scope of this paper to engage in a thorough analysis of Hegel's theory of contract. It is enough to point out that Hegel believes all exchanges are instances of the mutual alienation of determinate things, i.e. in which all duties of contractual performance are regarded as property,[45] and furthermore that he believes that parties to a contract exchange things of identical value,[46] to show that his theory is not without complications.

What is important here is that Hegel's ordering of alienation above use and possession as a manifestation of property permits him to overlook the fundamental features of property. In Chapter 4 I argued that exclusion, use, and alienation are all conceptual elements of the right of exclusive use, properly understood, but there is no basis upon which the last element should be raised above the others, for they all depend on the same basic 'recognition of other determinate wills', to use Hegel's terms. Contract is indeed a different matter, but not because it is the truth of property, but because it treats property as one object among others which can be the subject of an agreement. Agreements are a completely different realm of human interaction in their own right.

The Value of Hegel's Theory of Property

Clearly, the problem is one of properly taking account of the existence of the wills of others, i.e the existence of other persons. In order to make Hegel's theory of property work, one must reconceive the individual personality of abstract right not as an isolated individual surrounded by will-less things, but as an individual surrounded by a world populated both by will-less things *and* other wills. At the very least, in order to respect rights at all, the individual must be able to distinguish the other persons from the rest of the 'things' that surround him. Without that capacity, a person could not distinguish between his use of an animal as a beast of burden and his enslavement of a man. He would not be able to understand that the first is the rightful use of a thing and that the second is not right in any respect.

Hegel confuses two bases of autonomy. There is, first, the autonomy that is provided by a right of exclusive use, the right to determine the use of things, so far as a right of exclusion can do so. Secondly, though, there is the entirely different and powerful realm of autonomy created when persons are free to make agreements amongst themselves. The distinction between these two forms of autonomy is not formal but substantial. They concern different aspects of human relations. The former can become the subject of the latter,

[44] Ibid., para. 72.
[45] See, *e.g.* ibid., paras. 79, 79R.
[46] See ibid., paras. 63 and 77.

when contractual exchanges of property occur. And the latter can become the subject of the former, when contractual rights, such as those in negotiable instruments or shares, become alienable and the relationship between the original parties becomes de-personalized. This interactive capability, however, does not just render contract and property formal variants of the same thing. To vary the last example slightly, given Hegel's conception of contract and property, it is difficult to maintain a distinction between my temporary use of a beast of burden and my contractual right to the services of another person. Both are regarded simply as rights to things.

If the distinction between persons and things is properly taken account of at the outset, however, Hegel's theory provides a wonderful insight into the right of exclusive use. Hegel's notion of a will 'filling a thing' makes sense of the right of exclusive use. Property is the manifestation of autonomous decision-making: the *will* of the owner fills a thing in the sense that he determines what is to be done with it, so far as mere exclusion of others, the exclusion of their wills and designs on the thing, can do so. This does not mean that a person must use a thing alone, in isolation from others. He can share it, or engage in joint ownership should he, with another, determine that only an agreement of their wills shall determine the use of a thing.

What we should take from Hegel is the barest justification for property that there is, and it is the correct one. Persons are categorically different from things, by virtue of having personalities, one constitutive facet of which is their free will. By virtue of that, they may determine the use of things. They may do this either with others or singly, but it must be remembered that doing this with others may involve the further element of human agreements of a contractual nature.

The respect for the right of exclusive use derives precisely from the respect for others as autonomous agents in the context of a social situation in which there must be some relations of right between persons that are not substantially personal. Any society which is complex enough to be faced with having to acknowlege an *in rem/in personam* distinction in their various practices, rights, and duties will evince a property practice. But this practice is only one aspect of human relations and, being in some sense basic or fundamental, does not entail any priority in moral reasoning. The morality of dealing with the needs of others, with one's interests in living under a State, in raising a family, in making agreements, etc., may all ultimately demand higher allegiance. Indeed, property can be justified instrumentally because the right to things facilitates so much that is done in the name of these interests. The State cannot tax unless there is property, nor redistribute wealth (*as* property) to the worse off. Neither may the goods in a family be shared, nor a contract for wages performed.

Brudner's Characterization of Hegel

Before leaving this topic, it is worth examining another recent analysis of Hegel's discussion of property in *The Philosophy of Right*. Professor Brudner's ambitious article, 'The Unity of Property Law',[47] draws largely on Hegel's views. Brudner's article is a complex analysis of the common law of property which attempts to show how the various moments of Hegel's system, Abstract right, Morality, and Ethical Life, are reflected, respectively, in the common law of property, in equitable doctrines, and in the fusion of law and equity and in advances in corporate and labour relations law. I will not touch on these overarching themes of his paper. What is relevant here is Brudner's characterization of Hegel's notions of property in Abstract right. Because Brudner emphasizes the isolation of the individual owner of property before the advent of alienation in exchange, he stands as a contemporary example of one who, like Hegel, not only de-emphasizes the foundation of the property right in the recognition accorded owners in the duty of non-interference, but would also entangle property with contract to the detriment of understanding either.

As is apparent from the foregoing, there is much support for this approach in Hegel's discussion of property in *The Philosophy of Right*, and Brudner can claim to be modernizing Hegel's own view of property. On the other hand, while acknowledging a debt to Hegel, Brudner presents his theory as valid in its own right, not simply as an 'Hegelian' theory of property.[48]

In discussing the level of personality which characterizes Abstract Right, Brudner argues that this will, stripped of all its particular inclinations, must be conceived as an isolated individual.

> This conception of the essential reality as a self shorn of individuating features is paradoxically determined by an individualistic premise. Specifically, it is determined by the assumption that the individual's isolated or pre-social condition is its natural one, or that the atomistic individual has a fixed and stable reality.[49]

I think this is badly mistaken. Though there is no 'natural community'[50] at this stage, this only means that Abstract Right is not characterized in terms of the actual effects, good or bad, of the actions individuals perform, just so long as they abide by the rights individuals have simply by virtue of their having personality. It does not mean, and it cannot mean, that individuals are self-regarding in the sense that they cannot distinguish other persons from things in the external world which they confront. It is this ability to discriminate between persons and things, and to make sense of that distinction if only in the rudimentary and perhaps unsympathetic way of recognizing other people to be determinate wills, which underlies the capacity for these persons to have rights at all.

[47] Brudner 1991. [48] Brudner 1991, 3–8, and 8, n. 13. [49] Ibid., 19. [50] Ibid.

This vision of the individual at the stage of Abstract Right permits Brudner to say: '[w]e can understand property, . . . as the objectively realized claim of *the person* [N.B. not each person or all persons] to be the end of things.'[51] But rights can only be objectively realized in societies of some kind, and so the Idea of right must be structured to make sense of that reality. To the extent Brudner treats the objectively realized claim of property as the claim of the individual in isolation from others, as surrounded only by willless things, this claim is not what is objectively realized in the institution of property. Property must be understood as the objectively realized claim of person*s* to be the end of things, *and* of all persons to be (at least partly) their own ends. That this view is (one of) Hegel's is evident from the injunction that abstract right entails, '[b]e a person and respect others as persons', which is stated prior to his discussion of property.[52] Only if the distinction between individual persons is borne in mind along with the distinction between persons and things can sense be made of property.

Brudner follows the preceding quotation with this:

> property is here essentially private or exclusive, because it is the embodiment of the self of the atomistic individual, external and *indifferent* to others. At this stage the being of things is the *particular* self, the self of the discrete individual, a self that therefore excludes the self of other individuals.[53]

In contrast to this view and, as I have pointed out rather unrelentingly, the right of exclusive use entails nothing of selfishness or acting like a hermit: under it all property could be jointly held, and much is. The point about exclusion is not that it's every man for himself, but rather that it will rarely be all men for everyone. There is nothing about this stage of right which leads to the view that the individual's determinate uses of his property will be selfish. All that is entailed is that the person's determination of the use of a thing is justified whatever the size of ownership, from individual ownership to joint ownership with many joint owners.

By this depiction of the selfish, isolated individual, Brudner is able to minimize the recognition of others' rights implicit in the practice of not interfering with others' property. Like Hegel, Brudner wishes to reveal 'the intimate connection between property and contract',[54] and to show 'that contract must be understood not as the arbitrary transfer of a property juridically complete prior to exchange, but rather as itself the immanent and perpetually re-enacted completion of property'.[55]

[51] Ibid., 21.
[52] Hegel 1942, para. 36.
[53] Brudner 1991, 21, first instance of italics mine.
[54] Ibid., 34.
[55] Ibid., 34–5. Brudner goes on to say that this is also the view of the common law. He states: 'I have no property prior to exchange in the value of the thing nor in the profit it generates, both of which may be lawfully diminished by my neighbour. That is to say, I have no pre-socially fulfilled property in that which is essentially constituted as property through the unity of mutual assent of abstract wills. Moreover, the doctrine that something is worthy of judicial protection as property only if it has exchange value is now comprehensible as a

This connection is explained as follows: in the first place, the isolated individual does not merely have the right to appropriate any unowned thing by virtue of his having a will and a thing not having one. The apparent independence of unappropriated objects causes the will to seek to validate its primacy, its superiority over things, by seeking to appropriate all things. Each individual determinate will has this presumptive right to unlimited appropriation.[56] But since each act of appropriation denies the equal right of all others, since everyone, obviously, cannot all at the same time appropriate everything, an act of appropriation 'fails as an objectively valid conquest of the thing'.[57] A general consent by everyone to a right to appropriate will not make these appropriations valid. 'No person could rationally, that is, consistently with his claim to be an end, consent to a unilateral and exclusive appropriation by another, for such a consent would be one to his perpetual exclusion from the thing.'[58] The solution is a form of recognition in which individual ownership is recognized, but at the same time the prospect of perpetual exclusion from a thing is nullified.

> In exchange, I recognize the other's right to exclusive possession by giving him in return an equal value; yet I do not hereby foreclose my opportunities for *unlimited acquisition*, for I recognize his right to the thing only insofar as it becomes available to me (only insofar as he ceases to be the owner), while he recognizes mine under the same proviso. Furthermore, in alienating my possession, I resolve the contradiction between my putative mastery of the thing and my actual dependence on it; for now I demonstrate its nothingness in relation to my will by disdainfully abandoning it. By getting rid of the thing, I show conclusively that it belongs to me rather than I to it. If I abandon it as a *res nullius*, however, I lack objective confirmation for my claim of right to dispose of it according to my will. If I alienate it as a gift, I obtain recognition from the donee who accepts it as such; but because the donee does not assert himself in the transaction as an equal and owning person, his recognition cannot satisfyingly confirm my possession as objectively mine. Only in exchange am I recognized as an end by someone who, because he is simultaneously recognized by me as an end, can authoritatively validate my claim to exclusive control of the object.[59]

This ingenious argument is flawed in several respects. In the first place, the will acquisitive of everything is incoherent as described. If the will is concerned that things without wills are putting up a show of independence, challenging the superior status of the free will, and so must be revealed as the inferiors they are, then their ownership *by anyone* should be sufficient for the purpose. It is reasonable to suppose that the personality of Abstract Right is secured in its superior status by the demonstration that all things

statement that something is property only if it is already recognized as such by persons engaged in competitive acts of accumulation. The court simply makes explicit what is already implicitly accomplished by the market': ibid., 35.

[56] Ibid., 32–3.
[57] Ibid., 33.
[58] Ibid.
[59] Ibid., 35 (italics mine).

are owned, and thus that the determinate will is superior, regardless of the fact that many different persons are engaged in the process. Indeed, one may go further. Given that personality is as abstract as it is at this stage and that, by necessity, any individual determinate will must recognize the existence of other determinate wills for any of this to get off the ground, the burden of proof should be on someone who insists that this show of superiority is available to the determinate will only if it itself does the appropriating. The security comes from the demonstration that no thing can withstand the determinate will's acquisitive impulse; it is the show of determinate will as Idea, as an existent in the world that is important, not any particular manifestation of it. Indeed, given that the ownership of a thing requires some manifestation, through use, marking, and so on, that is, some actual presence of the determinate will, it is quite plain that one determinate will is not in the position to appropriate everything, and so could not make this status of superiority secure.[60] Without the presence of others, some large measure of the things that exist really would have an independent existence; some would always escape the determinate will's grasp, dancing out of the way to ridicule the very idea of their subservience.

So much, I would have thought, for the individual determinate will's going it alone. But there is a darker side to all of this. If the validation or show of superiority that the determinate will really seeks is a manifestation of its *own* individual superiority to what it is not, then this requires not merely a presumptive right to appropriate all things, but to appropriate *all* that is external to it, including other persons. The world has a sufficiently long history of conquest not only of lands but of peoples to recognize the plausibility of this sort of urge for a show of primacy.

Either of these two pictures of the will's urge to reveal itself as superior is coherent as a motivational account of the will of Abstract Right. But one cannot combine them to produce a will that both recognizes the equal status of other wills yet at the same time is fundamentally unsatisfied by those other wills' appropriations as manifestations of the will's superiority over things.

It is certainly the case that the presence of others will mean that many persons will be unable to appropriate as much as they particularly *desire*. But that is a different matter, as Hegel's distinction between Abstract Right and Morality seems to indicate. Desires, in the sense of subjective motivations to enhance one's welfare or good characterize in part the will as a moral, existential subject. It seems fairly clear that the clash of individuals' interests in their own welfare drives the inquiry into the justice of the distribution of property. But at the stage of Abstract Right, these desires have no standing,

[60] And some things, like 'air, events, or ideas' are not appropriable at all. Since these things retain their independence from the acquisitive will, the will's ambition to utterly destroy the independence of things through acquisition will be unrealized: see ibid., 25.

and so cannot upset the view that one will's appropriation is as good as any other's to show the will's superiority.

Secondly, even if one accepts Brudner's characterization of the will at this stage, it is not convincing to say that contract rather than abandonment or gift is a superior resolution of the problem of too many owners and too little property, that is, scarcity. The point of the resolution, it seems, is that, given alienability, there is always the possibility at least that one may become owner of any thing in the world, and so in principle, then, nothing is removed from the class of things that any individual might own. Now exchange is clearly not the same manifestation of *consent* as abandonment is, or gift is. Perhaps it is a better manifestation of that, because exchanges, being agreements, comprise mutual consent, while abandonment and gift are unilateral. But it is no better manifestation of alienation. All three represent the withdrawal of the will from a thing, and thus present the opportunity for the subsequent ownership of a thing by another. It is the recognition of that which permits one to treat all three as types of alienation, as alienations of property. Since all that is at stake is the possibility that my recognition of the ownership of another does not entail my permanent exclusion from what he owns, any alienation will do. Contract has no special status.

Finally, the whole idea behind this argument, that the alienability of property serves to circumvent the problem of a Lockean proviso,[61] i.e. the problem of extracting some plausible notion of consent to the appropriation of some leaving less than enough and as good for others, seems far-fetched. Certainly, given the fact that property is alienable, hypothetically I might be able to own any thing on earth. But that possibility hardly seems to stand as a justification of the fact that property may be held in various amounts, and that particular rare or unique things will be held by particular persons. Indeed, the fact that property is alienable, right down to one's only pair of shoes and the baby's cot, may be seen to be a part of the problem, for only if a person can be stripped of his property can he be made poor through injudicious contractual dealing or kleptocratic expropriation, or impoverish himself through profligate largesse, to say nothing of theft or robbery. Alienability is very much a two-sided coin. The possibility that I can have any thing and many things means that I may also have nothing.

[61] See Ch. 9. Brudner formulates the Lockean proviso thus: 'a unilateral appropriation becomes property if and only if it is made consistent with the right of others to an unlimited accumulation': ibid., 34.

9

Property and Contract III: Locke and the Consent to a Market Distribution

I have, I suppose, rather dwelled upon how understanding property tells us little about how we would go about justifying any particular distribution of property, or of wealth generally. It is time to return to what can plausibly be regarded as the source, in the Western philosophical tradition, for the idea that it may.

The twenty-seven paragraphs of Chapter V of the *Second Treatise of Civil Government*, 'Of Property', are generally taken as the initial foundation of at least three theories which purport to explain and justify the rights of private property, and not just property rights *per se*, but the sort of distribution of property rights one encounters in a place like England, i.e. an advanced industrial society with a market economy. It would be a tedious waste of time to elaborate those different theories here, or say why they are all faulty in some respect. There must be hundreds of books and articles which can do just that for an ignorant reader who earnestly desires enlightenment. On the assumptions, however, that anyone who is still with me following the much more abstract last chapter can certainly understand this one whether he knows the rudiments of Locke or not, and that anyone with a passing familiarity with the Locke literature will put this book down forever rather than drag himself through another tired recitation of it all, I shall start my discussion somewhat *in medias res*, as it were.

The argument I have been peddling off and on throughout this work is that the distribution of anything of value which is not an inalienable right is not determined by the practice of property, but by the different sorts of economy operating in a society. All property does is determine the nature of one kind of valuable right, the right of exclusive use over things. But I must admit that I am, and may remain, in a distinct minority in this view, perhaps a minority of one. It is worthwhile then, in the hopes of shifting the odds somewhat more in my favour, to see precisely how Locke has contributed to the view that a theory of property is also a theory of distribution. The moral I shall draw is the familiar one that, like many others, Locke confuses the right to property with the right to contract. He does so, however, in a particularly interesting way: Locke frames the right to property, and thus, by his lights, the right to the particular distribution of property that one may attain under a private property system, by employing a notion of consent. As we have seen, however, consent is a creature of agreement, not property, and so it is much better caged in the law of contract.

What I shall do is this: I shall construct an argument from Locke's assertions in 'Of Property', and show where Locke's own argument about the transition from a state of nature to a money economy goes awry. This will show how equating the ownership of things with the right to control one's own labour gives rise to a typical misjustification of property rights. After constructing the best argument that can be made of these premisses and showing its flaws, I will alter Locke's assertions slightly, to devise a better one, one which is more truly reflective of Locke's general orientation to the distribution of property. Unfortunately, this better argument is devoted entirely to the justice of making contracts in respect of one's labour; in other words, it has almost nothing to do with property.

If one reviews 'Of Property' and extracts the various premisses of Locke's discussion, one may, rather than follow Locke's own path of argumentation, see whether one can form a more coherent description and justification of property than he does himself. That is what I shall attempt below. Clearly then, I am not concerned to interpret 'Of Property' to show what Locke himself took his argument to be. My interest is to construct the best theory out of the points he makes. I leave it to the individual reader to determine whether this version sits well with his own impression of what Locke was trying to say, if indeed the reader has one.

This 'constructed' argument owes much to Macpherson's discussion in *The Political Theory of Possessive Individualism*[1] and to Cohen's discussion in 'Self-ownership, World Ownership, and Equality: Part II'.[2] They both emphasize that Locke's theory must rely on a notion of self-possession of some kind. Macpherson, for example, defines a version of self-possession in this way: '[t]he individual is essentially proprietor of his own person and capacities, for which he owes nothing to society'.[3] The purpose of the constructed argument is to show that even the most plausible justification of property that relies on Locke's several assertions fails, because it can only justify property as an expression of one's right to control, or 'possess', one's ability to act.

It is submitted that the various points that Locke makes in 'Of Property' can be fairly summarized as follows:

(1) Persons have a right to preserve their own lives, and this will require some appropriation from the common stock, particularly food.[4]

(2) A person's labour is his own, and this should be taken to include the claim that the value of a person's labour is value that he properly owns.[5]

[1] Macpherson 1962, 194–222. [2] Cohen 1986.
[3] Macpherson 1962, 263.
[4] Locke 1946, paras. 25, 26, 28.
[5] Ibid., paras. 27, 28, 44.

(3) A person's labour can be 'mixed in' or 'joined to' a thing, or as a result of labour have something 'annexed to it' that it previously did not.[6] While this is certainly obscure, it should probably be taken to include at least these two meanings: (a) that labour increases the value of a thing, implying that if it had zero value before the labouring, the total value of the thing is the result of labour;[7] and (b) that labour serves to indicate the extent of appropriation; it serves as a marker of what the appropriator intends to take from the common.[8]

(4) A person may justifiably appropriate only where enough and as good is left in the common stock for others.[9]

(5) A person may only appropriate to the extent that he does not waste his acquisitions or allow them to spoil.[10] Perhaps because Locke turns to the invention of money in fairly short order, which arises because there are things, particularly gold, which do *not* spoil, Locke is not rigorous in his definition of waste and spoilage. For example, is holding without using waste? In the context of land and the fruits of the earth, it is fair to say that Locke's non-waste provision should be construed as a requirement of positive use or enjoyment.[11] Locke does not consider using land as a hunting ground, or a park, which do not require labour in any significant way, and with respect to which it is difficult to apply concepts of waste or spoilage. Yet when he gets to money, his argument does not seem to depend on our getting any use out of gold or silver or diamonds, just that they can be held without spoiling.[12]

(6) There is enough land in the world for everyone to have as much land as he could make use of (so long as waste is not allowed), and anyone's land is as good as anyone else's.[13] (Incidentally, labour increases the amount of use-value that can be extracted from any particular piece of land, and so enclosure for cultivation actually increases the common supply of land, because cultivation permits any individual to require less in the way of land.[14])

[6] Ibid., para. 27.

[7] 'For it is labour indeed that puts the difference of value on everything'; '[n]ay, the extent of ground is of so little value without labour': ibid., paras. 40, 36, respectively. See also ibid., paras. 37, 41–3.

[8] In ibid., para. 28, before Locke discusses the value that labour adds, he says '[t]hat labour put a distinction between them and the common; that added something to them more than nature, the common mother of all had done, and so they became his private right. . . . The labour that was mine removing them out of the common state they were in, hath fixed my property in them': see Becker 1977, 33–4.

[9] Locke 1946, paras. 27, 33, 35.

[10] Ibid., para. 31, 37, 38.

[11] Ibid., paras. 31–3 and 36: '[n]o man's labour could subdue or appropriate all; *nor could his enjoyment consume more than a small part*' (italics mine). Locke certainly thought land could be wasted, and this seems to be tied to the effect of one's actually using it by tilling it; see ibid., para. 38.

[12] He does mention that a man may be pleased with the colour of gold, and that a pebble or diamond may sparkle (ibid., para. 46), but he does not emphasize this enjoyment value: see ibid., paras. 46, 47.

[13] Ibid., para. 36.

[14] Ibid., para. 37.

(7) The overwhelming part of the value of any thing is a result of the labour that has been 'joined' to it.[15]

(8) The invention of money occurs because people consent to value things, such as gold, which do not spoil. Thus an industrious person is able to trade the surplus perishable goods he produces for gold, or diamonds, and heap up as much of these as he may, because they do not spoil.[16] 'And as different degrees of industry were apt to give men possessions in different proportions, so this invention of money gave them the opportunity to continue and enlarge them.'[17] Hence acquisition of more land than any individual can make use of is facilitated, and thus all land can be owned, leaving none held in common. Yet this acquisition is still justified, for it depends on the mutual consent of people to the use of money, and thus the enlarging of possessions.[18]

At the outset, one can dismiss the first assertion from further consideration. It is an argument from necessity that cannot be extended beyond necessity to justify the appropriation of things which are not strictly required to preserve life. Even if we extend our concept of necessity to cover the acquisition of those things necessary for a fulfilling life in modern society, whatever *that* is, the point remains the same. What we are seeking a justification for is the ownership of things that we see today in a place like England, which is quite divorced from need.

There are essentially three stages to the constructed argument. The first applies to appropriation in conditions before a money economy, where there is no scarcity. The second stage is an argument about the value embodied in things as a result of labour, which is independent of background conditions. The third stage concerns the justice of unequal holdings of property after the advent of a money economy. All have a 'negative' quality, for the argument is not that a man ought to go out and appropriate and own, but rather that, if he does, no one is entitled to interfere with his holdings. Locke does try to give the argument a positive colour by quoting Scriptural passages, but these can be put to one side for our purposes.[19]

In the first stage, when all things are plentiful, the justification of property rests entirely on assertion (4), the 'enough and as good' provision, and on (3b), the assertion that labour marks off what one intends to appropriate. In conditions of plenty, merely getting access to a thing allows one to use it, and this action thus represents the total cost of holding a thing, and thus represents the total value of holding it. On these premisses, the value of a thing corresponds entirely to the effort involved in picking it up. This is of course false, because things have value of their own, that is, use value. So the cost of the effort involved in obtaining a thing does not equal its use-value. But it is true to the extent that one is interested in *exchange*-value: the thing one

[15] Ibid., paras. 40–3.
[16] Ibid., paras. 46, 47.
[17] Ibid., para. 48.
[18] Ibid., paras. 49–50.
[19] See ibid., para. 32.

holds has no use-value greater than any other thing of the same type, and since these things lie about in abundance, there is no conceivable reason why anyone should feel that any particular thing one holds has any special use-value and thus, if anyone wishes to possess such a thing, he should just pick one up for himself. The exchange value of a thing to any particular person corresponds to the cost of getting it. But note, this does not mean the picking up value, the exchange-value, will be equal for all persons, for some may be more skilled or able acquirers, and they may be differently skilled regarding the acquisition of different things. Tall people have an easier time with apples, while the fleet of foot may be able to capture rabbits. So nothing in this circumstance rules out bartering. One barters to gain the value of the effort in acquiring a particular thing, or rather to save oneself the cost of doing so, and since everyone will not have equal skills and abilities, some may get more of the valuable things than others. But of course one has no basis for a complaint simply because someone has taken some thing from the common, because there is enough and as good left. In that respect, it is as if the appropriator did nothing at all. Hence the 'right to appropriate' justified here is essentially no more than a prohibition against interference with a person's use or holding of things. If one has cause for complaint, it is with God or nature for making one short or slow. Of course, if we deny possessive individualism and treat our talents and abilities as not necessarily our own, then the common is expanded to include all 'things' of value, including those. But this must be regarded as dealing with a broader concern of justice than we could conceivably say Locke was addressing.

The second argument is about the way labour enhances the value of things, and it follows from assertions (2), (3a), and (7): since (i) a man owns the value of his labour, (ii) the value of labour enters into things laboured on, and (iii) the labour value put into a thing is the only significant value a thing has, it follows that a person owns the entire value of a thing.

The reason this argument works is that the thing in this instance is considered nothing more than the embodiment of the value of the labour put into it. Because one owns, i.e controls, one's labour value, in this special case this is equal in value to the control, i.e. the ownership, of a thing, since that thing's value is no more than the labour value. In other words, the labourer merely transforms one sort of value that he controls into another, through putting the value of his labour into worthless things. What this aspect of the argument shows is how necessary the state of plenty is to justified individual appropriation before some sort of consent amongst persons in some way or other permits the recognition of ownership in scarce things. (The consent Locke relies upon, and to which we will turn in a moment, is the consent to value money.) In a state of nature without any social compact or consent, plenty permits individual appropriation, for all it permits people to do is capture the value of their labour now embodied in things. Where things are not plentiful, the enough and as good condition constrains the capturing of labour value to the extent that it is in any way embodied in things or dependent on the use of things.[20]

We must again bear in mind the nature of the enough and as good condition. It refers to enough and as good *things*, not enough and as good *values*, which may in fact be largely created by human labour. A, an industrious soul, may live a much better life than B, an undisciplined layabout, though they live in the same world of plenty. The values each is able to realize are not merely the intrinsic values of the things in abundance, but result from their own efforts. There is nothing in the hypothesis of a plenty of things that it be like the Garden of Eden. There may be plenty of raw materials for food which can only be consumed after arduous work. This still counts as plenty on the hypothesis. Indeed, paradoxically, 'plenty' is more easily ensured the more difficult it is to work the raw materials in the environment into some useable or consumable form. The more arduous and time-consuming it is to get the value out of things, the more easily the enough and as good condition is met, for there will be greater limits on the amount any individual can make use of. In such circumstances, of course, differences in the abilities of persons to exploit the environment will become the paramount determinant of wealth and poverty. It is quite evident that Locke did not pursue this line of reasoning. There is nothing in 'Of Property' which suggests that differences in ability (as opposed to levels of industriousness) might be the most significant determinant of the values individuals are able to realize. This is clear when we look at the final stage of the argument.

The final stage depends on the last assertion, (8), regarding the consent of men to value things such as gold which do not spoil; this permits an exchange economy, indeed a money economy. Now there is something immediately remarkable about this assertion, because it represents such an odd transition from a state of plenty. Recall assertion (6), that there is still enough land to go around if its appropriation is limited by how much any person can use without its spoiling. So, presumably, land is still plentiful in the relevant sense. But for hoards of gold to have value, regardless of any consent to value it, it must be the case that gold, at least, is scarce. For there would be no point in hoarding it, whether it spoiled or not, if there was always an abundant supply of it at hand. So for a transition to a money economy, there must be at least *one* thing which is scarce that people value. This odd situation, in which a few things are scarce but most are plentiful is one flaw in Locke's argument which I will discuss below, but for now I accept it as one of his (implicit) premisses. One might easily explain the appearance of one 'scarce' thing by arguing that only certain individuals have the ability to acquire it or make use of something which is in abundance but, as I have said, this is not Locke's method.

[20] See Cohen 1986, 82–7.

The constructed argument for the justification of unequal property holdings in conditions of scarcity is this: men consent to value something which is scarce, and thus they will exchange the things they hold for it. Since this scarce thing does not spoil, it can be hoarded up, and the only limit to a person's accumulation of it will be his industry in enhancing the value of plentiful things. In other words, the value of a person's labour can now be stored and traded, rather than being subject to the spoilage proviso, since his efforts can be enjoyed by others when he transfers them to others in exchange for money. His own limit of consumption of the perishable fruits of the earth no longer sets a restriction on what he can appropriate to himself, and therefore he can appropriate as much as he can enhance with his labours. This enhanced capacity for employing one's labours results in the appropriation of all the land, and thus land becomes scarce. Yet this scarcity is not supposed to diminish the justice of anyone's holdings, for this appropriation of all land, and one might as well add at this point, all other things, is the logical consequence of consenting to value scarce non-spoiling things, i.e. money. This is the importance of the second stage of the argument and assertion (6). The second stage showed that, even if the value of a individual's labour is his own, this does not justify the ownership of things. But if he is justified in owning them anyway, if he can trade them he can effectively trade the value of his labours. Assertion (6) is that if there was no money, there would still be an abundance of land, at least. So, at least as regards land, any person's labours on it would even now be his own, were there no money, because he is entitled to all the land he can labour on. Now, if all people together consent to value money, then in the first stage of trading at least, individuals are only trading the value of their labours, because land is plentiful. But the result of money is that industrious types will be able to use much more land because they can part with the labour put into it, rather than having to use it themselves or let it spoil. Soon enough, land will be scarce.[21]

The important question is whether the coming of scarcity, and its consequent effects, undermines the consent of the original valuation of money, which leads to it. This problem is not recognized by Locke, at least not explicitly, for he never states that the consent to value money extinguishes the 'enough and as good' condition.

Macpherson argues that Locke handles this problem in either of two ways. The first is simply that he assumes that consent to money is consent to its consequences.[22] The second solution is to assert, as in the parenthetical statement to assertion (6), that labour increases the effective supply of land, and to assume that this increase is distributed even to the worst off, so that even they cannot complain that they may no longer appropriate as much land as they can use on their own. '[A] king of a large and fruitful territory

[21] Locke 1946, para. 50. [22] Macpherson 1962, 211.

[in America], feeds, lodges, and is clad worse than a day-labourer in England.'[23] Neither of these will do, however. The first simply begs the question. The second does not show that the enough and as good condition is properly extinguished, but rather changes its nature to a right to a certain level of welfare, as Macpherson recognizes.[24] The right to veto appropriations that do not leave enough things that are as good as those sought to be appropriated is transformed into the right to veto appropriations which do not provide the same access to the same amount of value, the illegitimacy of which manœuvre has been well exposed.[25]

It can be shown quite easily that the kind of consent Locke describes, that is, to value money, is not able to extinguish convincingly the 'enough and as good' condition, which is easily one of the most intuitively plausible premises Locke comes up with. Some form of consent to its extinction seems the obvious path to pursue, but Locke rules out consent by compact, i.e. some sort of real, historical consent, which, given the only quasi-historical nature of the argument, makes sense. There has obviously never been such a great collective agreement. One might propose the sort of consent that Macpherson does above, that consent to something is a consent to its consequences, no matter how unforeseeable they may be, but although this may seem to follow from Locke's failure explicitly to address the issue, it is so flawed in its own right we should look elsewhere.

The consent that Locke needs and which he seeks to provide is not really 'consent' as that term is normally understood at all, but is rather the predictable taking of a valuable opportunity by persons, given their human nature, once they realize it is there, or once they realize its advantages. This kind of 'consent' has the ring of a realization of an advantage to be gained by changing one's behaviour, the advantage of which is apparent as soon as it is realized. It is not really consent at all, but then real consent could not serve Locke's purposes. The universality of the consent that he requires is more like a standard reaction to the way things are, or the normal realization of the possibilities inherent in a situation. It must be as natural as the 'consent' to use language, once language appears on the scene. Who would hold out from linguistic communication once it appeared, even if, as is probably the case, some would benefit more from language than others? Consider this: for Locke, people come to realize that things that have intrinsic value have a different kind of value when they are scarce. Not everyone will be able to have them, and thus they conceive of exchange and exchange value. People realize that the opportunity of exchanging things provides them with the opportunity to have what is scarce, and they take advantage of it. Individuals will trade the only other value that they can muster in exchange for these

[23] Locke 1946, para. 41; quoted in Macpherson 1962, 212.
[24] Macpherson 1962, 213.
[25] See Cohen 1985, 95–102; E. J. Weinrib 1989, 1293–7.

scarce things, which is the product of their labours, their collected plums, the fruits of their tilling the soil. The exchange of his labour value, embodied in non-scarce things, for durable scarce collectables will allow a person to store up his labour.

This account is obviously multiply faulty. As soon as labour value can be embodied in things, at least those labour-enhanced things are scarce. So there is no need for the appearance of the scarce durable on the scene for people to get the idea of exchange. But, more fundamentally, this 'consent' does nothing to alter the status of the 'enough and as good' condition. Such valuable, scarce goods are immediately off-limits for individual appropriation, since any appropriation will only increase the scarcity of them, violating the enough and as good condition. Indeed, if anything, the appearance of these scarce, valuable things in a world of plenty would seem to *give rise* to the enough and as good condition, for here would be the first place that it would have a practical effect. Locke's particular solution by 'consent' fails.

On the other hand, there is one that is much more plausible. Very little of what Locke asserts has to be changed in order to generate this argument, and what is changed is changed for the better. The consent that is required is the realization by men that they can control their own labour power, and that they can take advantage of this by dealing with others in respect of *their* own control of *their* labour power. What this realization permits cannot be over-emphasized: *it underpins social co-operation itself*—it permits the move from a solitary, atomized existence at a subsistence level to the social organization of the production of value, to life in society itself. This 'consent', or realization, transforms a prohibition against one individual's interference with another, as embodied in the 'enough and as good' condition, into the *de facto* right of an individual to his due in society.

This realization is of course as historically fanciful as Locke's abundant state of nature and the consent to value money. If the state of nature has any value it lies in its abstracting particular morally salient features of the human condition. My suggestion is to re-situate the point of the fundamental realization, or 'consent', which moves us out of the abstract state of nature Locke describes to somewhere resembling our actual situation. Rather than a transition from some kind of civil society where there is nothing that can retain its value if stored for any length of time to a state in which money permits labour value to be exchanged, I propose a transition from the atomized existence of individuals, whose labour is solitary, to a state of civil society where co-operation between individuals is the norm. If we re-examine 'Of Property' along this line, it appears that there is much latent in Locke's words which supports this version of the fundamental 'consent'. More importantly, though, it does much better justice to his plausible assertions than does his own final argument.

All of Locke's examples of appropriation and labour are clearly those of individuals acting alone, save for the anomalous phrase 'the turfs my servant has cut' in paragraph 28, the significance of which is disputed.[26] To the extent that it imports an element of social co-operation in original appropriation, I think it should be disregarded as anomalous, even if it is revealing in some way of Locke's thought. But note that even here there is not necessarily the idea of co-operative labour. It is not servant*s*, but *a* servant, who cut the turf. Furthermore, some of his examples of labour in isolation, like digging ore and tilling land[27], are activities which one would normally assume involve the co-operative efforts of several persons; yet he renders them as the labours of individuals. This might all just follow from the task Locke sets himself, to justify individual appropriation relying solely on the significance of the individual's action or labour. But that he construes his task in this way is itself pertinent. Locke, like so many others, seems to think that the use of things by individuals on their own is the hallmark of property; but, as I have stated often enough, the importance of the right of exclusive use lies in the exclusion of everyone from the determination of how property is to be used, except for the owner *or owners*, and nothing requires an owner to use his property on his own. Had Locke paid more attention to this, he would have realized that his desire to show that appropriation is justified without the consent of mankind did not require that he show that people do not consent amongst themselves to anything else, such as co-operative production. In any case, it seems plain that, besides abundance, a second characteristic of Locke's state of nature is the total absence of co-operation amongst individuals.

The focus on the individual has advantages, but is essentially an impediment to making the most out of Locke's insights. It is advantageous for the simple reason that dealing with individuals alone simplifies matters, especially when one's particular concern is the actual content of the right of exclusive use in things appropriated from a plentiful supply, which is a prohibition against interference. This right is crystallized in the imagination much more effectively by the picture of one individual's assaulting another for his possessions—non-interference is visualized as no contact. This can become blurred in the context of the co-operative use of things, for then we have to distinguish between those outside the co-operative group who may not interfere with or use a thing and those in the group who may. Locke's choice of the individual also integrates his work with that of Hobbes, whom he answers in a sense. Locke's prohibition against interference embodied in the right of original appropriation provides a standard of justice which disengages 'solitary' and 'poor' from 'nasty, brutish, and short' in Hobbes's description of life in the state of nature. Locke accepts the first: individuals

[26] I do not propose to contribute to the dispute. Waldron 1988, 225–32 discusses the opposing claims of Macpherson 1962, 215–18, and Tully 1980, 137–42.
[27] Locke 1946, paras. 28, 32.

toil alone, and perhaps the second, that although they can have as much as they can work on and use it may not amount to much. But the natural right of non-interference shows that a standard of justice applies even to life in the state of nature, which, if followed by rational individuals, would prevent its necessarily being 'nasty, brutish and short.'

Yet the choice of the isolated individual sets a trap, which Locke falls into: his first image of social contact is individuals coming together to barter, which he mentions as the immediate prelude to the use of money.[28]

The notion that barter should stand as a paradigm of initial social interaction is extremely flawed, if not sociopathic. Some notion of mutual co-operation evincing consent to a course of action is perfectly reasonable, but barter assumes that persons first come together to exchange things. It presumes that bargaining to exchange things is conceptually prior to any other kind of bargain, for example a bargain that trades obligations to perform tasks, and that exchange, or bargaining, conceptually precedes giving. Both assumptions are insupportable. It is not that agreements concerning matters other than the transfer of property are prior to exchanges, or that giving is prior to barter; it is that there is no reason to believe that there is a priority amongst these at all. As with the argument that interfering with others is wrong whether or not they happen to be using some thing, agreeing on a course of action involves the idea of two autonomous individuals with human dignity crystallizing their intentions and trust, regardless of whether those intentions concern the use of things. Similarly, there is no reason to believe that people conceive their interests as being determined solely by their interests *in themselves*, rather than being determined by their interests *in themselves and in others*. Isolating barter as the initial form of social interaction, Locke heads straight not only into a market economy, but into a money economy to boot, proposing that the consent to value money is the fundamental shift which transfers us from the state of nature into the real world of unequal property holdings in the midst of scarcity. All this despite the fact Locke says nothing to support the claim that individuals may no longer press the 'enough and as good' condition.

Given Locke's depiction of atomized individuals, it is not surprising that he characterizes people in the state of nature as realizing the value of scarce things before they realize the possibilities of social co-operation. For if individuals are isolated they are only likely naturally to recognize the relationship of themselves to things as a relationship of value, not the relationship of themselves to others. So Locke's move out of the state of nature depends on the rational realization of the value of scarce things that do not spoil. The problem is that this realization does not ground the manœuvre he needs; he needs a realization which can ground the social interaction upon which exchange relies.

[28] Ibid., para. 46.

The appropriate realization is embodied in Locke's assertion that I have numbered (2), that the value of a person's labour is his own. This should be taken to mean that the value of a person's labour is his to dispose of or, in other words, that a person has the right to determine how he will employ his labour, and thus how his labour will benefit people. We may call this definition of autonomy 'self-possession'.[29] Self-possession means that there is a significant set of actions that an individual may undertake which affect others, but are neither morally required nor morally prohibited. They are morally justified, in that they either result in benefits, so there is reason to undertake them, or result in no harm, so there is no reason of one important kind not to undertake them, but in either case one is under no obligation to undertake them. In the language of norms, they would be protected by rights to liberties or by permissions.[30]

The realization of self-possession is pertinent with respect to labour and property in the following way. In general, actions which generate value, or 'labour', fall into the category of actions that are morally justifiable but not obligatory. Thus a person has the right to choose whether or not and how he will labour, and thus produce value. Any coercion of a person in order to make him labour interferes with this right and is unjustifiable, and so is any attempt to capture the value of someone's labouring after the fact. Self-possession is akin to ownership in that, like the right of exclusive use, the right to choose how to act can be restated as the right to determine how one will deal with one's capabilities for action. This will encompass the determination of who shall benefit from one's actions, to the extent that those benefits can be practically distributed.

Thus the justice in Locke's vision is embodied in the idea that a person's riches are nothing more than embodied free actions, his industry made material. The accumulation of those riches is only possible because the spoilage proviso is avoided through trade, and trade is only possible because there is a realization that what gives a non-scarce thing its value is nothing more than the labour expended on it, and that dealing with this labour value involves dealing with the source and agent of that labour value as the one who has the right to determine its disposition. Therefore, framing Locke's insights in their best light yields not a theory which justifies property, or even really the market distribution of property; it justifies the contractual or market distribution of the fruits of labour. If for Hegel, property is perfected by contract, for Locke it is transformed into contract.

Unfortunately, the problem with things remains, as Cohen points out. The

[29] I am not adopting the concepts of 'self-ownership' or 'possessive individualism' as defined by Cohen and Macpherson, respectively, to make the claims I do here, although there are of course clear parallels.

[30] See Ch. 2.

value that is created through labouring often, and perhaps always,[31] involves the use of things. So if we want to respect the right to choose how to act, we must also permit some measure of control over the things required for any particular action. There must be a right to determine how things are to be used, so that individuals, acting singly or in concert, have a meaningful right to determine how they will act.[32] Yet if the 'enough and as good' condition is valid, then we are at an impasse in conditions of scarcity, for any use of things will ultimately require collective agreement. This impasse is well described by Cohen:

> how can I be said to own myself if I may do nothing without the agreement of others? . . . Does not joint world ownership entitle a person to prohibit another's wholly harmless use of an external resource, such as taking some water from a superabundant stream, and is it not, therefore, inconsistent with the most minimal self-ownership (and independently indefensible to boot)?[33]

Clearly, either self-possession or collective determination must give.

What does is collective determination, in so far as it is embodied in the 'enough and as good' condition. Once it is realized that self-possession permits social interaction, i.e. that persons can live together only if they may still act significantly in their own right, it is also realized that the 'enough and as good' condition is a limitation of justice which is pertinent only to the realm of isolated individuals. Why is this so?

The logical import of the 'enough and as good' condition is not that where there is scarcity there will, or ought to be, collective determination of use. The condition is wholly negative as far as co-operation is concerned; it provides no basis for it. Indeed it impedes it, by proclaiming that any appropriation, save perhaps those made out of strict necessity, violates justice, and therefore presumably is violable. This is not to say that *violent* interference with another's use of a thing is required by justice, only that interference is permitted by justice. Since the 'enough and as good' condition is by definition pre-social, i.e. not depending on any actual positive social compact or organization, it follows that this interference need not have any legal or social imprimatur. The taking of things by individuals to release back into the common for any reason expresses their veto and satisfies the condition. The 'enough and as good' condition is wholly inappropriate as a standard of justice once people are no longer conceived as isolated, entirely self-reliant, unco-operating individuals. It must be jettisoned as soon as Man is conceived as a social being, capable of acting in concert with others on a consensual basis. Once this conception holds sway, the terms of justice must derive from the basis of that conception, not an abstract, hypothetical state of nature.

The problem of the needs of others, i.e. the question of what moral duties

[31] Cohen states: 'all human action requires space, which is jointly owned if the world is. (Even the mental activity of an immobile agent requires the space he occupies)': Cohen 1986, 84.

[32] See ibid., 83–4.

[33] Ibid., 83.

arise from them, cannot be cast in terms of the 'enough and as good' condition where there is actual society amongst individuals. The existence of society severs the determination of what duties are owed to the needy from the justification of the system of property rights.

In the first place, it must be remembered that the 'enough and as good' condition and even abundance, for that matter, are poor guarantees that needs will be met, for when they are in place an isolated individual's prosperity will entirely depend upon his own abilities to reap benefits from the raw materials of the earth. Society provides for the needy much better, but it goes about it in a different way.

In a society founded upon the realization of individual self-possession, some notion of desert or what one is due will be the basis upon which duties to the needy are recognized; therefore what counts as a need which gives rise to a moral duty will be intertwined with a concept of what a person is due, or deserves. It is beyond what I want to say here to determine what moral duties to the needy arise in a society founded purely on the notion of self-possession, except to say that 'none' is probably incorrect. Such a society is not necessarily a dog-eat-dog marketplace of exploitation; even if 'what one is due' is conceived of entirely as a matter of what an individual can obtain through contract, so that all one 'needs' is that bargains be enforced, self-possession presumably requires that the system of agreements which are based upon it must have standards of fairness and justice which do not allow agreements which violate it. For example, it would at first glance seem that a contract of slavery would not preserve self-possession, and would not be permitted. Furthermore, 'what one is due' presumably encompasses those necessaries which make one capable of entering just or fair agreements in the first place, and those necessaries would reflect the sophistication of the society in which the bargains are made, so, for example, education might count. Remember that self-possession is intended to apply universally. For any Lockean consent-based distribution to be acceptable, everybody must be on board; there's no room for a version of 'self-possession' which leaves any significant number of people unpossessed of themselves. In any case, I want to restrict my claim here to this: in a society which is partly or wholly based on co-operative practices, approaches to such moral duties which start from premisses like the 'enough and as good' condition will be totally inappropriate, since they only make sense from the point of view of atomized individuals who by hypothesis exist outside of a society of any kind.

Nevertheless, even my revised characterization of Locke's theory presents us with the central flaw in Lockean analyses and justifications of property generally, which is that they bind together property with self-possession in a way that is hardly persuasive if we consider that the right to property is not intrinsically linked to the right*s* either to labour or to make bargains. I am, of course, not denying that what Locke says may have a great deal of weight in justifying certain aspects of the present distribution of property, specifically the distribution of property through bargain exchanges. But since there are many other sorts of relations in evidence between the members of societies we know, this justification is at best partial, and at worst completely mistaken.

10
The Role of Property

'Property' denotes both a practice and the objects or things which are subject to it. As we have seen, the idea of property not only distributes the value of objects, by defining the limits of the rights an owner has in the particular things he owns, but distributes the practice, as it were, only to those things which are appropriately treated in this way. It is the latter aspect on which I want to dwell in this final chapter. Consider the following from Birks, which precisely captures what I am aiming at: '[t]hings either fall within the sphere of private ownership or they do not. The way in which the line is drawn goes far to determining the character of a society.'[1] But consider the lines that follow, which I think fundamentally, but typically, obscure this vital insight: '[m]ove it a little to one side, to exclude the means of production, and you have communism; a little to the other, and you accept property in human beings, in short slavery.'[2] The word 'private' in the first quotation is the source of the problem, because it allows Birks to treat the two variations in which the 'line of property' is drawn as variations of the same kind, and they are not.

Whether a society allows the means of production to be held privately or only by the State does tell us much about that society. It tells us whether it has a strong belief in collective ownership. But it tells us nothing special, or nothing different from a Western private property society, about what it treats *as* property. The Muscovite on the street had pretty much the same duty of non-interference with the factory he passed in 1980 as did his counterpart in London.[3] In both systems the means of production were objects of property. The only difference was the distributional implications of that ownership. In stark contrast, the ownership of human beings is not principally a matter of the justice of distribution of property (except in so far as slaves do not own any). The line that is drawn here, to put it in terms of 'distribution', is the distribution of the practice of property over the range of

[1] Birks 1989, 61.

[2] Ibid.

[3] As I said above in Ch. 2, to the extent that there is only one owner this duty appears more *in personam* than *in rem*, but collective ownership is not ownership by one individual, and the State is not an individual at all. The intended beneficiaries of state ownership of particular segments of the means of production are principally those individuals whose lives are most connected to those enterprises. The overarching social goal of distributing the value created by those enterprises, and the ultimate central control, should not blind us to the fact that in communist systems property is parcelled out; there is no single owner in the sense required in Ch. 3.

different kinds of things that exist. It is this latter kind of distribution which a property practice displays which reveals the idea of property a society has. The differing distribution of the same kind of property rights, say between Soviet Russia and the West, tells us about its attitude to the legitimacy of various economic transactions, in particular its attitudes to commands versus contracts. But it tells us nothing of their ideas of property, which are fundamentally the same.

Before turning to the important line that property draws, i.e. around the kinds of things it takes into the practice, it is worthwhile examining the claim that the distribution of property among particular owners or classes of owners is of the essence of the idea of property. It is, after all, a fair old puzzle understanding exactly what *legitimate* interests we have in using *particular* things to advance our lives, for it is quite obvious that there may not be enough of the world to go round if we all wish to serve our interests in every way we might want. What I want to do here is to situate the concern for the distribution of property in a way which shows the minimal significance it has for understanding the nature of property itself. I will do so by looking at one aspect of the dispute over the well-known Lockean justification of property rights, now that we have seen the general picture of Locke's argument.

Distributive Justice

As we saw in Chapter 9, there does not seem to be a way of making Locke's argument work from his first principles. I suggested that the best route he can take is to frame the transition from the state of nature to a market economy, where clearly there may not be as good and enough for others, as the transition from the situation where individuals are isolated to a state of society in which everyone's self-possession is recognized. This allows people to trade the fruits of their labours, and the industrious and those who strike good bargains will become very much better off than their fellows. But the general point was that once society is constituted in some way, the 'enough and as good' condition on the appropriation of things is quite out of place as a premiss upon which the duties to those less well off may be based. It embodies a meagre view of justice, what we might call the 'equal opportunity of the atomized to scarcity' approach, which conceives the duties that one person may owe another as confined to the sphere of their appropriation of things. But once there is society, the social connections become much more intricate and involved, and there are much greater opportunities to ensure that no one is left in a miserable state.

There is, perhaps, nothing wrong about abstracting from the human condition to produce a model of the state of nature, in much the same way as a scientist makes various simplifying assumptions in framing a hypothesis. But this is an artificial exercise that can go awry, and the Lockean state-of-nature tradition with its isolated individuals is a case in point. What kind of humans are these? Does no one in the state of nature have a mum? Regardless of the attachments that particular people have to particular things, when we are born we enter a world where we ourselves are already attached to particular people; to our mothers most obviously, but to our families, clans, tribes, communities, and nations, and to every living soul on earth if we are being catholic about our humanity. Such attachments situate us within a framework of personal relationships, and it is therefore a nonsense to organize a theory about what one person may demand to meet his essential needs which does not explicate the nature and consequence of these various attachments.[4]

It is hardly part of my remit to discuss in general the claims individuals in need have on their fellows. I should just make two points. Need is an irredeemably dreary and short-sighted focus if we wish to understand the claims others may make upon us, and the duties and interests we may have in directing our attentions to others. Anybody familiar with the kind of sensitive and circumspect view of individual autonomy and the ways in which others can contribute to one's well-being that Raz presents in *The Morality of Freedom*, to whose views I am clearly indebted, is likely to be sceptical of the role that the distribution of property *per se* is going to play in making people well off.[5] This is not in any way to deny that there is a rational, human interest in exclusively determining the use of things. That is the foundation for property. But it is to deny that our understanding of that gives us a ground for determining the extent and the character of need. Drawing on what might be regarded as the nature of property alone to deal with such quests for the 'justifiable' minimum that all should have is both misguided in principle and fraught in practice.

It is misguided in principle because need only captures part of the interest we have in the exclusive use of things. Certainly we are interested in things to meet the basic requirements of life, and those basic requirements may extend to some measure of adequate participation in culture, so that even theatre tickets, for example, should be affordable by the worst off. But the interest in property, no less than our interest in anything else, is an interest in creating values and forming relationships and experiencing delights which together make for the good life. The interest comprises more than an interest in simply surviving. Therefore considering the interest in exclusively

[4] If we recall the analysis of rights from Ch. 2, we remember that a right is not framed purely in terms of one's interests, but in terms of the relationships with others which would justify imposing a duty on them to serve or protect those interests.

[5] Raz 1986a, chs. 9, 14, 15.

determining the use of things on its own will not generate any guidelines as to a minimum amount of property.

It is fraught in practice, for the notion of a minimum in any meaningful sense is not a minimum of property, but a minimum kind of situation from which people may engage the world to pursue their actual projects. The interest in property is always to be set against, or considered in light of, other interests we have which together in various combinations suited to different individuals may be served to generate the good life. The minimum, or even a point well beyond it, may not require the ownership of any property at all. If I choose the life of contemplation, for instance, a room, regular meals, access to a good library, and the company of others who share my intellectual interests are what I *need*, not any property. This is intended to be an extreme example, but the point it makes is tolerably clear. A minimum of property will be a minimum which depends on a person's cultural situation, and will vary accordingly. It will thus form an extremely variable component in the minimum resources which must be available to a person for him to pursue an acceptable life. Consider these words of Munzer:

> People should have property rights in articles for personal use, such as clothing, grooming equipment, and some modest furniture. They should have property rights in things that foster control, privacy, and individuality. In a private property system these things will include a wider range of clothing and furniture, as well as books, cars, money, and *probably* homes.[6]

I wonder whether the reader finds this list as strange as I do. While it is not intended to be a general statement of the minimum property an individual requires,[7] it clearly appears to be based on some idea of what property a person needs to get on in the (Western) world. Yet the whole list shows a very idiosyncratic specificity, and I suspect any other list of the particular items of property that someone supposedly needs would do the same. Only someone who lives in Los Angeles could argue that one definitely needs a car but only probably a home. Furthermore, I consider myself part of the Western world and to have got by reasonably well, and yet I doubt whether I have ever had more than 'some modest furniture', to say nothing of the adequacy of my grooming equipment.

A similar scepticism may be appropriate when we consider Radin's claim that we should divide property into two kinds, or at least array it along a continuum between what she idiosyncratically calls 'personal' property and 'fungible' property.[8] The former is property which we become attached to, like our wedding rings or our houses, and which in some sense contributes to our very identities, and in that sense can be regarded as something necessary.

[6] Munzer 1990, 209 (italics mine).

[7] It is, according to Munzer, a list of the private property justified by the principles of efficiency and utility: ibid.

[8] Radin 1993, ch. 1.

Fungible property, paradigmatically money, is replaceable by property of similar value. Whether or not our attachments to individual items of property are as constitutive as Radin claims, she appears blind to the constitutive value of fungible property, in particular, property we just consume. Some people shape their lives very largely around the delights of the table. Moreover, I would have thought that the constitutivity of the relationship to fungible or personal property varies considerably over the course of one's life. Take the case of a university student. He might need no 'personal' property whatsoever to lead a perfectly fulfilling life, but if he had none of the fungible stuff, in particular money which he could exchange for other fungible stuff like cigarettes and alcohol, he might lead a very sad existence indeed. Similarly, while the gifts of possessions treasured by their former owners are often very meaningful, gifts are standardly made precisely because the property is fungible and the donee may get more out of it than the donor. But that use of fungible property is typically very constitutive of very significant relationships. Which examples of ownership are so constitutive as to be necessary is difficult to assess and, as with any list of necessary goods, likely to vary with individuals.

The general point is that concerns about the distribution of property, in which an essential minimum or a constitutive kind are to be given some kind of established basis in the idea of property itself, are generally completely swamped by broader considerations of a person's well-being. In a sense I am making a similar point to one of Ryan's, but from the opposite perspective. Ryan argues that the concept of 'self-ownership' has proved next to useless in resolving disputes in political theory, largely because there is no common sense of what ownership of oneself actually consists in. As a result 'self-ownership' in the hands of one person will entail a massive realm of non-interference, while in the hands of another it will prove no barrier to the most invasive redistribution of every kind of valuable right an individual has.[9] This is the unsurprising result of trying to square the 'ownership' of oneself with the 'ownership' of a pair of boots.[10] In these pages I have tried to develop a concept of property which, tied to the legal system as it is, is unable to be so promiscuous in its ramblings. But the picture I present draws us to the same conclusion. If Ryan is right, as I think he is, to argue that the project of political morality will not be advanced by addressing every question in terms of the scope of ownership, then it will also not be advanced by presuming that the justice of any particular distribution of property rights is a major, if not the most important, problem of economic justice. The legitimacy of property rights *per se* strikes me as well nigh indisputable, for the practice of property protects a liberty, i.e. exclusively to determine the use of things, that has proved marvellously productive in contributing to the good

[9] Ryan 1994, especially at 254–8.
[10] Ibid. 247–54.

life of many. Determining the justice of any distribution of property, on the other hand, should draw our attention to those distributional mechanisms themselves, such as gifts and contracts and commands, all of which distribute a much broader set of goods than property rights.

Gifts, Contracts, and Commanded Transfers

I should say a few more words about these different modes of transfer. As I have said, gifts count as an owner's own disposition of his property in a special way, and it is an open question whether, like contract or command transfers, an economy might be largely constituted by gifts, or more exactly, gratuitous transactions, to include gratuitous provisions of services as well as gifts of property. I rather doubt it, for if gifts serve the donor's interest because his interests are significantly linked to the interests of his donee, then that imposes severe limits on the scope of economic transactions in which any one individual could take part. While many people have many friends, it is quite clear that one's interests are not in any significant way linked with the vast majority of other individuals *as individuals* in a modern society. We should take extreme care in suggesting that an entire economy could run along the lines of the National Health Service blood donor service described in Titmuss's justly famous *The Gift Relationship*.[11] Titmuss's point in that book was that we can create economic institutions which positively engender social solidarity and which are as, if not more efficient than, the market alternative.[12] This kind of 'altruistic' gift, in which the particular interests of the donor are not significantly implicated by the benefits which the gift accords to the particular donee, is an entirely praiseworthy sort of thing, and my point is not to criticize it; these gifts are akin to charitable gifts, in which the donor serves his own interest, and the interests of others, in the creation of a decent, enlightened, cultured and humane society, by no means a trivial interest. Any sane society would, to the extent society can design itself, arrange to maximise those spheres in which this mode of economy could operate. But we should heartily resist any suggestion that this might become the picture of an entire economy, since it denies the importance and justice of contractual and command transactions.

Nowhere in this book has my purpose been to trash contracts, but only to distinguish them from property and, in particular, gifts of property. Contractual transactions have a nobility all their own. In a contract, it is true, one looks out for one's own interests, but this is not to say that one ignores or subverts the interests of the other party; rather, the agreement creates obligations or transfers property causing each side precisely to serve the interest of the other party. Contracts create a division of responsibility in the

[11] Titmuss 1970. [12] Ibid., ch. 12.

service of our interests; each side determines whether an agreement serves his own interests and only enters it if it does.[13] In this way contracts allow us to serve our interests and the interests of others without having to get involved with the party and figure out what his interests are. In view of this, there is no good reason to think that a total gift economy would be able to serve our interests as effectively as a mixed economy which included contract. Would anyone really want their economic situation to be determined by gifts from other people most of whom did not know one at all well, if at all? If our goal at the end of the day is to serve our interests, then different modes of doing so suited to our different relationships with others, i.e. whether they are reasonably close or entirely impersonal, will each have a role to play.

An economy of total command transactions is best described by Mauss in his justly famous book, *The Gift*.[14] I know the book is called 'The Gift', but he mistitled it. Indeed, he doubly mistitled it, because the subtitle of the book is 'The Form and Reason for *Exchange* in Archaic Societies', which might have given his readers a clue as to the book's true subject. In a nutshell, Mauss describes customary or traditional *command* economies. The societies he describes are committed to a cyclical transfer of goods which in large part determines their social, hierarchical, and religious character. Gifts they are most definitely not. As Mauss says, '[t]hese total services and counter-services are committed to in a somewhat voluntary form by presents and gifts, though in the final analysis they are strictly compulsory, on pain of private or public warfare.'[15] Not only that. Consider, for a moment, the idea of a gift that enslaves.

> The punishment for failure to reciprocate is slavery for debt. At least, this functions among the Kwakiutl, the Haida, and the Tsimshian. . . . The individual unable to repay the loan or reciprocate the potlatch loses his rank and even his status as a free man. Among the Kwakiutl, when an individual whose credit is poor borrows, he is said to 'sell a slave'.

These are not command economies in the sense that there is a central authority which dictates particular gifts, but command economies in the sense that the traditional laws or rules of the society dictate the participation, timing, and form of these gifts and counter-gifts. As the first quotation above indicates, participation is not voluntary; it is commanded, or demanded, by custom.

I am aware that Mauss is widely interpreted as showing that there is no such thing as a 'free gift' such as I have described between a donor and a donee whose interests he shares.[16] On this view, all gifts of whatever kind engender obligations on the donee to reciprocate. I just hate this idea. When

[13] See Penner forthcoming-b. [14] Mauss 1990.
[15] Ibid., 5. [16] Ibid., vii–viii (foreword by Mary Douglas).

I introduced my analysis of gifts in Chapter 4 I said that such a view was plainly cynical, and it is, because in essence it denies the possibility that my interests can extend beyond my own self-interest construed in the narrowest way. I hope, however, that the preceding brief characterization of Mauss's anthropology shows that one has a great deal of explaining to do before easily assuming that what he calls 'gifts' in *The Gift* bears more than a passing resemblance to the transactions I was speaking about.

There is no question, however, that these customary, reciprocal obligations are vitally important to the running of these societies, in particular the avoidance of warfare.[17] In the last chapter of his book,[18] Mauss argues for a return to elemental, social ideals in the economic order, which might be expressed in, for example, a social insurance scheme, on the basis that reciprocal bonds engender mutuality of interest, co-operation, and solidarity. Whether we like Mauss's version of the good economy or not, and, more to the point, whether it follows in any way from the gift-exchange transactions he finds in primitive and archaic societies, we can draw a more general conclusion. To the extent that we have obligations to contribute to social projects, in particular to the provision of public goods, and it is difficult to believe we do not (how else could one justify taxation?), then commands of various kinds to do so will be entirely appropriate. Call these transfers 'gifts' if you want, but they are definitely commanded, and must be distinguished from the real thing. No one in their right mind would remove the 'command' element from this kind of transaction. Given human nature, it would be a matter of social suicide were a large country like England to rely upon giving to secure what is presently collected through taxation. The fact, however, that practical reason indicates that the law should make these transfers compulsory does not detract from their moral validity. If these transfers comply with valid obligations, they are validly demanded of us. Meeting them is as much a morally significant act as giving the true voluntary gift.

There is one final point that might be addressed, as a matter of balance, perhaps. We have discussed the problem of a necessary minimum of property, but what characteristically exercises people in the distribution debate as much as the desperation of the poor is the extravagance of the rich. Gifts, in particular testamentary gifts, often come in for a thrashing here, since it is common to have in mind the wastrel youth squandering his way through one small fortune after another on the backs of his more industrious or, at least, frugal forbears. As a question of distribution, this animosity seems misplaced, for if one is concerned about extravagance or waste, surely the wastrel celebrity or businessman, i.e. a person who had made his money through contract, who builds himself a private zoo, or who hires an African country for his birthday party deserves our opprobrium just as much. In any

[17] Ibid,, 5–6, 37–43. [18] Ibid., ch. 4.

case, such worries, I suggest, involve concerns which are much broader than the distribution of property. In particular, they call into question the moral status of anyone, quite independently of how much property he has, who uses the means at his disposal to consume much but contribute little. In contrast stands the person, wealthy or not, who devotes a huge proportion of his wealth and energy contributing to the public enterprise. Waste, or selfishness, therefore, is only in the most attenuated way a problem about the 'distribution of property'. The rich will always be with us in one guise or another, and those concerned with profligacy and extravagance should consider sumptuary laws rather than immediately leaping to the (false) conclusion that the institution of property needs fixing.

The Distribution of the Practice—What Counts as Property?

We can now turn to what the idea of property in any particular legal system might tell us, by looking at what the system treats as a suitable object of property. I shall discuss applications of the practice of property: property in humans, i.e. slavery, principally in antiquity; medieval property interests under the English feudal system, and the modern tendency to equate property with wealth or income.

The ownership of humans, slavery, is particularly suggestive. The idea of property I have elaborated suggests that the treatment of humans as property requires a depersonalization of the relationship between a master and his slave such that, like a debt and unlike a contract of employment, the master does not feel any aspect of his personality to be involved with the slave's personality (which is not to say that his identity may not be bound up with the ownership of slaves *per se*); his relationship becomes as contingent as that to any other 'thing'. I also suggested that slavery may take two forms, either chattel ownership or a kind of status relationship. It would not be surprising, therefore, to find that treating people as property in these two different ways will draw on different justifications. Consider the following passage from Arendt:

> The opinion that labor and work were despised in [Greek] antiquity because only slaves were engaged in them is a prejudice of modern historians. The ancients argued the other way around and felt it necessary to possess slaves because of the slavish nature of all occupations that served the needs for the maintenance of life. It was precisely on these grounds that the institution of slavery was defended and justified. To labor meant to be enslaved by necessity, and this enslavement was inherent in the conditions of human life. Because men were dominated by the necessities of life, they could win their freedom only through the domination of those whom they subjected to necessity by force. The slave's degradation was a blow of fate and a fate worse than death, because it carried with it a metamorphosis of

man into something akin to a tame animal. A change in a slave's status, therefore, such as manumission by his master or a change in general political circumstance that elevated certain occupations to public relevance, automatically entailed a change in the slave's 'nature'.

> The institution of slavery in antiquity, though not in later times, was not a device for cheap labor or an instrument of exploitation for profit but rather the attempt to exclude labor from the conditions of man's life. What men share with all other forms of life was not considered to be human.[19]

To the extent that Man was the political animal whose very humanity depended on the escape from the labours of keeping himself alive, the status of the slave labourer could hardly be considered human at all. As Arendt points out, such slaves were akin to tame animals, and therefore chattels in the scheme of property rights. By contrast, the picture is much more complicated in the case of the many different slave situations which existed in imperial Rome.[20] Some slaves were undoubtedly worked as cruelly and to the same purpose as any beast of burden, while others lived lives which surpassed those of many free men. The status of the slave could not, therefore, be equated with the nature of his exploitation, for a rich and powerful slave who himself had slaves was still, at the end of the day, a slave. The guiding distinction, which was not free of confusion, appears to have been that between Roman citizen and foreigner.[21] In other words, the distinction did not turn on the de-humanizing of the slave *per se*, but in a moral and political constitution by which severe inequalities of status between persons was regarded as fundamental to the order of things, just part of the *donee*, as it were. This conception of slavery permits the most intricate forms of servile participation in the world, since the slave might do anything his master might, while all the time being ultimately in thrall to the wishes and purposes of that master. The case of the slavery of blacks in the colonies of America and in the United States was typically justified in a different way again, on racist assumptions about the slave's natural inferiority. Here the slave's nature is not servile because of the labour he performs, as in ancient Athens, but rather he performs the labour he does because this is what he is fit for.

It is difficult not to believe that each of these justifications must have been swallowed with a lot of bad faith by contemporary proponents of the institution of slavery. But what is most interesting about the application of property to humans in these cases is the different insights they generate into what was regarded as at least superficially plausible as a justification. We get a sense of the Athenian's immense pride in the achievement of the polis as the first true cradle of culture, but at the same time of his very real appreciation of its cost, and the fear that fate might make him the payer. Similarly evocative are the Roman's outlook on human society in terms of the inescapable relation

[19] Arendt 1958, 83–4. See also Thebert 1993, 139, 164–5.
[20] See Thebert 1993.
[21] Ibid. 164 ff.

of the conquerors to the conquered, and the almost hysterical insistence of the white slave-owner that the dominance of Europe and Europeans could not merely be the result of the fickle tides of history, but must have deeper roots in the different bloods of different races. It is perhaps worth pointing out that each of these arguments has been applied in a modified form to justify the subjection of women. The woman's role as the bearer of children and keeper of the private realm is necessary for men to engage in the business of the world, the conduct of politics and war, and the life of contemplation. The woman's role is merely an expression of the natural order of things; to question the superior status of some, men, to others, women, is to question the only possible social constitution. And, of course, claiming natural inferiority is as tried and true an approach to defending inequality as one is likely to find.

Jumping several centuries to feudal England, we see property to encompass a myriad of incorporeal things which we would not recognize as property, in particular, offices. They, and their 'thinglikeness', are importantly connected to the development of property in land in feudal law. Interests in land became property in English law fairly quickly after the Conquest,[22] as the personal right to hold land of the King hardened into the right to an 'estate'[23] in the land. Nevertheless, the feudal hierarchy was maintained through a system of 'tenures'[24] of land, essentially a system by which different tenants had hierarchical rights in the same land. At the top was the King, at the bottom the person actually in possession of the land, and in between there might be any number of lords who took their places on this feudal ladder. It was essentially a pyramid scheme. Each tenant, starting with the one in possession who through his serfs would produce agricultural goods, passed the wealth of the land upward by doing 'rent-service' of various kinds to the lord immediately above him, and so on up to the King. Thus although a person might have an estate in the land, it was as likely to be a seigneury, i.e. the right to a rent from a tenant immediately below on the feudal ladder, as it was to be an estate in possession of the land itself. Thus the ownership of estates in land themselves was in a very real sense the ownership of something incorporeal. As Pollock and Maitland write:

[T]he line between the corporeal and the incorporeal thing is by no means so clear in medieval law as we might have expected it to be. . . We must return to the case in which a lord has a freehold tenant [i.e. a tenant in possession of the land] and that tenant has been duly performing his services. Shall we say that he [possesses] the tenant's homage and fealty and services, or shall we say that he [possesses] the

[22] Simpson 1986, ch. I, 49–54.

[23] An amount of time for which the land could be held. In the greatest estate, the fee simple, the estate was given to 'A and his heirs', and so was essentially perpetual. See ibid,, 49–54, ch.IV.

[24] Simpson 1986, chs. I, III.

land? We may take whatever course we please; but if we say that he is [possesses] the land, we ought to say that he [possesses] it in service. On the other hand, if we say that he [possesses] the services, we must understand that these services are a thing, and a thing that is exceedingly like an acre of land.[25]

Given both this abstract characterization of the possession of 'things' like services relating to land, and remembering as well that one's position in the feudal ladder was essentially an indicator of one's status, it is not surprising that offices, i.e. positions of authority, which attached to land in the sense that the profits or payments of the office were raised from a particular locality or estate, were no less things for the medieval lawyer. Speaking of a *corody*, the obligation of a religious house to supply a person with some commodities at regular intervals in return for some benefit or service, Pollock and Maitland contrast the medieval outlook with the modern:

If an annual supply of victuals or other necessaries is to be received in some certain place, the right to receive it is to be treated like land. To us this treatment of what in our eyes is but the benefit of a contract may seem very awkward. . . . If rights that appear to us to be merely contractual are thus dealt with, we shall not be surprised to find that where the contractual element is wanting, incorporeal things are very easily created. If 'offices', [such as 'the wardenship of woods, parks, chases, warrens and gates'[26]] are to fall within the private law at all, if they are heritable and vendible, perhaps we can not do better than treat them as being very like pieces of land.[27]

Such offices were clearly unlike contracts of employment between individuals. They were bought and sold on the supposition that the personal character of the occupant could not affect the nature of holding that position, any more that it could one's holding land. If the holder of a corody was not receiving his entitlement, the law gave him an action which allowed him to 'complain of his ejectment from his free tenement; they sent the jurors to view the monastery whence the corody issued'.[28] As Pollock and Maitland say, '[a] better example of medieval realism could hardly be given.'[29] But yet it all makes sense. Where for any person of status all value was received directly or indirectly from the land, the things of economic value which could be given and exchanged were various 'shares', as it were, in the profits of different pieces of land. And the shares in which the services were paid were much more tangible than the money dividends which a company shareholder today receives. As particular goods they very much were things, fruits of the land itself. In such a feudal hierarchy, the performance of the necessary duties so that these services would be delivered was not a matter of continual bargaining. From serfs all the way up these services were a function of one's status, and essentially taken for granted. Anyone in principle of the right class could fit into any particular slot.

25 Pollock and Maitland 1968, 125.
26 Ibid. 135.
27 Ibid.
28 Ibid.
29 Ibid.

Jumping a few centuries further, I wish now to finish by discussing some aspects of our own application of the practice of property to particular things. The thread that runs through this discussion is the extent to which our application of the practice of property is now largely shaped by a view of ourselves in which our principal economic motivation is to control income for the purposes of consumption.

Ever since Berle and Means wrote *The Modern Corporation and Private Property*[30] the distinction between 'ownership' and 'control' of corporations has been the focus of academic inquiry. The idea is quite simple. Before the corporate form of business enterprise took hold, the owner of a business both invested his property in it, managed it, and took the income which was generated. The corporation, however, separates the functions of management and ownership. Investors hold their shares merely as sources of income and capital growth in expectation of the company doing well. By contrast, the directors of the company who control the running of the enterprise need not be shareholders at all, and although they generally are, in the case of large enterprises it is exceedingly unlikely that they will themselves own more than a small fraction of the total shares. Thus, at least in respect of large business enterprises, the ownership of a share is akin to the feudal ownership of an incorporeal right to services from the land. Like the feudal corody or office, it is an impersonal stake in an economic enterprise. What the shareholder owns is not any tangible piece of the corporation's property, but a right to the income stream. Similarly, the shareholder does not have anything truly like a contract with the directors and officers of the corporation. While the directors are, of course, put in place by the votes of the shareholders, the directors' management of the company is not governed by the obligations of contract. Rather, their behaviour is regulated only by their own self-interest, which one hopes coincides at least for the most part with the shareholders',[31] and by the rules of company law.[32] Thus in both cases the owner's right is a right to a stream of income in an economic enterprise which is organized by a structure of obligations which is the creature of law, not the result of any personal contract of service as between the individual owner and those who serve to generate the income, the directors. As Berle and Means saw it, the great power of the modern corporation gives those who sit atop the enterprise powers and status which resemble very much the picture of feudal nobility, which therefore must be made subject to public control.[33] Regardless of the actual cogency of this view, it does capture in the most complete way the 'thingness' of the share itself, in parallel to the incorporeal thing of medieval law. Of course we do not subscribe to a

[30] Berle and Means 1933.

[31] Although this is disputed by Berle and Means 1933, 8–9.

[32] Company directors are also regarded by equity as fiduciaries, which should govern their behaviour with greater strictness, especially in situations of conflict of interest.

[33] Ibid., 352–7.

doctrine of estates and tenures in the general economic enterprise, in which one's shareholdings turned on one's political status and personal relationship to a king. If we did, however, we would indeed have a modern feudal system.

The notion of income rights as property rights is a particularly interesting one. In the case of the corporation, the idea that one earns income by participating in some real way in the enterprise is extinguished by the idea that one sells one's money to a company for a time. One participates in it only in the sense that one might have used the money elsewhere. There is nothing personal about the involvement, and so the right to the return naturally falls into that class of incorporeal rights which are objects of property. It appears that our society is willing to consider income interests of various kinds as property in a way in which those of an earlier generation might not have. For example, Reich argued in 1964 that various state benefits, like welfare entitlements, ought to be treated as property.[34] This seems perfectly reasonable if we treat the State as a kind of public enterprise in which people have various income rights, but seems much less plausible if we regard the state as being somehow involved at a personal level in the lives of those who require its support. The proprietary character of benefit entitlements, i.e. the extent to which the claimant may say that the benefit is his, depends very largely on the extent to which the benefit is guaranteed by a fixed set of rules rather than on the shifting course of bureaucratic attitudes and administrative policies, so it is difficult to say whether the idea of a 'new' property of this kind has really taken hold in our way of thinking about these entitlements. Nevertheless, there may be something in the mere fact that such rights to income appear to us as plausible candidates for objects of property.

If we once again consider Arendt, we see one way of characterizing an income-dominated approach to the classifications of things.

> The profound connection between private and public, manifest on its most elementary level in the question of private property, is likely to be misunderstood today because of the modern equation of property and wealth on the one side and propertylessness and poverty on the other. . . .[W]ealth and property, far from being the same, are of an entirely different nature. The present emergence everywhere of actually or potentially very wealthy societies which are at the same time essentially propertyless, because the wealth of any single individual consists of his share in the annual income of a society as a whole, clearly shows how little these two things are connected.[35]

In very rough terms, Arendt closely associates property with privacy, as a realm in which an individual and his family engages in the use of tangible things to provide the necessaries of life, but which also captures the mortal

[34] Reich 1964. [35] Arendt 1958, 61.

and mysterious side of a person's existence: '[t]he sacredness of this privacy was like the sacredness of the hidden, namely of birth and death, the beginning and end of all mortals who, like all living creatures, grow out of and return to the darkness of an underworld.'[36] Such a realm is a necessary condition or counterpart of the engagement in the public sphere. Property therefore is a kind of necessary contrast to, and base from which a person could enter, the public realm. This is all to be sharply contrasted with wealth. Wealth is merely economic power, undifferentiated and unrealized. Wealth is necessary to sustain property and thus the private realm, but it is not to be exalted for its own sake.[37] The maintenance of property and the private realm, and thus the maintenance of the public realm, is in turn bound up with a quest for immortality, the transcendence of one's own limited time on earth.

Only the existence of a public realm and the world's subsequent transformation into a community of things which gathers men together and relates them to each other depends entirely on permanence. If the world is to contain a public space, it cannot be erected for one generation and planned for the living only; it must transcend the life-span of mortal men. . . . Through many ages before us—but not now any more—men entered the public realm because they wanted something of their own or something they had in common with others to be more permanent than their earthly lives. . . . There is perhaps no clearer testimony to the loss of the public realm in the modern age than the almost complete loss of authentic concern with immortality, a loss somewhat overshadowed by the simultaneous loss of the metaphysical concern with eternity.[38]

Arendt argues that modernity has witnessed the dissolution of the true public and private realms, and that this is intimately connected with the diminution of property and the ascendance of wealth.

The dissolution [of the public and private] may most conveniently be watched in the progressing transformation of immobile into mobile property until eventually the distinction between property and wealth, between the *fungibles* and the *consumptibles* of Roman law, loses all significance because every tangible, 'fungible' thing has become an object of consumption; it lost its private use value which was determined by its location and acquired an exclusively social value determined through its ever-changing exchangeability whose fluctuation could itself be fixed only temporarily by relating it to the common denominator of money.[39]

Arendt sees in this change from property to wealth a significant shift of perspective, which we can frame in terms of a shift in our classification of the 'things' which can be held as property. The striking feature of the pre-wealth society is that it is the engagement with the actual property itself which seems to underpin the interest in the use of things; it is an interest in the long-term use-value of particular property, and so the property itself must

[36] Ibid., 62. [37] Ibid., 66–7. [38] Ibid., 55. [39] Ibid., 69.

be of the kind to sustain such uses, principally land and durable chattels. Only such an emphasis on the continuing engagement with the material world will secure the realm of the private, and create the walls outside which a person may act in the public sphere. In the case of the wealth society, property is largely regarded as income, i.e. as amounts of stored use-value which are to be realized or cashed in for property which is immediately consumed and passes away.

Now the point of raising this distinction is not to say that in Arendt's pre-wealth property culture there will not be forms of property like money or choses in action which represent stored use-value, to be later cashed in. Not at all. Rather, such kinds of property are used in a particular way, that is to sustain what she calls property, i.e. the actual use of tangible items of property, in ways which have an effect upon the permanent world or, rather, which create the permanent private and public environments. In this culture, wealth serves property. In the income society, wealth serves consumption.

If Arendt is right, then we see that there is a kind of bias in an income society against the use of property which generates value only when we actively participate in *creating* something with it. Rather we have an interest in 'participating' in our property only in so far as we can *consume* it. Now, of course, consciousness of the ills which afflict a consumer society have become part of the *Zeitgeist*, and I have no ambition to discuss them here. But I would like to suggest that the emphasis on income may have a particular effect on the way we characterize those things which we regard as suitable objects of property.

There are two elements to this argument. For the first, recall the characterization of the economic analysis of property in Chapter 3. On that view, a property right was essentially any exclusive entitlement which could be traded in a market. Secondly, recall my characterization of the way that interests in property are represented in bargain exchanges and in gifts. In bargain exchanges, I relinquish my interest in a thing to the other party whereas, in the case of gifts, I take on board or share the donee's interests in the disposition of the property. This contractual/gratuitous distinction can be applied to distinguish kinds of agreements, not just kinds of transfers of property. We can have mutual agreements, which are like joint projects in that the agreement is intended to serve our joint interests, wherein I conceive your interests as mine, and you conceive mine as yours. There are also bargain agreements, of course, the paradigmatic example of which might be the exchange of property, where one party's interests partake not at all of the interests of the other party. We simply transfer our own interests in one piece of property to another.

Now, if we frame the serving of our interests in terms of 'income' or 'consumption use', we see that in a bargain the income we achieve is the serving of our own interests, rather than serving our interests by taking on board the interests of others, or serving what we take to be true joint interests. If, therefore, we allow the economist's emphasis on contract predominantly to shape our concept of income and interest, we will regard everything as property which will serve our interests through the making of contracts. Why?

In the case of gifts and mutual agreements, an individual takes on board or participates in the interests of others. Thus these transactions necessarily involve the personal participation of those involved. Thus gifts and mutual agreements create relationships which cannot themselves be regarded as contingent impersonal attachments. They therefore cannot be treated as property. On the other hand, if we tend to look at the world through contractual spectacles, these personal connections by definition drop out of place. In consequence, we may look at certain kinds of benefits or interests as goods which are exchanged, *transforming* them into property, whereas their real defining characteristic is that they are relational goods between persons, like friendships, professional collaborations, family relationships, and so on, which are achieved through the mutual participation of individuals; as relational goods of this kind they are not, or should not be, property, but the contractual spectacles allow us to see them as such.

Any number of examples supports our familiarity with this kind of transformation. To the extent that we regard an employment contract as merely the exchange of income streams, in which either party could as easily be replaced with another so little do any really personal involvements dictate its course, then our jobs are property, and the contracts we have with employees are, too. On the other hand to the extent that our employment or occupation requires us to engage faculties which reflect something of ourselves, so that our occupation or employment becomes an aspect of our own personal history and identity in a significant way, and which may indeed result in something both public and lasting, then the relationship is not one of mere ownership of a office and the correlative ownership of a service.

More frightening is the reduction to property status of personal relationships and interactions like friendship, love, and sexual intercourse. The last, of course, is most likely to fall prey to the reduction, since sexual intercourse is regularly the subject of contractual exchange. It hardly needs saying that a prostitute and his purchaser are not engaged in a project to serve any joint interest, but to exchange values which serve their individual interests. This is not to say that a prostitute cannot enjoy his work, but if he does that bonus accrues as function of his own 'income', not as a function of his sharing in his purchaser's. Of course we recognize the darker side of this depersonalization. If sex is just a service we can exchange, rather than a joint activity which both engages and serves the mutual interests of the participants, then coercing the service by rape must be regarded as akin to 'robbery', like threatening a hotel keeper to give us a room without any intention of paying the bill.[40]

We can now tie this up with Arendt's distinction between property and wealth. To the extent we no longer participate personally in any meaningful way in our property except in so far as we consume it, we may lose the sense that the use of property is a kind of meaningful engagement with the thing itself. It is perhaps not too fanciful to describe the meaningful engagement with a mere thing as a kind of joint enterprise with it. An artist enters into a kind of dialogue with his materials, as does an architect with the land he builds on and the materials he uses. There are obviously different forms of this engagement. As Tully points out, the colonial settlers in America engaged the land to subdue it and create an agricultural enterprise in a way which was distinctly different from the way the native Americans engaged the land.[41] When the native Americans said that the land did not belong to them, but rather they belonged to the land, they were capturing the way in which their ways of living involved their adapting to the demands of the land in contrast to the way that the settlers demanded that, as far as possible, the land adapted to their purposes. Nevertheless, for both colonists and natives it was meaningful engagement of a kind.

Now it may be the case that the attitudes and motivations required to learn how skilfully to engage the things of this world are not dissimilar to the attitudes and motivations required to learn how skilfully to engage the people of this world, perhaps particularly in the more impersonal public realm. If, as Hegel would have it, we make ourselves real by reducing the mere potentiality of our existence to actuality by making an effect on the external world, perhaps this external world should be considered to some extent as of a piece. My point is obviously not that we should treat people as things. The point I am suggesting is that only by drawing upon our creative capacity to work sincerely with all the materials outside us, both people and things, may we learn the capacity to distinguish the two, and appreciate their separate merits. If everything is merely a source of income, including our relationships and interactions with others, then there is no basis for not treating all our rights as 'income' rights.

The possibility of the 'incomization' of the category of 'things' to which property applies does not threaten to alter the idea of property in law as I have described it. If this shift took place it would only alter the distribution of the practice, through the depersonalization, or 'thingification' of relationships conventionally regarded as significantly engaging the personalities of those in the relationship. It is difficult to state the extent of the influence of the income model of the character of things on the way we perceive the scope of property, since as we have seen, property theorists have tended to

[40] See also Radin 1993, 201–2.
[41] Tully 1993, ch. 5.

link property to contract constitutively, treating all exchanged values as property of a kind, which confuses the issue. But perhaps Munzer's view that rights to things which we can only give away are 'weak' property rights, while rights to those which we can sell are 'strong' property rights[42] might suggest that the 'contractual income' characterization of what counts as property may be very influential, not only among economists, but among lawyers as well. I should point out that my purpose here has not been to criticize the economic definition of property, but rather to distinguish it from the legal idea of property while at the same time showing how the economist's viewpoint, if it became general or natural to us, would influence the character of the actual property practice we have.

I realize that these remarks have only scratched the surface of the role that property plays in the characterization of a society through its categorization of things as fit or unfit objects of the practice. I hope however to have shown how the idea of property in law provides a guide for doing so.

I am also extremely conscious of the scores of issues in property law which this book might have addressed, and even of the suspicion that a learned lawyer may have that, had I done so, much of what I have said might be undone. But I stand by the effort these pages represent: to say something in general about an idea of property which has a passing chance of capturing the way in which things are dealt with under existing legal systems. The book is intended primarily as a theoretical examination of the idea of property, which I hope exposes some common mistakes in past approaches, and makes some headway in areas heretofore insufficiently explored. A vindication of these ideas through the examination of the rules and doctrines of the property law in different jurisdictions, cultures, and historical periods is the subject of a different book which must await another day, so I shall stop here.

[42] Munzer 1990, 49.

Bibliography

ACKERMAN, B. (1977), *Private Property and the Constitution* (Yale University Press, New Haven, Conn., 1977).

AMERICAN LAW INSTITUTE (1936), *Restatement of the Law of Property, Volume I* (American Law Institute, St. Paul, Minn., 1936).

ARENDT, H. (1958), *The Human Condition* (University of Chicago Press, Chicago, 1958).

ATIYAH, P. S. (1978), 'Contracts, Promises and the Law of Obligations' (1978) 94 *Law Quarterly Review* 193.

—— (1981), *Promises, Morals, and Law* (Clarendon Press, Oxford, 1981).

—— (1986), *Essays on Contract* (Clarendon Press, Oxford, 1986).

BAILEY, S. J. (1931–2), 'Assignments of Debts in England from the Twelfth to the Twentieth Century' (in three parts) (1931) 47 *Law Quarterly Review* 516; (1932) 48 *Law Quarterly Review* 248, 547.

BAIRD, D. G. (1983), 'Common Law Intellectual Property and the Legacy of *International News Service* v. *Associated Press*', 50 *University of Chicago Law Review* 411 (1983).

BARKER, K. (1995), 'Unjust Enrichment: Containing the Beast' (1995) 15 *Oxford Journal of Legal Studies* 457.

BARTON, J. L. (1976), 'The Rise of the Fee Simple' (1976) 92 *Law Quarterly Review* 108.

BEATSON, J. (1991), 'Benefit, Reliance, and the Structure of Unjust Enrichment' in *The Use and Abuse of Unjust Enrichment* (Clarendon Press, Oxford, 1991), 21.

Becker, L. C. (1977), *Property Rights: Philosophic Foundations* (Routledge and Kegan Paul, Boston, Mass., 1977).

—— (1980), 'The Moral Basis of Property Rights', in J. R. Pennock and J. W. Chapman (eds.), *Nomos XXII: Property* (New York University Press, New York, 1980), 187.

—— (1992), 'Too Much Property' (1992) 21 *Philosophy and Public Affairs* 196.

BELL, A.P. (1989), *The Modern Law of Personal Property in England and Ireland* (Butterworths, London, 1989).

BENSON, P. (1989), 'Abstract Right and the Possibility of a Nondistributive Conception of Contract: Hegel and Contemporary Contract Theory', 10 *Cardozo Law Review* 1077 (1989).

BENTHAM, J. (1970), Appendix B, parts I and II of *Of Laws in General* (H.L.A. Hart ed.) (Athlone Press, London, 1970), 251..

BERLE, A. A. and MEANS, G. C. (1933), *The Modern Corporation and Private Property* (Macmillan, New York, 1933).

BERLIN, I. (1969), *Four Essays on Liberty* (Oxford University Press, Oxford, 1969).

BIRKS, P. B. H. (1985), *An Introduction to the Law of Restitution* (Clarendon Press, Oxford, 1985 (reprinted with revisions, 1989)).

—— (1989), 'An Unacceptable Face of Human Property', in P. Birks (ed.), *New Perspectives in the Roman Law of Property* (Clarendon Press, Oxford, 1989), 61.

BIRKS, P. B. H. (1990), 'The Independence of Restitutionary Causes of Action', 16 *University of Queensland Law Journal* 1 (1990).
—— (1991a), Book Review, 70 *Canadian Bar Review* 814 (1991).
—— (1991b), 'In Defence of Free Acceptance' in Andrew Burrows (ed.), *Essays on the Law of Restitution* (Clarendon Press, Oxford, 1991), 105.
—— (1992a), *Restitution—The Future* (The Federation Press, Sydney, Australia, 1992).
—— (ed.) (1992b), *Examining the Law Syllabus: The Core* (Oxford University Press, Oxford, 1992).
—— (1993), 'No Consideration: Restitution After Void Contracts' (1993) 23 *Western Australian Law Review* 195.
—— (1994), 'Adjudication and Interpretation in the Common Law: A Century of Change' (1994) 14 *Legal Studies*, 156.
—— (1995), 'The Foundations of Legal Rationality in Scotland', in R. Evans-Jones (ed.), *The Civil Law Tradition in Scotland* (The Stair Society, Edinburgh, 1995), 81.
—— and CHAMBERS, R. (1994), 'Restitution Research Resource 1994' (1994) *Restitution Law Review,* Supplement.
BLACKSTONE, W. (1766), *Commentaries on the Laws of England* (Dawsons, London, reprinted 1966).
BRODHURST, S. (1895), 'Is Copyright a Chose in Action?' (1895) 11 *Law Quarterly Review* 61.
BROWDER, O. L. (1977), 'Giving or Leaving: What is a Will', 75 *Michigan Law Review*, 845 (1977).
BRUDNER, A. (1989), 'Hegel and the Crisis of Private Law', 10 *Cardozo Law Review* 949 (1989).
—— (1991), 'The Unity of Property Law' (1991) 4 *Canadian Journal of Law and Jurisprudence* 3.
BUCKLAND, W. W. and MCNAIR, A. D. (1965), *Roman Law and Common Law* (2nd edn. revised by F. H. Lawson. Cambridge University Press, Cambridge, 1965).
BURN, E. H. (1994), *Cheshire and Burn's Modern Law of Real Propert,* 15th edn.. Butterworths, London, 1994).
BURROWS, A. (1983), 'Contract, Tort and Restitution—A Satisfactory Division or Not?' (1983) 99 *Law Quarterly Review* 217.
—— (1988), 'Free Acceptance and the Law of Restitution' (1988) 104 *Law Quarterly Review* 576.
—— (1993), *The Law of Restitution* (Butterworths, London, 1993).
CALABRESI, G. and MELAMED, A. D. (1972), 'Property Rules, Liability Rules, and Inalienability: One View of the Cathedral', 85 *Harvard Law Review* 1089 (1972).
CAMPBELL, K. (1979), *The Concept of Rights* (D.Phil. Thesis, Oxford, 1979).
—— (1992), 'On the General Nature of Property Rights' (1992) 3 *King's College Law Journal* 79.
CHRISTMAN, J. (1994a), *The Myth of Property* (Oxford University Press, New York, 1994).
—— (1994b), 'Distributive Justice and the Complex Structure of Ownership' (1994) 23 *Philosophy and Public Affairs* 225.
COHEN, F. S. (1954), 'Dialogue on Private Property' 9 *Rutgers Law Review* 357 (1994).
COHEN, G. A. (1985), 'Nozick on Appropriation' (1985) 150 *New Left Review* 89.

COHEN, G. A. (1986), 'Self-Ownership, World Ownership, and Equality: Part II' (1986) 3 *Social Philosophy and Policy* 77.

COLLINS, H. (1993), *The Law of Contract* (2nd edn., Butterworths, London, 1993).

COULTER, M. (1991), *Property in Ideas* (Thomas Jefferson University Press, Kirksville, Miss., 1991).

COVAL, S., SMITH, J. C., and COVAL, S. (1986), 'The Foundations of Property and Property Law' (1986) 45 *Cambridge Law Journal* 457.

CRASWELL, R. (1989), 'Contract Law, Default Rules, and the Philosophy of Promising', 88 *Michigan Law Review* 489 (1989).

DEMSETZ, H. (1967), 'Toward a Theory of Property Rights', 57 *American Economic Review (Proceedings)* 347 (1967).

DENMAN, D. (1978), *The Place of Property* (Geographical Publications Limited, Berkhamsted, Herts., 1978).

DWORKIN, R. (1987), *Taking Rights Seriously* (Duckworth, London, 1987).

ELPHINSTONE, H. W. (1893), 'What is a Chose in Action?' (1983) 9 *Law Quarterly Review* 311.

EPSTEIN, R. A. (1979), 'Possession as the Root of Title', 13 *Georgia Law Journal* 1221 (1979).

—— (1985a), 'Why Restrain Alienation?', 85 *Columbia Law Review* 970 (1985).

—— (1985b), *Takings: Private Property and the Power of Eminent Domain* (Harvard University Press, Cambridge, Mass., 1985).

FINNIS, J. (1971–2), 'Some Professorial Fallacies about Rights' (1972–2) 4 *Adelaide Law Review* 377.

—— (1980), *Natural Law and Natural Rights* (Clarendon Press, Oxford, 1980).

FOX, H. G. (1947), *Monopolies and Patents* (University of Toronto Press, Toronto, 1947).

FRIED, C. (1981), *Contract as Promise: A Theory of Contractual Obligations* (Harvard University Press, Cambridge, Mass., 1981).

FRIEDMAN, L. M. (1966), 'The Law of the Living, The Law of the Dead: Property, Succession, and Society' [1966] *Wisconsin Law Review* 340.

FRIEDMANN, D. (1989), 'The Efficient Breach Fallacy' (1989) 18 *Journal of Legal Studies* 1.

—— (1991), 'Valid, Voidable, Qualified, and Non-existing Obligations: An Alternative Perspective on the Law of Restitution', in A. Burrows (ed.), *Essays on the Law of Restitution* (Clarendon Press, Oxford, 1991), 247.

FRYFOGLE, E. T. (1989), 'Context and Accomodation in Modern Property Law', 41 *Stanford Law Review* 1529 (1989).

FULLER, F. (1958), 'Postivism and Fidelity to Law—A Reply to Professor Hart', 71 *Harvard Law Review* 630 (1958) .

GARDNER, S. (1990), *An Introduction to the Law of Trusts* (Clarendon Press, Oxford, 1990).

GAUS, G. F. (1994), 'Property, Rights, and Freedom' (1994) 11 *Social Philosophy and Policy* 209.

GOODE, R. M. (1976), 'The Right to Trace and its Impact in Commercial Transactions—I and II' (1976) 92 *Law Quarterly Review* 360, 528.

—— (1987), 'Ownership and Obligation in Commercial Transactions' (1987) 103 *Law Quarterly Review* 433.

GOODE, R. M. (1991), 'Property and Unjust Enrichment', in A. Burrows (ed.), *Essays on the Law of Restitution* (Clarendon Press, Oxford, 1991), 215.
GORDON, W. J. (1993), 'A Property Right in Self-Expression: Equality and Individualism in the Natural Law of Intellectual Property', 102 *Yale Law Journal* 1533 (1993).
GRAY, K. (1991), 'Property in Thin Air' (1991) 51 *Cambridge Law Journal* 252.
—— (1993), *Elements of Land Law* (2nd edn., Butterworths, London, 1993).
GREY, T. C. (1980), 'The Disintegration of Property' in J. R. Pennock and J. W. Chapman (eds.), *Nomos XXII: Property* (New York University Press, New York, 1980), 69.
HACKNEY, J. (1987), *Understanding Equity and Trusts* (Fontana, London, 1987).
HAMMOND, R. G. (1984), 'Theft of Information' (1984) 100 *Law Quarterly Review* 252.
—— (1990), *Personal Property: Commentary and Materials* (Oxford University Press, Auckland, New Zealand, 1990).
HARGREAVES, A. D. (1956), 'Modern Real Property' (1956) 19 *Modern Law Review* 14.
HARRIS, D. R. (1961), 'The Concept of Possession in English Land Law', in A. G. Guest (ed.), *Oxford Essays in Jurisprudence* (Clarendon Press, Oxford, 1961), 69.
HARRIS, J. W. (1979), *Law and Legal Science: An Inquiry into the Concepts 'Legal Rule' and 'Legal System'* (Clarendon Press, Oxford, 1979).
—— (1986), 'Ownership of Land in English Law', in N. MacCormick and P. Birks (eds.), *The Legal Mind: Essays for Tony Honoré* (Clarendon Press, Oxford, 1986), 143.
—— (1987), 'Legal Doctrine and Interests in Land', in J. Eekelaar and J. Bell (eds.), *Oxford Essays in Jurisprudence, Third Series* (Clarendon Press, Oxford, 1987), 167.
—— (1989), 'Unger's Critique of Formalism in Legal Reasoning: Hero, Hercules, and Humdrum' (1989) 52 *Modern Law Review* 42.
—— (1991), review of S. R. Munzer, *A Theory of Property* (1990), (1991) 107 *Law Quarterly Review* 340.
—— (1995), 'Private and Non-Private Property: What is the Difference?' (1995) 111 *Law Quarterly Review* 421.
—— (1996), 'Who Owns My Body?' (1966) 16 *Oxford Journal of Legal Studies* 55.
HART, H. L. A. (1954), 'Definition and Theory in Jurisprudence' (1954) 70 *Law Quarterly Review* 37.
—— (1958), 'Postivism and the Separation of Law and Morals', 71 *Harvard Law Review* 593 (1958) .
—— (1961), *The Concept of Law* (Clarendon Press, Oxford, 1961).
—— (1963a), 'The Ascription of Responsibility and Rights', in A. G. N. Flew (ed.), *Logic and Language, 1st Series* (Basil Blackwell, Oxford, 1963), 145.
—— (1963b), 'Kelsen Visited', 10 *UCLA Law Review* 709 (1963).
—— (1982), *Essays on Bentham* (Clarendon Press, Oxford, 1982).
—— (1984), 'Are there any Natural Rights', in J. Waldron (ed.), *Theories of Rights* (Oxford University Press, Oxford, 1984), 77.
HAYTON, D. J. (1991), *Hayton and Marshall: Cases and Commentary on the Law of Trusts (9th edn.,* Sweet & Maxwell, London, 1991).
—— (1993), *The Law of Trusts* (2nd edn., Sweet & Maxwell, London, 1993).

HEDLEY, S. (1988), 'Contract, Tort and Restitution: Or, On Cutting the Legal System Down to Size' (1988) 8 *Legal Studies* 137.

HEGEL, G. W. F. (1942), *The Philosophy of Right* (translated with notes by T. M. Knox) (Clarendon Press, Oxford, 1942).

HETTINGER, E. C. (1989), 'Justifying Intellectual Property' (1989) 18 *Philosophy and Public Affairs* 31.

HOBBES, T. (1651), *Leviathan* (Michael Oakshott (ed.), (Basil Blackwell, Oxford, 1946).

HOFFMASTER, B. (1992), 'Between the Sacred and the Profane: Bodies, Property, and Patents in the *Moore* Case' (1992) 7 *Intellectual Property Journal* 115.

HOHFELD, W. N. (1923), *Fundamental Legal Conceptions* (Yale University Press, New Haven, Conn., 1923).

HOLDSWORTH, W. S. (1923a), *A History of English Law,* Volume III (3rd edn., re-written, Methuen & Co. Ltd, London, 1923), chs. I, II.

—— (1923b), *A History of English Law, Volume II* (3rd edn., rewritten, Methuen & Co. Ltd, London, 1923), ch. 1.

—— (1937), *A History of English Law, Volume VII* (2nd edn., Methuen & Co. Ltd and Sweet and Maxwell, London, 1937), ch. II.

HONORÉ, A. M. (1960), 'Rights of Exclusion and Immunities Against Divesting', 34 *Tulane Law Review* 453 (1960).

—— (1961), 'Ownership', in A. G. Guest (ed.), *Oxford Essays in Jurisprudence* (Clarendon Press, Oxford, 1961), 104.

—— (1987), *Making Law Bind* (Clarendon Press, Oxford, 1987).

HOROWITZ, M. J. (1973), 'Transformation in the Conception of Property in American Law, 1780–1860', 40 *University of Chicago Law Review* 248 (1973).

HUDSON, A. H. (1984), 'Is Divesting Abandonment Possible at Common Law?' (1984) 100 *Law Quarterly Review* 110.

HUGHES, J. (1988), 'The Philosophy of Intellectual Property', 77 *Georgetown Law Journal* 287 (1988).

JAFFEY, P. (1995), 'Restitutionary Damages and Disgorgement' [1995] *Restitution Law Review* 30.

KAPLOW, L. (1986), 'An Economic Analysis of Legal Transitions', 99 *Harvard Law Review* 509 (1986).

LAWSON, F. H. and RUDDEN, B. (1982), *The Law of Property* (2nd edn., Clarendon Press, Oxford, 1982).

LIBLING, D. F. (1978), 'The Concept of Property: Property in Intangibles' (1978) 94 *Law Quarterly Review* 103.

LLEWELLYN, K. (1931), 'What Price Contract—An Essay in Perspective', 40 *Yale Law Journal* 704 (1931).

LOCKE, J., (1946), *The Second Treatise of Civil Government and a Letter Concerning Toleration* (J. W. Gough (ed.), Basil Blackwell, Oxford, 1946).

LUCAS, J.R. (1980), *On Justice* (Clarendon Press, Oxford, 1980).

MACCORMICK, D. N. (1977), 'Rights in Legislation', in P. M. S. Hacker and J. Raz (eds.), *Law, Morality and Society* (Clarendon Press, Oxford, 1977), 189.

—— (1982), 'Children's Rights: A Test Case For Theories of Right', in *Legal Right and Social Democracy* (Clarendon Press, Oxford, 1982), 155.

—— (1990), 'Rights', in *The Laws of Scotland; Stair Memorial Encyclopedia* (The Stair Society, Edinburgh, 1990), Vol. II, 1073.

MacNeil, Kent (1989), *Common Law Aboriginal Title* (Clarendon Press, Oxford, 1989).

Macpherson, C. B. (1962), *From Hobbes to Locke: The Theory of Possessive Individualism* (Oxford University Press, Oxford, 1962).

—— (ed.) (1978), *Property: Mainstream and Critical Positions* (Basil Blackwell, Oxford, 1978).

Maitland, F. W. (1885), 'The Seisin of Chattels' (1885) 1 *Law Quarterly Review* 324.

—— (1886), 'The Mystery of Seisin' (1886) 2 *Law Quarterly Review* 481.

—— (1926), *Equity* (Cambridge University Press, Cambridge, 1926).

Mann, F. A. (1992), *The Legal Aspect of Money* (5th edn., Clarendon Press, Oxford, 1992).

Marshall, G. (1973), 'Rights, Options and Settlements' in A. W. B. Simpson (ed.), *Oxford Essays in Jurisprudence, Second Series* (Clarendon Press, Oxford, 1973), 228.

Martin, J. E. (1993), *Hanbury and Martin: Modern Equity* (14th edn., Sweet & Maxwell, London, 1993).

Mathews, P. (1981), 'Proprietary Claims at Common Law for Mixed and Improved Goods' [1981] *Current Legal Problems* 159.

—— (1983), 'Whose Body? People as Property' [1983] *Current Legal Problems* 193.

Mauss, M. (1990), *The Gift: The Form and Reason for Exchange in Archaic Societies* (trans. W. D. Wallace) (Routledge, London, 1990).

McBride, N. (1994), 'A Fifth Common Law Obligation' (1994) 14 *Legal Studies* 35.

McKendrick, E. (1990), *Contract Law* (Macmillan, Basingstoke, Hants., 1990).

Megarry, R. and Wade, H. W. R. (1984), *The Law of Real Property* (5th edn., Stevens & Sons Limited, London, 1984).

Milsom, S. F. C. (1981), *Historical Foundations of the Common Law* (2nd edn., Butterworths, London, 1981).

Mincke, W. (1993), 'Property: Assets or Power?: Objects or Relations as Substrates of Property Rights', in *Collected Papers* (W. G. Hart Legal Workshop 1993, Institute of Advanced Legal Studies, London, 1993).

Moffat, G. (1994), *Trusts Law: Texts and Materials* (Butterworths, London, 1994).

Munzer, S. R. (1990), *A Theory of Property* (Cambridge University Press, Cambridge, 1990).

—— (1991), 'The Acquisition of Property Rights', 66 *Notre Dame Law Review* 661 (1991).

—— (1994), 'An Uneasy Case Against Property Rights in Body Parts' (1994) 11 *Social Philosophy and Policy* 259.

Mure, G. R. G. (1965), *The Philosophy of Hegel* (Oxford University Press, London, 1965).

Murphy, W. T. and Roberts, S. (1994), *Understanding Property Law* (2nd edn., Fontana, London, 1994).

Nicholas, B. (1962), *An Introduction to Roman Law* (Clarendon Press, Oxford, 1962).

Nozick, R. (1974), *Anarchy, State, and Utopia* (Basil Blackwell, Oxford, 1974).

Paul, A. and Flanagan, T. (eds.) (1979), *Theories of Property: Aristotle to the Present* (Wilfrid Laurier University Press, Waterloo, Ontario, 1979).

Pelczynski, Z. A. (1971), *Hegel's Political Philosophy: problems and perspectives* (Cambridge University Press, Cambridge, 1971).

PENNER, J. E. (1993), 'Nuisance and the Character of the Neighbourhood' (1993) 5 *Journal of Environmental Law* 1.
—— (1996), 'The 'Bundle of Rights' Picture of Property', 43 *UCLA Law Review* 711 (1996).
—— (forthcoming–a), 'The Analysis of Rights', *Ratio Juris*..
—— (forthcoming–b), 'Voluntary Obligations and the Scope of the Law of Contract' 2 *Legal Theory*.
—— (1997), 'Basic Obligations' in P. B. H. Birks (ed.), *Extending Obligations* (Oxford University Press, Oxford, 1997).
PENNOCK, J. R. and CHAPMAN, J. W. (eds.) (1980), *Nomos XXII: Property* (New York University Press, New York, 1980).
POLINSKY, A. M. (1979), 'Controlling Externalities and Protecting Entitlements' (1979) 8 *Journal of Legal Studies* 1.
POLLOCK, F. (1894), 'What is a Thing?' (1894) 10 *Law Quarterly Review* 318.
—— and MAITLAND, F. W. (1968), *The History of English Law (2nd edn.,* Cambridge University Press, Cambridge, 1968), Vol. II.
POSNER, R. A. (1981), *The Economics of Justice* (Harvard University Press, Cambridge Mass., 1981).
—— (1986), *Economic Analysis of Law* (3rd edn., Little, Brown & Co., Boston, Mass., 1986).
POTTAGE, A. (1990), 'Property: Re-Appropriating Hegel' (1990) 53 *Modern Law Review* 259.
—— (1994), 'The Measure of Land' (1994) 57 *Modern Law Review* 361.
—— (1995), 'The Originality of Registration' (1995) 15 *Oxford Journal of Legal Studies* 371.
RADIN, M. J. (1993), *Reinterpreting Property* (University of Chicago Press, Chicago, Ill., 1993).
RAZ, J. (1972), 'Legal Principles and the Limits of Law', 81 *Yale Law Journal* 823 (1972).
—— (1977), 'Promises and Obligations', in P. M. S. Hacker and J. Raz (eds.), *Law, Morality and Society* (Clarendon Press, Oxford, 1977), 210.
—— (1979), *The Authority of Law* (Clarendon Press, Oxford, 1979).
—— (1980), *The Concept of a Legal System* (2nd edn., Clarendon Press, Oxford, 1980).
—— (1982), 'Promises in Morality and Law', 95 *Harvard Law Review* 916 (1982).
—— (1984a), 'On the Nature of Rights' (1984) 93 *Mind* 194.
—— (1984b), 'Legal Rights' (1984) 4 *Oxford Journal of Legal Studies* 1.
—— (1986a), *The Morality of Freedom* (Clarendon Press, Oxford, 1986).
—— (1986b), 'Dworkin: A New Link in the Chain', 74 *California Law Review* 1103 (1986).
—— (1990), *Practical Reason and Norms* (2nd edn., Princeton University Press, Princeton, N.J., 1990).
—— (1994), *Ethics in the Public Domain* (Clarendon Press, Oxford, 1994).
REEVE, A. (1986), *Property* (MacMillan, Basingstoke, Hants., 1986).
REICH, C. (1964), 'The New Property', 73 *Yale Law Journal* 733 (1964).
ROSE, C. M. (1985), 'Possession as the Origin of Property', 52 *University of Chicago Law Review* 73 (1985).

ROSE-ACKERMAN, S. (1985), 'Inalienability and the Theory of Property Rights', 85 *Columbia Law Review* 931 (1985).

RUDDEN, B. (1980), 'Notes Toward a Grammar of Property' [1980] *The Conveyancer* 325.

—— (1987), 'Economic Theory *v.* Property Theory: The *Numerous Clausus* Problem', in J. Eekelaar and J. Bell (eds.), *Oxford Essays in Jurisprudence, Third Series* (Clarendon Press, Oxford, 1987), 239.

—— (1994), 'Things as Things and Things as Wealth' (1994) 14 *Oxford Journal of Legal Studies* 81.

RYAN, A. (1984), *Property and Political Theory* (Basil Blackwell, Oxford, 1984).

—— (1994), 'Self-Ownership, Autonomy, and Property Rights' (1994) 11 *Social Philosophy and Property* 241.

SALTER, M. (1987), 'Justifying Private Property Rights: A Message from Hegel's Jurisprudential Writings' (1987) 7 *Legal Studies* 245.

SAMUEL, G. (1994), 'Property Notions in the Law of Obligations' (1994) 53 *Cambridge Law Journal* 524.

SCHROEDER, J. L. (1994), 'Chix Nix Bundle-O-Stix: A Feminist Critique of the Disaggregation of Property', 93 *Michigan Law Review* 239 (1994).

SHAVELL, S. (1991), 'An Economic Analysis of Altruism and Deferred Gifts' (1991) 20 *Journal of Legal Studies* 401.

SIMPSON, A. W. B. (1964), 'The Analysis of Legal Concepts' (1964) 80 *Law Quarterly Review* 535.

—— (1986), *A History of the Land Law (2nd edn.,* Clarendon Press, Oxford, 1986).

—— (1987), *Legal Theory and Legal History: Essays on the Common Law* (Hambledon Press, London, 1987).

SINGER, J. W. (1991), 'Sovereignty and Property', 86 *Northwestern University Law Review* 1 (1991).

SMITH, J. C. (1993), *The Law of Theft* (7th edn., Butterworths, London, 1993).

SNARE, F. (1972), 'The Concept of Property', 9 *American Philosophical Quarterly* 200.

STILLMAN, P. G. (1989), 'Hegel's Analysis of Property in the *Philosophy of Right*', 10 *Cardozo Law Review* 1031 (1989).

SUCHMAN, M. C. (1989), 'Invention and Ritual: Notes on the Interrelationship of Magic and Intellectual Property in Pre-literate Societies', 89 *Columbia Law Review* 1264 (1989).

SUGARMAN, D. (1986), 'Legal Theory, the Common Law Mind, and the Making of the Textbook Tradition', in W. Twining (ed.), *Legal Theory and Common Law* (Basil Blackwell, Oxford, 1986), 26.

SUMNER, L. (1987), *The Moral Foundations of Rights* (Clarendon Press, Oxford, 1987).

SWEET, C. (1894), 'Choses in Action' (1894) 10 *Law Quarterly Review* 303.

—— (1895), 'Choses in Action' (1895) 11 *Law Quarterly Review* 238.

TAY, A. E. and KAMENKA, E. (1988), 'Introduction: Some Theses on Property' (1988) 11 *University of New South Wales Law Journal* 1.

TAYLOR, C. (1979), *Hegel and Modern Society* (Cambridge University Press, Cambridge, 1979).

—— (1985), *Philosophy and the Human Sciences: Philosophical Papers 2* (Cambridge University Press, Cambridge, 1985).

THEBERT, Y. (1993), 'The Slave', in A. Giardina (ed.) and L. G. Cochrance (trans.), *The Romans* (University of Chicago Press, Chicago, Ill., 1993), 138.

TITMUSS, R. M. (1970), *The Gift Relationship* (George Allen & Unwin Ltd., London, 1970).

TREITEL, G. H. (1991), *The Law of Contract* (8th edn., Stevens & Sons, London, 1991).

TULLY, J. (1980), *A Discourse on Property: John Locke and his Adversaries* (Cambridge University Press, Cambridge, 1980).

—— (1993), *An Approach to Political Philosophy: Locke in Contexts* (Cambridge University Press, Cambridge, 1993).

TURNER, J. C. W. (1941), 'Some Reflections on Ownership in English Law', 19 *Canadian Bar Review* 342 (1941).

UNDERKUFFLER, L. S. (1990), 'On Property: An Essay', 100 *Yale Law Journal*, 127 (1990).

VANDEVELDE, K. J. (1980), 'The New Property of the Nineteenth Century: The Development of the Modern Concept of Property', 29 *Buffalo Law Review* 325 (1980).

WADE, H. W. R. (1948), 'What is a licence' (1948) 64 *Law Quarterly Review* 57.

WALDRON, J. (ed.) (1984), *Theories of Rights* (Oxford University Press, Oxford, 1984).

—— (1988), *The Right to Private Property* (Clarendon Press, Oxford, 1988).

WATERS, D. W. M. (1967), 'The Nature of the Trust Beneficiary's Interest', 45 *Canadian Bar Review* 219 (1967).

WATTS, P. (1995), 'Restitution—A Property Principle and a Services Principle' [1995] *Restitution Law Review* 49.

WEINRIB, A. S. (1988), 'Information and Property', 38 *University of Toronto Law Journal* 117 (1988).

WEINRIB, E. J. (1989), 'Right and Advantage in Private Law', 10 *Cardozo Law Review* 1283 (1989).

—— (1995), *The Idea of Private Law* (Harvard University Press, Cambridge, Mass, 1995).

WELLMAN, C. (1985), *A Theory of Rights: Persons Under Laws, Instititions, and Morals* (Rowman & Allenheld, Totowa, N.J, 1985).

WHITE, A. R. (1984), *Rights* (Clarendon Press, Oxford, 1984).

Williams, P. J. (1994), 'Spare Parts, Family Values, Old Children, Cheap', 28 *New England Law Review* 913 (1994).

WILLIAMS, T. C. (1894), 'Is a Right of Action in Tort a Chose in Action?' (1894) 10 *Law Quarterly Review* 143.

ZIEGEL, J. S., GEVA B., and CUMING, R. C. C. (1987), *Commercial and Consumer Transactions: Cases, Text and Materials* (2nd edn., Edmond Montgomery, Toronto, 1987).

ZIMMERMAN, R. (1995), 'Unjustified Enrichment: The Modern Civilian Approach' (1995) 15 *Oxford Journal of Legal Studies* 403.

Index